THE LAST ESCAPE

THE LAST ESCAPE

JOHN KILLICK

THE MAN BEHIND THE MOST DARING JAILBREAK IN AUSTRALIAN HISTORY

First published in 2017 by New Holland Publishers
Sydney

Level 1, 178 Fox Valley Road, Wahroonga, NSW 2076, Australia

newhollandpublishers.com

A record of this book is held at the National Library of Australia.

ISBN 9781760796501

Managing Director: Fiona Schultz
Project Editor: Simona Hill
Designer: Andrew Davies
Production Director: Arlene Gippert
Printed in China

10 9 8 7 6 5 4 3 2 1

Keep up with New Holland Publishers:

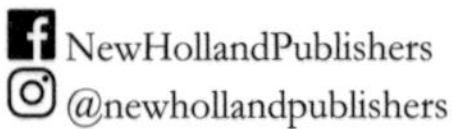
NewHollandPublishers
@newhollandpublishers

CONTENTS

FOREWORD

As I wrote this book, warts and all, I often became depressed. There were times when I had to put it aside and try to focus on something else.

When you look back over a long life, and are confronted with some of the stupid and criminal acts you have committed, you ask yourself: 'Can I do anything about it now? I know I can't take back what I've done. Can I redeem myself?'

The answer is yes and no. Redemption is not a tangible thing.

If I turn my life around it doesn't help the victims. What's done is done. You can't take it back.

But I can use this book to get the message across loud and clear to young men and women, who might already be caught up in a life of crime or on the fringes of it, that crime does not pay. A lot of people get hurt through criminal acts, sometimes physically, sometimes psychologically and emotionally. When we become criminals our families also suffer and are often left to pick up the pieces while struggling with their own lives. And then we have the victims. Not only are many of them traumatised for years, but often their families and even friends suffer as well.

When I was young I looked at the world as though everything was either black or white. And I acted appropriately. Now I look at it as a kaleidoscope of colour.

You can't categorise people or groups. You have to look at the individuals. Not all criminals are bad. Some have made mistakes but remain good, decent human beings who have done and will do good things. There is no denying that some are bad. I have even met a few whom I would class as evil. Are they a product of their environment? When I see young men caught up on the treadmill of the criminal justice system, repeatedly coming into prison for often senseless crimes, I see kids who haven't had a chance and are definitely products of their disadvantaged origins. But there are others who come from privileged backgrounds. Environment is often a factor leading to criminality but it would be too simplistic to say it is the main reason behind criminality. I'm often criticised by my criminal peers because I am not anti-police. Why should I be? Police stand on the line between us and anarchy. Where would we be without police? Show me an honest cop and I'll point to a person I respect. Show me a corrupt cop and I say lock the bastard up. Why not?

I've criticised prison officers in this book and often referred to them as 'guards' because that's the way I felt during tough times in prisons when I and others were bashed, brutalised and psychologically tormented. But a lot of prison officers are decent human beings simply doing a job that has to be done. I have met a lot who I would be happy to have a beer with. It is the brutal, corrupt and sometimes sadistic prison 'guards' who spoil it for everyone. They are in the minority. But it only takes one to make life difficult for a prisoner.

My experiences have taught me that there is good and bad in all of us.

You know it's true.

BAD DAY AT BOWRAL

Let us start with 20 January 1999. I am about to rob a bank. Which bank? This time I had chosen the National in Bowral, a leafy little town in the Southern Highlands 120 kilometres south of Sydney.

You could say I was a pro. I robbed my first bank, Commonwealth of course, in January 1966 – exactly thirty-three years ago. At the time, I was twenty-three and I was a fast runner. There have been many banks since then. Now at fifty-six, I have slowed down some. If I get chased I'm in trouble.

I'm like an old boxer. I think I've still got it, not as fast, not as fit, but I'm counting on experience. And just like the boxer who psyches himself before he gets into the ring, I have to psych myself before I walk into a bank to rob it.

I really don't want to be doing this. But for reasons which I will go into later, I feel I have no choice.

Wearing a cap, a blonde wig and a stocking I was about to pull down over my face, I entered the bank brandishing an eight-shot .32 self-loading Colt pistol. Inside, there were four or five customers and three tellers.

I always try to be in and out inside a minute in case one of the tellers presses a silent alarm alerting police.

I spoke loudly, but calmly. 'This is a hold-up! Everyone stay calm and no one will get hurt'. I pointed the pistol in the direction of the tellers, all of them female.

'Put all the money on the counter, large notes only – no fives!' I knew a guy who had robbed a bank and was caught when a dye bomb exploded, covering him in purple dye. He told me it had been hidden in a pack of five-dollar notes.

Apart from the tellers, I had to keep an eye on the customers in case one of them decided to jump me. What do I do if someone does come at me? Do I shoot? My mindset is no, I am not a killer, I work on bluff. I figure people don't argue with a man with a gun. But people don't really know what they will do until they are put to the test. In the past, I had never been put to the test – but that was about to change.

I scooped up the money from the counter and placed it in an overnight bag. There looked to be more than $20,000 there. (The actual amount tabled in court was $23,800).

'Don't come after me!' I yelled to no one in particular as I turned and hurried towards the exit. Adjusting the stocking back under my cap, I stepped outside.

To my left I noticed a youngish, dark haired guy standing by a teller machine staring at me. He was with another guy. I started to run and he came after me. After about 100 metres I glanced around. He was about ten metres behind. Two other guys were also giving chase, but they were some distance back and they didn't look to be trying to bridge the gap. One of them was the bank manager who had been alerted by staff. Apart from the chasers, I had another problem. Red smoke began to billow from my bag. One of the tellers had planted a dye bomb inside one of the bundles of notes! Sneaky little thing! Movement sets them off. I was in trouble.

Never had I been tricked into leaving a bank with a dye bomb planted in the money. So much for leave the fives! Things change: I was a criminal dinosaur trying to make a comeback and I was failing miserably.

I ran around the corner into Station Street which paralleled the railway line. Stopping, I turned, pistol in hand, and confronted my pursuer. He ducked behind a parked car, picked up a rock about the size of my fist and hurled it at me. If I hadn't dodged, it would have hit me square in the head.

'Don't be a hero, this is a real gun!' I yelled. 'It's a toy!' he said, picking up another rock.

I fired a shot over his head. 'You think that's a fucking toy!' The red smoke continued to billow out from the bag. Cars drove past, slowing down to see what all the fuss was about. Maybe they thought we were doing a scene for a movie. Though they would have had a problem trying to recognize the actors.

Thinking I might have scared the rock thrower off, I started to run towards where I had parked my rental car in the railway car park, about another 500 metres away. I couldn't see my two other pursuers, the gunshot had probably scared them off.

But I hadn't scared the rock thrower. I later learned that his name was Richard Rostron, an off-duty senior constable stationed at Bowral. Cursing, I ran towards the railway line and jumped over a small fence down onto the tracks. Rostron still came after me. I could hear sirens everywhere. Houdini couldn't get out of this mess – but I had to try. I ran back to the fence, scrambled over it and looked for Rostron. He wasn't far away. I fired a shot into the ground near him, kicking up dust.

'See, it's real!' I yelled.

He stared at me and retreated. I fired another one in the air. This time he took refuge behind an upholstery building. Near exhaustion, I was running on adrenaline as I made it to the car. As far as I could discern no one was following me.

At this stage, I had discarded the overnight bag with its contents. I had red dye on my hands and I figured the money would also be covered in it – it was worthless. As I drove out of the carpark a police car drove by. I decided I had no chance of driving out of Bowral because they would have the exits blocked. Driving up a side street, I turned left into a lane situated directly behind the main street of shops. I calculated that if I could get changed and slip into the shopping centre I had a chance – they would be looking for a young blonde-haired guy dressed in jeans, not a grey-haired guy in his fifties wearing a suit.

Parking in a driveway behind one of the shops, I took off my jeans and struggled into my suit. I could hear the sirens blaring. There was no time to change shoes. I slipped the pistol into my suit coat pocket and got out of the car, totally unaware that a woman had seen me changing clothes and had contacted police.

I was halfway down the lane when a police car pulled up alongside me and two plainclothes detectives got out and asked me who I was. They didn't appear to be armed. It flashed through my mind that I could hold them at gunpoint and drive off in their car. But then what? I was trapped in a bloody country town. I saw two other police cars coming up the lane. I had to try one last bluff.

'I'm John Reardon,' I said. 'What's the problem?'

They stepped either side of me. Their names were MacDonald and Pascoe.

'Take your hands out of your pockets,' MacDonald, who had ginger hair, said.

The two police cars had stopped behind the first vehicle. This was a classic case of being caught red-handed.

'You've got me,' I said showing them my hands stained with red dye. 'The gun's inside my coat pocket.'

I was quickly handcuffed before they took the pistol. It was also covered in red dye.

'Where's the money?' Pascoe asked.

'I tossed it. Red smoke coming out, dye everywhere.'

'Where did you toss it?'

'Near the railway.'

Under heavy police escort, I was taken to where I told them I had thrown away the overnight bag. It wasn't there. 'Maybe the rock thrower picked it up,' I said.

'He's a police officer,' MacDonald said. 'You were lucky he wasn't armed.'

'Who did you give the money to?' Pascoe asked.

'No one. I did this on my own. Some opportunist has picked it up. Look for a local with red hands. He could be wearing a police uniform.'

With cops everywhere they got me to backtrack the route I had taken. A photographer followed us with a video camera.

Senior Constable Rostron approached us. Later, he would be praised by the judge for his bravery. I call it foolhardiness. 'If I was a killer, you'd be dead, mate!' I said.

He didn't reply. He knew it was true.

As they took me to the police station I wondered what Lucy would do when she learnt of my arrest.

• • •

'Killick wanted for a visit!' a voice bellowed over the loudspeaker.

It was the call I had been waiting for. It was three days after the disastrous bank robbery in Bowral. I was now in the maximum security Metropolitan Remand and Reception Centre (MRRC) in Silverwater. It was the largest prison in Australia, holding over 900 prisoners.

Before being allowed into the visiting room I was strip-searched and given a pair of white overalls – two sizes too large – which were zipped at the back and padlocked by the guard. The prisoners called these pocketless overalls 'zoot suits'.

As I entered the visiting room I immediately saw Lucy. Dressed in a long white dress and black high-heeled shoes, she stood out among all the other visitors. Her small, delicate features, obviously Slavic, were proof of her upper-middle-class Russian heritage. She wasn't beautiful, but radiated a femininity that attracted most men to her, including me. Although forty, she looked ten years younger.

Smiling, she rushed forward and hugged me.

I was surprised and disappointed to see that she had cut her long blonde hair to shoulder length.

As we walked to a table I asked her why. 'It's a Russian thing,' she said.

'What are you talking about?'

She looked at me, hurt and sadness in her eyes. 'You are here, I am out there. I will grow my hair long when you are with me again.'

This was typical Lucy logic. I didn't pursue it.

It was a large room with dozens of tables and chairs concreted to the floor. There were a few vending machines that dispensed overpriced drinks and confectionery. The visiting area extended to an outside section with grass, plants and flowers. Pleasant enough if you could ignore where you actually were and why you were there.

'Boy,' Lucy said. She always called me 'Boy'. 'Will they give you bail?'

'Not a chance. I'm charged with two bank robberies and shooting with intent to avoid arrest.'

Pausing, I held her hand. 'I'm going to be in here for a long time, Luce.

We might have to call it quits.'

She stared at me. 'What do you mean?'

'It might be best for you to go your own way. We can't have a relationship with me in here.'

'Tell me Boy, how long?'

I shrugged. 'At least ten years.'

She withdrew her hand and stared at the table. 'This should never have happened.'

'I know. But it did. That's the reality.'

She grabbed my hand again and gave me an intense look. 'Do you remember that night when we walked across the bridge?'

I nodded. 'Yes. We made a pact.'

'I told you, one in, both in. Till the death.' I smiled. 'Luckily, I'm the only one in.'

'I'm serious, Boy. We are in together. I will get you out.'

'Luce, they have already told me I'm high security.'

'Jackie got you out, I'll get you out.'

History was repeating itself. In May 1984, I'd been arrested in Queensland and charged with four bank robberies. My then girlfriend, Jackie, had visited me in the notorious Boggo Road Gaol and swore she would get me out. And she did. (More on that later.)

'That's the problem, they know about that escape. Now, when I go to court or hospital or anywhere outside the gaol I will be escorted by special squad guards armed and trained to prevent escapes. I will have a security belt around my waist with my hands cuffed to it at the front. They may even put ankle cuffs on me.'

She looked distressed. 'What do we do, Boy?'

'I honestly don't know. I don't want to lose you, but trying to wait years for me while I am in here will destroy both of us.'

'Then it is settled, I will find a way to get you out.'

I knew Lucy. She meant it. 'Let's wait and see,' I said. 'I will look around, try to find a flaw in their security.'

'We will do it, Boy.'

I looked around me at all the prisoners with their visitors. Was anyone else talking about trying to escape? I doubted it. This was a modern maximum security gaol. The assistant commissioner, Ron Woodham, a stickler for security, was on record as stating Silverwater was escape proof. Was he right? Surely there must be a way. All we had to do was find it.

I squeezed her hand and met her gaze. 'Okay, we'll find a way.' She brightened. "Whatever it takes, Boy. I'm there."

There was no bravado with her. Just a statement of fact. No matter what the risk, I could count on her being there.

That was a huge plus.

THE EARLY YEARS

1942–1960

We need to start at the beginning.

I was born in Sydney, Australia in February 1942, only a few months after the Japanese bombed Pearl Harbour and a few days before they first attacked the Australian mainland, where 180 Japanese planes dropped more tonnage of bombs on Darwin than on Pearl Harbour. We were in the middle of World War II and after the attack on Darwin and the recent fall of Singapore, many Australians were fearful that the Japanese would soon overrun us. They were tough times.

I have no memory of my birth parents. I was handed over for adoption as a baby. My adoptive parents, Reg and Laurie Killick, were poor. Reg was a truck driver who spent a lot of his wages on beer, often coming home drunk and abusive, usually towards my mother. But sometimes he would focus on me, calling me a little black bastard. My brother David, three years younger than me and also adopted, was his favourite. But when Reg was in one of his drunken rages, David was also fearful of him. Reg had been the 1932 middleweight champion of Balmain and had the trophy to prove it. The neighbours knew not to mess with Reg Killick.

Sometimes he was so out of control that my mother, David and I would hide under the house or walk the streets until the early hours of the morning then creep back inside when he had fallen into a drunken sleep. One day I watched her come at him with a kitchen knife. He backhanded her, knocking her to the ground. I lived in dread that one of them would kill the other. But when he was sober, he was a good and decent man.

By the time I was thirteen we had moved from Bronte to Rozelle to North Ryde, back to Rozelle and then to Fairfield. Apart from coming down with most of the childhood illnesses at the time, I also suffered from asthma. Sometimes the attacks were so bad that I had great difficulty breathing and thought I was going to die. I was a sickly, puny kid who retreated into a world of fantasy. Comics, books and radio serials were my world. I wasn't interested in sport. On my first attempt at playing rugby league I had my left arm broken.

But I was a good storyteller. When we lived in Rozelle the kids from around the neighbourhood would come and ask me to tell them a story. Sometimes I had a dozen kids sitting around on the grass as I regaled them with stories about heroes, baddies and monsters. I had a vivid imagination and had no difficulty in making it up as I went along.

For my twelfth birthday, I received a second-hand bicycle. I began riding it around Rozelle and Balmain where there were a lot of steep hills and after a few months I gained a level of fitness that helped my asthma attacks to disappear. I was a naturally fast runner and my fitness now enabled me to beat all the kids in the neighbourhood. I delighted in giving them a start and dashing past them near the finish. This ability to run fast would prove to be a great asset later in life when I was being chased by police, store detectives, bank tellers, bookmakers and assorted angry people.

In early 1955, we moved to Fairfield in the south-western suburbs of Sydney. I started at Fairfield High School two months behind and never caught up. My schoolwork deteriorated. I rarely did homework and often I didn't bother to go to school. Mum would always write me a note stating I was sick. The teachers never questioned the veracity of the numerous notes I presented them. At exam time, I generally finished near the bottom of the class in most subjects except English and Maths. I had a natural flair for mathematics and due to all the reading I did, I was always top of the class in English and Spelling. At the time, in the third year of high school, students had to pass the Intermediate Certificate examination to go on to Leaving Certificate and from there to university. I fell at the first hurdle, failing the Intermediate despite a brilliant pass in English.

Rather than repeat, I immediately left school and took a job with Coles Variety Store in Auburn. It was late 1957. (It wasn't until 1960 that Coles opened its first supermarket in Australia.)

A few months after starting at Coles, I began dating a pretty, dark-haired girl named Sonia. I had also taken up tennis and went on to win a few trophies in the local Fairfield competitions. I'd become extremely fit, riding my bike from Fairfield to Auburn six days a week and playing tennis four times weekly.

I also started gambling, placing small bets with the local SP bookmaker. In those days, there were no TABs. Starting price (SP) bookies flourished, mainly operating from their homes and hotels. Most Australians loved to bet and I never tired of that feeling. But at that stage I always bet within my means. For a while I probably won more than I lost. I loved the thrill of listening to a race and hearing my horse win. It wasn't until my early twenties that my gambling got out of control.

After about seven months of working at Coles I resigned, explaining to the perplexed manager that I wanted to play Saturday morning competition tennis. Shortly afterwards Sonia and I split up.

I began working for a dog biscuit factory, Wrenches, in Lidcombe. I worked twelve-hour shifts, earning nearly twice as much as I had been getting at Coles.

Sonia and I rekindled our romance but she broke it off for good when I went to the races instead of turning up for a date. My excuse was that there were no phones on the racecourse for me to ring her explaining why I couldn't make it but it didn't dissuade her. She had met someone else. A nice butcher. Why stay with a dog biscuit maker when she could get the best meat in town from her new beau? I was out of the running – just like some of the horses I backed.

Working twelve-hour shifts interfered with my social life, particularly playing tennis. I stuck it out for seven months then resigned. When the boss asked me why I was leaving I told him that when girls found out I baked dog biscuits for a living, I couldn't get a date. It wasn't far from the truth, but I was restless.

After that I took a few different jobs before resigning within weeks. I didn't like working in factories or behind counters serving people, but I wasn't qualified to do anything else. My employment history was deplorable and finding a job became increasingly difficult.

In late June 1959, after years of abuse, my mother took an overdose of sleeping pills. When she fell out of her bed at about 2.00am Dad heard it and called out to David and I that she was in a bad way. We didn't have a car or a phone so I rode my bike to the nearest phonebox to call our regular doctor. In those days doctors made house calls even, in an emergency, in the early hours of the morning. But the first phone I tried was disconnected – vandals had struck again. I rode half a mile to the next one – aware that in this situation time was the enemy. This time I was able to ring Doctor Ferguson's number. His wife answered the phone. After I explained the dire situation to her she told me the doctor was asleep and I would have to call another one. Then she hung up. I suspected that she knew mum owed the doctor money. How could she pay for a 2.00am emergency call? I didn't have any coins to ring again. More stressed than I had ever been in my life, I rang the operator and begged her to put me through to a doctor. She did so and when I gave him a hurried account of what had happened he told me he would drive over immediately. When I returned Dad was angry at the amount of time I had taken. I briefly told him why.

This made him angrier. 'Bloody Ferguson has been giving her all these pills and now she has taken too many of them and the bastard won't come because she owes him money!'

I hurried to Mum's bedroom. Dad had placed her on the bed. She was unconscious. I felt her pulse, it was very faint and slow. I knew my mother was close to death.

When the doctor came he immediately ordered an ambulance. But too much time had been wasted. The emergency team at the hospital tried in vain to save her.

The mother I loved was dead at forty-three. And inside of me something also died. Until that day I had always believed that if you are good, everything will turn out all right. My mother had been a good woman in every way and life had given her little. Her death shocked me into a state of depression. Blaming my father for her death, I left home that day and rented a share-room in a boarding house in Burwood.

I was bitter and determined that from that day it would be me against the world. I broke away from my friends and family. After my roommate, a big weightlifter, tried to sexually assault me, I forged his signature and withdrew money from his account. I was the obvious suspect and was soon arrested. Up to that point I had never stolen anything. Technically, it was my first bank robbery.

I was taken to the Albion Street Boys' Remand Centre. More depressed than ever, I think I relegated most of the experience to my subconscious. I recall eating dinner at a large table with a lot of other kids, most of them younger and smaller than me. Then we were taken to the showers, six at a time and ordered to strip off and have a shower while a couple of our minders watched. I had never experienced anything like this before and I was extremely embarrassed about showering naked with other boys.

After dressing in pyjamas, we were taken to a dormitory which contained about twenty beds. As soon as the lights were turned off I began to cry into my pillow. I cried for my mother who had only been dead a month. I cried for what might have been.

A month ago, the world had been a totally different place...

The following morning my father, accompanied by David, came and bailed me out. I had no option other than to return home with them.

I knew Dad was trying to redeem himself as a father but it was too late. At that stage, my resentment towards him was overpowering. He was on lifetime compensation after permanently injuring his back loading and unloading goods for twenty years for Yellow Express. He had no hobbies other than going to the pub and drinking. When he couldn't afford that he stayed home. It didn't take long before we began arguing over trivialities. Although I regretted leaving David alone with him I soon moved out again, renting a room with an Italian family in Guildford.

I was given a twelve-month good behaviour bond for the forgery. I wasn't remorseful.

Until my mother had died I had been a good kid. Polite and respectful to others, I was never in trouble at school except for a couple of fights which I didn't start. I was never dishonest and I was always kind to animals, even spending my pocket money on scrap meat for stray dogs – of which there were a lot in those days.

After my mother died I couldn't get it out of my mind that if we hadn't owed the doctor money, or we had have had a car or even a phone we would have managed to get her to the hospital in time. Being poor had cost my mother her life. If I baked dog biscuits for a living or worked in a factory I would always be poor. My father, an honest man, had worked hard all his life but we had nothing. I had no qualifications but I would find a way to get ahead. If that meant breaking all the rules along the way, then so be it.

I teamed up with a guy my own age named Jim. He was a habitual thief from the western country town of Orange. We spent our days stealing from shops and selling the items in hotels. I could say Jim was a bad influence on me but I took to stealing like a duck to water. I was chased many times but I was never caught. One night, while Jim waited down the street, I snatched a large amount of money from an SP bookmaker's place in Newtown, one of the toughest suburbs in Sydney. Angry punters – perhaps fearing the bookie wouldn't be able to pay them if they won – chased me. If they had have caught me they may well have kicked me to death.

Another time I went to Canley Vale railway station with the intention of robbing it with a replica pistol. Again, Jim waited across the street citing his lack of speed if pursued as the reason, rather than lack of intestinal fortitude. But while I was waiting in the toilet for the railway employee to come out, a little guy in a suit stepped out of a toilet cubicle and offered me money for oral sex. When I invited him to suck the barrel of my pistol he declined. Instead of robbing the railway I relieved him of fifty-eight pounds. I had no qualms about that. To my mind he was just a deviate trying to corrupt boys.

It was only a matter of time before our luck ran out. In January 1960, the two of us and another fool named Albert from the country town of Blayney broke into a house in Burwood after Albert assured us that the champion jockey, Athol Mulley, lived there and he had a stack of money hidden away.

Whoever lived there wasn't Mulley – his pants would have fitted two jockeys inside. We stole some of the clothes and took them away in suitcases.

The next day Albert was arrested trying to pawn them and he told the police we had led him astray. The police believed him, arrested Jim and I and let Albert go.

Although I was still seventeen I was taken with Jim to Long Bay Penitentiary. The sentenced prisoners were given navy blue pants and jackets which had numbers sewn onto the backs and over the heart areas. These were the targets for guards to shoot at if someone tried to escape.

Because we were unconvicted prisoners, Jim and I were allowed to wear our civilian clothing. We were escorted to A Wing, one of six cell blocks, each containing two levels. Only remand prisoners were housed in A Wing.

Conditions were atrocious. Three men to a cell, coir mats for mattresses, no sheets or pillow slips – just two unwashed blankets per prisoner. A tin bucket containing a bit of disinfectant sufficed as a toilet for three. A tin jug of water was the only water available. There were no radios or televisions, no electrical appliances and the lights were switched off at 9.00pm. The meals were so bad that the previous year prisoners had rioted over the numerous stews, nicknamed the grey death, that were served up. A lot of the prisoners simply didn't eat most of the meals. In 1960 if you wanted to lose weight Long Bay Penitentiary was the place to come.

We shared a cell with a little wiry guy named Ted who was about fifty. He had been in gaol a few times and made a point of advising us of what we could do and what we shouldn't do in a prison society.

'If you see someone getting bashed or even stabbed you walk away, you don't see a thing.'

I looked at Jim as he paled.

'Does that happen very often?' he asked.

'There's a lot of fights, men cooped up like animals what do you expect?

Not a lot of stabbings, but it happens now and again.'

'Anyone killed?' I said.

'Not lately, although I reckon the screws will kill Simmons and Newcombe if they keep bashing them every night.'

Simmons and Newcombe had recently been recaptured after escaping from Long Bay in October and the next day going to Emu Plains prison camp where they killed a guard and took his rifle. The escape and killing had generated the biggest manhunt in Australian history.

'They've got them in the Observation cells,' Ted said. 'Away from everyone. But a bloke in the wing next to them told me he hears them screaming out every night when the screws go in and flog them.'

'They go to court a lot,' I said. 'Couldn't they complain to the judge?'

Ted gave me a look that implied I was an idiot. 'This is political, son: they committed the cardinal sin of killing a screw. No one will dare intervene. Least of all the judges who will give them life sentences down the track.'

Ted was only partly right. Although Simmonds was sentenced to life, Newcombe received fifteen years and served ten. In November 1966 Simmonds was found hanged in his cell in the punishment section of the notorious Grafton Gaol.

'One other thing,' Ted said. 'Talking about bashings, be careful when you go to the showers. A young bloke got knocked out and raped there recently and the screws saw nothing.'

I was shocked that someone would rape a boy! 'Did they catch the rapist?'

'No. The young bloke said he didn't see who it was. But he wouldn't have said who it was anyway. First rule in gaol: You don't give anyone up no matter what happens to you. And the same applies outside. We are criminals but we have a code of honour. Break it and you'll be branded a dog for the rest of your life.'

I discovered later in life that this code was more mythical than factual.

ON THE TREADMILL OF THE CRIMINAL JUSTICE SYSTEM

1960–1962

Within a week of my incarceration at Long Bay the inevitable happened: I was involved in a fight with an arrogant young German. I mention his heritage because he wasn't an Aussie or an Italian or a Greek, he was a German. When I beat him in a game of chess he hit me over the head with the chess board. I threw a punch at him but missed and he grabbed hold of me and wrestled me to the ground thumping my head against the concrete. After a bit of rolling around trying to strangle each other, we broke apart and jumped to our feet. He was no match for me in a fight and I hit him flush on the jaw felling him immediately. The fight was over. If the guards saw anything they ignored it. Ted told me they didn't mind us bashing each other as long as no weapons were used.

'Beating that Kraut won't do you any harm,' Ted said. 'Everyone saw it and the bullies now know you can handle yourself.'

His reference to the German as a 'Kraut' was significant of the times. We might deny it but in 1960 many Australians – including my father – were racists. To Dad anyone who wasn't an Aussie was a 'wog'. We still had the 'White Australia' policy that prevented Asians and Africans immigrating to Australia. Until 1967 our Indigenous people weren't permitted to vote. But from 1945 to 1959 1.5 million people, mainly from Europe and Britain, immigrated to Australia. These immigrants were a great asset to Australia and helped to contribute to the new booming economy of the 1950s.

After three months in Long Bay, Jim and I were taken to court and given bonds by the judge who warned us that next time we would remain in gaol.

Jim returned to Orange. I went to see Dad and found him in his favourite hotel. After we had a few drinks he started to lecture me about where I had gone wrong.

'You're the son of a working man, Johnny,' he said. 'Forget about all your fancy ideas and get a job in a factory.'

Maybe it was good advice, but I didn't think so. I caught a train to Orange where I met with Jim. He allowed me to share his flat with him. He had a job at the abattoirs and offered to get me some work there. Something I could never do. But I needed money and got a job digging up potatoes. It was hard labour and I knew Dad would approve.

Within a week of my arrival Jim was arrested for stealing a car. This time he was refused bail and sent to Bathurst Gaol. I arranged to take over the rental of his flat.

One of my potato digging buddies, Barry, had a nice-looking sister, Barbara. A talkative brunette with a shapely figure, she was a year older than me. Her parents approved of me and we began dating.

Barry had been in the Mittagong Boys' Home for stealing. When I told him about my stay at Long Bay he asked me if I would be interested in breaking into a local clothing shop with him. I figured we would soon get caught trying to hide a stash of stolen clothing in a country town and declined.

About a week later I spent the day in Bathurst and went into the Western Stores, reputedly the largest department store in the west. I noticed that the skylights weren't alarmed, nor were the jewellery cases. When I saw Barry, I mentioned it to him and we both agreed it would be an easy place to rob. But we didn't pursue it. A few days later Barry, tired of digging potatoes for a living, went to Sydney.

When he returned he had two friends with him. They intended to rob the Western Stores and as it had been my idea, they invited me along.

Explaining to the perplexed Barbara that my potato digging days were over, I set off with the three amigos to Bathurst.

Taffy, the driver of the car, looked to be in his late thirties. 'We have a fence in Sydney waiting to buy the goods for a quarter of their value,' he said.

He didn't tell me the car was stolen. The third guy, a thin-faced weasel type guy, was named Sparrow. He would go on to become a notorious pickpocket.

We arrived behind the Western Stores at about 11pm. After we climbed onto the roof we broke one of the skylights and the three of them lowered me down into the premises by a rope. I let them in via the back door which wasn't alarmed.

After cleaning out the jewellery cases we filled as many suitcases with clothes as we could fit into the vehicle. The total value of the property was in excess of £5000, the equivalent today of about $200,000.

But we didn't make it to Sydney. When we ran out of petrol at Lithgow, Taffy and Sparrow began to siphon some from a parked car when the police arrived. Taffy managed to escape; my two accomplices and I were taken to Lithgow Police Station.

Although it was 3.00am in the middle of July, we were ordered to strip naked. When Sparrow reluctantly took off his socks, three diamond rings fell on to the floor.

The cops laughed. Barry began to abuse him for stealing from his mates. I was shivering, depressed and wondering how the hell I'd gotten into this mess. I made a mental note never to trust Sparrow again.

We were charged with break, enter and steal and later that day taken before a magistrate who set bail at 500 pounds. There was no chance any of us could raise it and we were taken to Bathurst Gaol.

Although Bathurst Gaol was for convicted criminals who reoffend, it also held a few remand prisoners. We weren't permitted to mix with the sentenced prisoners so they put us in a small yard about the same size as a cell. We stayed there all day until they brought us back to the wing at about 3.00pm for dinner. We would be locked away in a cell until about 8.00am the next morning.

The meals were an improvement on those at Long Bay and each cell had a flush toilet as well as a tap and a washbowl. There was a radio receiver on the wall which was operated by the guards from a central switch. They always put the local station 2BS on. The highlight of the week was the hit parade when they played the top five songs. As usual Elvis was on top this time with 'It's Now or Never'.

A few days after we arrived, Taffy, sporting a black eye, joined us. He was adamant that one of us had told the cops where he lived and as I had no idea of where that might be, he had narrowed it down to either Sparrow or Barry. My money was on Sparrow, but he managed to convince Taffy that brilliant detective work was responsible for his arrest.

Barbara visited Barry and asked him to tell me that she didn't love me anymore. I could have kept my job digging up potatoes and we could have lived happily ever after. But I had to go and spoil it. So now she was going back to her old boyfriend, Bruce. He wouldn't let her down. She went on to marry Bruce but a few weeks later he was killed in a car smash.

While all that was going on I concluded that Bathurst wasn't for me. I decided to escape. Should be a piece of cake at court where a couple of county cops walked the four of us, without handcuffs, into and out of court. In those days, it didn't occur to country cops that someone might try to escape. Where would they go?

I put the plan to the three amigos. 'As we walk out of court into the lane we run for it and split into four different directions. They probably won't chase us but if they do they can only chase two of us.'

'Johnny,' Taffy said, 'I think it will work.'

'Count me in,' Barry said.

'Me too,' brave Sparrow said.

Experience later taught me that when it comes to escaping from gaol, a lot of prisoners will talk about it, but very few will attempt it – unless it involves walking off a prison farm or absconding from an external leave programme.

On the day of the escape conditions were auspicious. One of the escorting police officers was an old sergeant who looked like he couldn't run 10 metres; the other was an overweight detective.

As they led us out of the courthouse into the back lane, which led to the police cells, I shoved the old sergeant in the back, sending him stumbling forwards.

'Let's go!' I yelled and began to run towards the park.

'Good luck, Johnny!' Taffy yelled.

As the detective began to run after me the three amigos helped the old sergeant regain his composure and the four of them watched the chase.

When the detective realised that he couldn't catch a runaway from kindergarten let alone a fit young escapee running on adrenaline, he withdrew his pistol and tried to shoot me.

I heard the shot so I knew things were getting serious. I ran through the park across the main street and down into a side street. I knew the cops would come out in force trying to find me. I had to go to ground until it got dark. Jumping over a fence into a backyard I climbed inside a chook pen. If the chooks hadn't squawked at the intrusion I doubt the cops would have figured it out. But the old lady who owned the chooks saw me and maybe she thought I was trying to steal some of them because when she saw a cop she told him where I was.

When they took me back to the police station I complained to the overweight cop that I had cut my hand jumping over a fence and now it was bleeding. Could he get a bandage and some antiseptic?

He punched me in the head and when I fell down he lashed out with his boot, catching me on the elbow. That hurt.

Then they left me alone in the cell. Taffy, who was in another cell with the other two, sang out: 'Hey, Johnny! Are you okay?'

'No, I'm not. You are all a pack of weak bastards!'

'You moved too quick for us,' Barry yelled.

On returning to Bathurst gaol I was placed in a cell on my own. There was no radio or sheets, just blankets Long Bay style. This was the beginning of the punishment. The next morning, I was taken before the governor who stared at me as though they had brought a rat into his office. He told me that by escaping I had negated any chance of ever going to a minimum security prison.

'If you get ten years you will do it all in maximum security,' he said. 'But first you can spend a couple of days in the pound to give you time to ponder on your stupidity.'

Ten years! He must be joking. Murderers didn't get much more than that. I was taken to B Wing to where the guards unlocked a steel door. Inside there was a small area that led to another steel door. They unlocked it and told me to step inside, strip off and hand over my clothes. There were no lights, no windows, just a small air vent. There was no bed, chair or table. I noticed a tin bucket in the corner – my toilet.

As I took off my clothes and handed them to one of the guards he dropped them outside the cell. I stared at him. I wasn't embarrassed anymore about being naked in front of strangers and although I was vulnerable, I wasn't afraid. I was angry.

The guard's face softened. 'No one is going to hurt you son, remember that and you'll be okay.'

They locked the door and went away. I was in total darkness. It was August and even under normal conditions Bathurst was a cold place in winter. Being naked in a small, darkened concrete cell was nothing less than torture. I was eighteen, in solitary confinement in a maximum security gaol after being shot at and bashed. But I wasn't feeling sorry for myself, I knew I had brought it on myself. My attitude now was to make the best of a bad situation. I began to jog up and down in the small cell. One, two, three, four, five steps, push the wall, spin around and repeat... After a while I began to sweat. Then I walked up and down singing. The acoustics were good and I felt I was in the class of Elvis. What a hit I would be, singing naked to all the girls...

I had lost track of time when the guards opened the door and gave me dinner: half a loaf of dry bread and a jug of water. They also brought into the cell a coir mattress and a few blankets.

'Cut the singing out,' one of them said. 'We thought you were being murdered.'

Comedians, Bathurst country-style. Couldn't be funny to save their lives. I was tired and after wolfing down the bread I wrapped the blankets around me and soon managed to go to sleep on the mat. For a few moments when I woke up in the pitch darkness in the early hours of the morning I didn't know where I was. Then the reality of my situation sank in. I was a despised convict, an outcast of society. I could die in this cell and they wouldn't know until they came to take the mat and blankets away. And no one would care. Dad and David maybe, but no one else.

I was determined not to become depressed. My mother became depressed and died. To this stage my life hadn't been easy and I used the memories to fuel my anger. I didn't have to look too far for reasons to be a rebel. Stuff society and its niceties, it was all a sham.

The forty-eight hours in solitary seemed like a week. You have no idea of time. When they did come and let me out they again escorted me to the front yards.

Eventually I received eighteen months for the Western Stores robbery and an additional three months for the escape.

After about six weeks in those miserable yards I was taken to Long Bay for sentencing on my broken bond. I received two years for that.

While I was at Long Bay one of my cellmates sexually propositioned me. I told him I wasn't interested but he persisted. His name was Max. He was a few years older than me, about the same weight but shorter. I was confident I could take him in a fight but I was concerned about the third guy in the cell. If they both attacked me I was in trouble.

I tried to reason with him one more time. 'Look, I'm not that way inclined.'

'Well they shouldn't put good-looking boys in our cell.' He stepped towards me. 'Just give it a try.'

I hit him with a flurry of punches knocking him to the ground. Then I jumped on him and hit him again. The other guy jumped off his bed and grabbed hold of me.

'That's enough, mate!'

I shoved him away and went into a fighting stance. 'Do you want to try it too?'

'No, I don't, it's not my go.'

Max staggered to his feet. He was bleeding profusely. I had a slight cut over my left eye where he had managed to land a retaliatory blow.

'I'm sorry, mate. Gaol does this to you. I'm into girls outside.'

'So am I,' I said.

Suddenly the door opened. The guards had heard the commotion and arrived in force. There were five of them. When Max told them he fell over they thought it was funny. We were both charged with fighting.

The next morning the governor sent both of us to the pound for forty-eight hours. Déjà vu. The set up was much the same as that at Bathurst except this time I was permitted to wear my clothes minus the belt, shoes and socks.

I was virtually in a dungeon. The more I jogged and walked up and down the more the gnawing hunger increased. By the end of the day all I could think about was getting my half a loaf of bread. If the authorities thought this was the way to rehabilitate young men they were way off the mark. All it did was harden my spirit. At seventeen I had been a law-abiding, polite youth. Now I was a tough eighteen-year-old who could take anything they wanted to throw at me. And I was bitter that the law permitted, even condoned, this type of treatment simply because I had defended myself from being raped. Rules were rules and you couldn't break them regardless of the circumstances. That's the way the prison system was in 1960 and that is still the way it is today. Discretion and empathy are not in the dictionary of Corrective

Services as they now call themselves. The result is that the dehumanising process forces people to switch off and suppress their emotions. Some of them, when they are released back into the community, can't switch back on. Most sociopaths aren't born that way, they evolve through their environment and circumstances.

When I was released from the dungeon the punishment continued. I was confined to the front yards at Long Bay, which were identical to the ones in Bathurst. While I was there John F. Kennedy won the US election. I learnt about it months later. In the front yards, we received about as much information as a troglodyte would living in a cave in Siberia.

• • •

In January 1961, I was transferred to Goulburn Training Centre. At the time, it was a maximum security gaol for first-time offenders. But most murderers are first offenders. Murdering someone is often the only crime they will commit in their lives. They are usually model prisoners.

Goulburn was almost a twin gaol to Bathurst. But whereas Bathurst had flush toilets in the cells, Goulburn had the Long Bay style buckets for toilets.

When I arrived, I was given a job chopping and sawing wood on the wood heap. It wouldn't happen today where prisoners have to use plastic knives and forks in case they use a steel utensil to stab somebody with. But at Goulburn in 1961 I worked alongside murderers, rapists and thugs swinging axes while a couple of bored guards watched on, totally confident that no one would attack them. And no one did.

I was a good worker and after a few weeks I was given a job in the tailor shop making pyjamas on a sewing machine. My teacher was Dave Scanlon, nicknamed the 'Kingsgrove Slasher' because he had a proclivity for sneaking into houses at night and slashing the night dresses of women while they slept. He terrorised people in the Kingsgrove area for about eighteen months until he was caught. Apart from this flaw in his character, Dave was a lovely person who took it upon himself to be my mentor. He told me he would never slash another night dress and as far as I know after he was released he never climbed through another window.

While I was at Goulburn I met a lot of the murderers. One of them, John Leach, a grey-haired man of about fifty, worked in the tailor shop a few machines down from me. He was nicknamed 'Ratty Jack' due to the horrific nature of his crimes.

Dave told me the story: Leach raped and murdered two seven-year-old boys in a country town. While committing this horrific crime he mutilated the boys' genitals. He then hid their bodies in a cave. When they couldn't be found a search party was launched and Leach was one of the team. He went into the cave and ran out screaming: 'The rats have got them!'

He was sentenced to life imprisonment but in those days most lifers only served fourteen or fifteen years. There were, of course, exceptions for what were termed 'particularly heinous crimes'. You would think that Leach's crime would come under that category. The fact that he was able to walk around in the mainstream area of the gaol was significant of the times – particularly in a gaol for first offenders. Today Leach would be placed on strict protection from mainstream prisoners because if they could get to him he would die a horrible death.

Another high-profile murderer I met was a strange, tubby little guy named Kelly. He was nicknamed the 'Bega Bomber' due to blowing up a house with gelignite in 1957, killing a police officer, his wife and child. Apparently, he had been upset that the policeman issued fines for his tractor. Kelly's crime was classed as heinous and he served thirty years before being released. He died in 2007 aged eighty-nine.

Then there was Eric Thomas Turner. He was serving a life sentence for strangling his girlfriend before killing her father with an axe in 1948. He was the only prisoner prohibited from working on the wood heap. They released him in 1970 but he was back again in 1973 for killing his mother-in-law and his eleven-year-old stepson. He killed all four victims while he was heavily inebriated. He died in custody in 2008, setting the unenviable record of having spent fifty-seven of his last sixty years in prison.

The prisoner I despised the most at Goulburn was Stephen Leslie Bradley, a fat pig of a man who was disliked by everyone, not just for his crime but for his arrogant bullying manner. Bradley kidnapped eight-year-old Graeme Thorne shortly after his father had won the 100,000 pounds Opera House lottery. He rang Mr Thorne demanding 25,000 pounds for the safe return of his son. Thorne agreed to pay the ransom but he also called the police. Bradley didn't try to collect the money. Five weeks later the boy's body was found wrapped in a rug on a vacant lot in Seaforth. He had been strangled. Bradley fled the country but was arrested in Ceylon (now Sri Lanka) and extradited back to Australia.

In October 1968, aged forty-eight, he died of a heart attack after a game of tennis with the only person in the gaol he could beat – the governor. There were some who said he was poisoned.

• • •

Goulburn held four sporting carnivals a year, with prizes for the winners. At Easter, I was confident I could win the 440 consisting of one circuit around the inside perimeter of the gaol, which Dave estimated to be closer to 550 yards (about 500 metres). But there were about sixty runners lined up at the start. Most of them had run in these races before and I soon found myself shuffled back at the rear. This wasn't just an ordinary race among friends at the local picnic. I had thieves, murderers, rapists, conmen and one arsonist jostling for position early in the race. By the time I got a clear crack at the leaders, the bird had flown. An English conman won the race easily. I had bet two packets of tobacco on myself and was bitterly disappointed to have lost.

After that I trained in my cell every night, doing push-ups, sit-ups and running on the spot. At the Queen's Birthday event, I raced up near the lead and dashed past the Englishman on the final turn, racing away to win easily. After that I never lost a race while I was at Goulburn.

But I lost a fight. One night I must have made too much noise running up and down in my cell. The guy in the cell underneath was so upset he challenged me to a fight on the weekend. As luck would have it, he was Big Bruce, the best fighter in the gaol and a renowned bully. He was three years older than me and a lot bigger. Word got around the gaol about the coming fight and when asked I told everyone I was in with a chance. But I didn't believe it. I was scared.

At the time, a guard nicknamed Monkey Nuts (apart from his slight resemblance to the ape family I have no idea why people called him that) would allow prisoners to fight every Saturday morning while he supervised it. I think he got a kick out of seeing two baddies belting the hell out of each other.

The three of us went into the education area which was normally closed on weekends. Monkey Nuts locked the gate and said to us: 'It will be a fair fight. Any low punches and you will be charged with assault. If one of you gets knocked down, the other will step back and let him get back up.' My opponent was simply too big for me. He must have outweighed me by at least 20 kilograms. I put up a show and hurt him once, but he knocked me down five times. As I staggered to my feet, vision blurred, blood pouring from my nose and mouth, Monkey Nuts moved in and stopped the fight. I was done.

Later, Big Bruce boasted that he had knocked me down five times.

My good friend Dave, the Kingsgrove Slasher, said: 'Well, he must have kept getting back up again.'

I felt better then. If you go down, pick yourself up and try again. Win or lose, it is a good philosophy.

During my stay at Goulburn I was involved in two other fights, winning both. But my opponents weren't the calibre of Big Bruce. Still, after having received such a beating, the wins were good for my self-esteem.

In March 1962, I was released. Had I learnt anything? Was I rehabilitated? Well, I still thought it was okay to steal, just don't get caught. That was me, just turned twenty and headed for big trouble...

FIRST LOVE

1962–1963

For the first few weeks of my release I lived with Dad and David in a rented house in Canley Heights. For a while the three of us got along well. Dad wasn't drinking as much as he had in the past. He couldn't afford it. David, seventeen, had grown into a good-looking blond-haired youth.

He now had a girlfriend and spent a lot of time with her.

Although, in the past, I had been determined I would never work in a factory, my experience of working with murderers and thieves in the gaol tailor shop for seven shillings (70 cents) a week changed my attitude. I took a job working in a factory at Yennora for about 13 pounds (26 dollars) a week. But it was boring, tedious work and each day I had to force myself to go there.

For a while I began dating a young Russian girl named Irene. She was nice but her mother was very religious and didn't approve of me. The relationship ended the night I met Cathy Bishop. She was selling tickets for the Catholic Church at a bingo game. She had the biggest brown eyes and reminded me of a young Audrey Hepburn. It was love at first sight for me. She told me she was almost sixteen.

Her parents wouldn't let her date. I was so smitten with her that I began to meet her every day after school. It usually took us an hour to walk the less than two kilometres to her place. At this stage, I had resigned from my job and was selling raffle tickets during the day for a non-existent judo club. I bought a toy printing set and stamped each ticket to give them an authentic look. I went from door to door around various suburbs. I usually managed to sell two books of tickets a day, charging a shilling (10 cents) a ticket or three for two shillings. I was earning about 40 pounds a week tax-free – three times the amount I had been earning in the factory. But I didn't bank much. Some of it went on gambling but I spent most of it on clothes, shoes, movies, rent and eating in cafes and restaurants – something I had promised myself I'd do when I had been starving in solitary confinement. I had already moved out of Dad's place. We had started arguing again. Gaol had toughened me and when he became abusive I retorted in a similar manner. He didn't like it.

'No one talks to Reg Killick like that!' he said.

'I'm not no one,' I retorted. 'I'm your son, your adopted son. The little black bastard, remember?'

'Johnny, I want you out of here.'

I moved in with an old couple a few blocks away. They thought I was a nice young man. The old fellow, Bill, asked me what I did for a living. I told him I trudged the suburbs all day selling saucepans for the Mormon religion. You couldn't make something like that up. I actually did work for them trying to sell expensive saucepans door to door. After the first day, I resigned. People would slam the door in my face. But they didn't mind parting with a couple of shillings for some raffle tickets.

I rang Cathy every night and we would spend hours talking nonsense. Her father, Roland, an American, couldn't handle it. He relented and permitted me to come to their place most nights and see Cathy. He approved of the way I was always neatly dressed with spit-polished shoes – something I had learnt to do in gaol. Her mother, Mary, an Australian lady who was the same age as Roland, 39, was always nice to me. There were two sisters: Mildred, the youngest, was eleven and often teased Cathy about me. Patricia was eighteen. At first, we established a good rapport, but after a while she cooled towards me.

Five years previously these same three sisters, neatly dressed in their Catholic school uniforms including hats, would get on the bus that I usually took to go to school. Although I never took much notice of them, the bus always stopped near their place to pick them up. No way could I have foreseen that the little girl in the middle would become my first love.

In November 1962, I was arrested for illegally selling raffle tickets. They called it imposition. The magistrate declared me a rogue and a vagabond and sentenced me to six months. That night I found myself back in a cell at Long Bay with two other depressed prisoners.

A week later I was in Bathurst Gaol. Although normally serving a six month sentence I would have gone straight to a prison camp, my escape precluded that privilege. As the governor had delighted in telling me two years previously, I would spend all my gaol time in maximum security.

I was given a job of sweeping yards and cleaning locks. My wage was sixpence (5 cents) a week. They had to pay something so you couldn't be classed as a slave. I had to work two weeks to earn the price of one raffle ticket!

My main concern was Cathy. How would she handle my disappearance from her life? She would think I became bored with her and found another girl. Should I write to her? Her parents would probably get the letter first. 'Look, Roland, that nice young man who came here nearly every night to see our daughter is actually a rogue and a vagabond!'

Cathy would be humiliated. No, she would have to think I left her. I would straighten things out when I could go and see her.

With remissions for good behaviour I was released in early March 1963. I rented a room in Fairfield with a Russian family. They didn't speak much

English and as long as I paid the rent they weren't curious about my background or what I was doing.

When I rang Cathy, she told me she had given up on me. She was angry. Where had I been?

'I'll explain it all when I see you. I thought about you every day.'

'I find that hard to believe,' she said.

She agreed to meet me the next day. She had left school and was enrolled in a business college in the city. I waited for her at Wynyard station. When she saw me, she ran to me and we hugged. All was forgiven. She looked beautiful in a long white dress with high-heeled shoes.

During our traditional long walk home I told her I had been in gaol. She was shocked. 'Why would they put someone like you in gaol?'

About nine months previously during a talent quest at the Hotel Charles in Chatswood I had been involved in a fight and injured my opponent's eye, but it wasn't serious. (Thirty-seven years later *The Daily Telegraph* claimed in an article that I broke the guy's arm because he ridiculed my rendition of Roy Orbison's 'Crying'. Wrong, I sang Bachelor Boy and didn't touch his arm).

I couldn't admit to Cathy that I had been imprisoned for selling raffle tickets! So, I told her about the fight. 'His eye was damaged and they charged me with malicious injury.'

'That's terrible. It must have been horrible in gaol with all those criminals.'

'Well it got around that I was a good fighter so they left me alone.'

She gave me a look I could only regard as skeptical. 'You don't look like a fighter.'

I grinned. 'That's because I never get hit.'

'Still it was self-defence, they shouldn't have put you in gaol.'

'Well, it's done now.' I stopped and grabbed hold of her, pulling her close to me. 'I want you to think about whether you still want me to come around now you know I'm a hardened criminal.'

She held my gaze. 'Hardened criminal. I've watched television about prisons, and you aren't a criminal, let along hardened.' Those big brown eyes were so innocent. I hated deceiving her. 'I don't want to lose you, John. You don't know how much it hurt me when you stopped calling me and coming around.'

'I'm sorry, Cathy. I will never leave you again.'

And I meant it. I loved this girl. My problem was I had no job, no qualifications and a criminal record. Not a lot to offer a girl like her.

You would think that after being sent to gaol for selling raffle tickets I would try something new, but I didn't. I simply went to different areas to sell tickets for the non-existent judo club.

Things were becoming serious between Cathy and I. Her parents had accepted me back into their home without question. The entire family made me feel welcome. I hadn't experienced that feeling in a long time. My bitterness began to dissipate.

But I was a fake. The great pretender. Their daughter was involved with – despite what she believed – a hardened criminal who counted among his good friends the Kingsgrove Slasher. I sold raffle tickets for a living and didn't bother giving anyone a prize. I had put the barrel of a replica pistol in the mouth of a homosexual and robbed him. I had escaped from police and been shot at. I was not the type of guy you would want marrying your daughter.

I resolved to turn it around. I would go back to what I used to be – a decent human being. It wasn't too late, I was only twenty-one.

I began working in a factory in Enfield. My job consisted of carrying ladles of molten metal from a vat and pouring it into casts. It was hot, tough work. It also meant a drop in wages of sixty per cent. Selling raffle tickets was easier and more profitable but it felt good to be earning an honest living.

When I told Dad, he said: 'We are working people, Johnny. If we have to cart shit, we do it. You've found a good job, keep it.'

But it wasn't meant to be. In May, Roland dropped a bombshell when he announced that the family would be returning to America to live in Illinois.

Cathy was excited. 'I was born in the US,' she said. 'But I was too little to remember it.' She looked at me, the big eyes expectant. 'You'll come too, won't you, John?'

I was shattered. I knew that US had a 'no criminals allowed in' policy. And regardless of how others might regard me, my criminal record would preclude me from entering the United States.

'I guess I'll have to start saving for my fare,' I said. 'Then it's settled. John will come with us, everybody.'

Roland laughed. 'Give him a chance. You have bullied him into making a decision before he thinks it through. It's not a decision to make lightly.' He turned to me. 'There's plenty of time, John, we won't be leaving until November. You think about it for a while.'

Still in a state of shock, I nodded. 'Okay, Roland. But wherever Cathy goes, I won't be far behind.'

'She might find another boyfriend,' Mildred said, grinning. 'I will not,' Cathy said.

I went home depressed. The decision by Roland to take his family to America was to have such far reaching consequences that the ripple effect is still in play – fifty-four years later.

My motto is never give up. Sometimes the long shot gets in, the one everyone thought had no chance. I hired a solicitor to try to find a way for me to enter the

US. He came up with a huge negative. There was no way I would be permitted to legally gain entry.

Right. Legal is out, that leaves illegal. Already I was thinking illogically. Cathy's parents wouldn't agree to me going there illegally. So, I wouldn't tell them. Neither would I tell Cathy. I would get a false passport and travel a few weeks after them. What would I do when I arrived? I wouldn't be able to work. I suppose I could sell raffle tickets for the Chicago Judo Club...

Naturally I gave up my job. Back to the raffle tickets. But that wouldn't pay for a false passport, visa and ticket to America. I once read that wisdom is the ability to choose alternatives. I had a contingency plan. A guy I had met in Bathurst, Don, was getting out soon. He was interested in committing a robbery with me. Although originally, I had been keen to go ahead with it, I changed my mind when I began working in the factory. Now, robbery was back on the table.

We chose a jewellery store in Burwood. Because I was a fast runner I would go into the store, ask to see a few pads of expensive diamond rings and run off with them to where Don would be waiting in a stolen car. He had a fence (someone who buys stolen goods) prepared to pay us a third of the face value. We figured on receiving 1000 pounds each (2000 dollars). That would get me to America.

In early June, I talked Cathy into taking the day off college and spending it at her place. It was the day Pope John XXIII died, but although she was a Catholic she didn't pretend to be upset about the death of an old man on the other side of the world.

This was the day she told me she loved me and that if she lost me she didn't know what she would do. I told her truthfully that I loved her and that I wouldn't be able to cope if we parted.

She gripped my hand. 'We will go to America together, John. We'll never part.'

Oh boy. What I fake I was. Soon I would be risking everything. But what choice did I have? No way was I prepared to let her sail off to America and out of my life because they wouldn't let me into the country. What terrible crimes had I committed? Sold a few raffle tickets...broke into a store...forged a deviate's signature...I wasn't a murderer or a rapist.

I was angry, frustrated. Of all the girls I had to fall in love with, I pick this one.

The robbery didn't quite go the way we planned. Wearing sunglasses as a disguise, I told the female assistant that I was getting engaged and could I have a look at the two most expensive trays of diamond rings in the window? But she would only hand me one at a time, so I thanked her, dropped the tray into my bag and ran out to where Don was waiting in the car. He drove me to the rear of the railway station then, leaving the car there, he jumped onto his motorcycle and rode off with the rings. I caught a train.

When I met him the next morning he handed me 300 pounds. 'You said we get a third,' I said. 'That's 500 each for one tray.'

'Mate, the fence wasn't happy. He had arranged to sell two trays, I bring him one. We were lucky to get 300 each.'

'Fuck him! A deal's a deal. We take our business elsewhere. I need at least another 700. We'll have to do another one.'

'No problems. But wait a week or two until the heat dies down.'

Two days later I was arrested. Don had held out on me and kept three of the rings. You just can't trust crooks. When he was arrested during a fight in a hotel (a common occurrence in those days) he had the rings on him. He told the cops I was the culprit. So, they showed the girl from the jewellery store my photo and she identified me. Case solved. Don was free to go. They took most of my 300 pounds and put me in gaol. The money was never mentioned in court.

It was the end of my American dream. I wrote to Cathy and told her the truth. I didn't expect to hear from her again but she replied with a long, sad letter.

'The darkest hours are before the dawn,' she concluded.

Her parents also included a letter offering encouragement. Even Mildred offered to 'keep an eye on Cathy until you get out.'

A nice family. One I would have loved to have been a part of. But I had blown it and I knew it.

When Cathy wrote again, she wanted to visit me. Although I desperately wanted to see her, pride dictated my decision. I didn't want her last memory of me to be one where I was dressed in ill-fitting prison garments with us looking at each other through a metal grille while a guard listened to everything we had to say during the allocated twenty minutes. All mail was censored and I wasn't permitted to tell her these things. She saw my refusal as unreasonable and wrote again imploring me to reconsider. She reminded me that her departure date was drawing nearer, she needed to see me.

Again I refused, stating emphatically that under no circumstances would I accept a visit from her while I was in gaol.

She didn't write again.

I was sentenced to three years. With remissions for good behaviour I could be out in twenty-seven months. To me it might as well have been a lifetime. Soon Cathy would be 10,000 miles away. In twenty-seven months, I would be a distant memory.

• • •

While I was at Long Bay waiting to be transferred to Bathurst, I met the eighteen-year-old Arthur 'Neddy' Smith. Tall, blond and solidly built, he was a good style of a youth. But he had an arrogant, aggressive manner and was already on the way to becoming a standover man.

I got along okay with him and he described to me how he had been starved, beaten and brutalised in the Tamworth Boys' Home, a secondary punishment institution for juveniles. Boys were sent there for escaping or offences committed while at the Mount Penang Boys' Home.

'They starved me so often that I lost over three stone,' he told me.

This wasn't the first time, nor would it be the last, that a prisoner told me about the atrocities he had suffered in this hell hole. All of them went on to become serious violent criminals: Neddy Smith is now serving a life sentence for two murders; William Munday became a convicted murderer whose favourite pastime was abducting couples in cars, bashing the males and raping the females; Archibald McCafferty murdered three people and, while he was in gaol, he was convicted of the manslaughter of another prisoner; Peter Schneidas came to gaol for fraud and murdered a prison officer with a hammer; James Finch killed fifteen people during the firebombing of the Whiskey Au Go Go nightclub in Queensland; Kevin Crump, an evil double murderer, was also a victim of the Tamworth regime. George Freeman, the organised crime boss, was another who was brutalised at Tamworth in the name of the law.

In 1989 after a spate of suicides, this heinous institution, which by then was renamed Endeavour House, was closed down. The systematic brutalisation, undoubtedly unofficially condoned by the higher authorities, almost certainly contributed to these criminals and many others who went to Tamworth, violently unleashing their pent-up anger and frustration on mostly innocent people.

• • •

I was at Bathurst on the 22 November 1963, the day John F. Kennedy was assassinated in Dallas, Texas. In the gaol prisoners and guards were relaying the tragic news: 'Kennedy's been killed!'

I knew Cathy's ship had sailed from Sydney on 5 November. Had she arrived, or was she still in transit? I later learnt that they had arrived on the day of the assassination. An inauspicious time to be returning to the land of the free.

AN UN-REHABILITATED MAN

1963–1965

For me, 1964 dragged. I was angry and bitter. My communication with the outside world was almost nil. Prisoners were unable to make phone calls, I didn't receive visits and apart from an occasional letter from David or a note from Dad, I received no mail. Cathy had obviously given up on me. I had no idea where she was and hoped she would relent and send me a letter. When the guards handed out the mail and there was nothing from her, I was often depressed and in an aggressive mood. I was involved in numerous fights and the governor told me I was an incorrigible recidivist and banished me to working in the yards for sixpence a week until my release. This was the equivalent of $2.60 per annum.

We didn't get the newspapers and had no access to television. We received news from bulletins on the local radio station 2BS. Even in Bathurst The Beatles had replaced Elvis as number one on the hit parade. In fact, we were besieged by songs from the British bands: The Rolling Stones, Gerry and the Pacemakers, The Hollies, Herman's Hermits, The Animals, The Who and many others.

I remember hearing on the radio that over 300 people were killed during a riot at a soccer game in Chile when the referee disallowed a goal by Chile against Argentina with two minutes to go. Sheer madness. It was also the year that Nelson Mandela received a life sentence in South Africa for sabotage against the government.

One night my cellmate, Ray, hit the other cellmate on the head with a tin of jam while he was sleeping. It just missed the guy's temple. It wasn't as though the guy, who was from Broken Hill, didn't deserve it. He had been running to the guards complaining about us. A whack in the nose would have, in my opinion, been suffice retribution. To smash the guy on the forehead with a full tin of jam while he was sleeping was definitely an overreaction.

Fortunately, he survived. He had a little cry while we bandaged his head, then we all went to bed – me with one eye open.

The next morning, he ran to the guard's office complaining we had tried to kill him. One guard even suspected we had tried to rape him.

Fortunately for us at the time all the violence occurring in the system was hushed up by the authorities. People in the community had no idea about the rapes, bashings and standovers prevalent throughout the system. And most of them didn't care. So, the incident was recorded as minor and the guy was returned to Broken Hill. The three of us were lucky. If Ray had have killed him I undoubtedly would have gone down as an accessory and given a possible life sentence.

• • •

I was released in early September 1965. The world had changed. South Vietnam was losing the fight against Communist insurgents and North Vietnam. In an effort to turn the tide, the United States had started bombing the North. Australia, which already had troops in Vietnam in an advisory role since 1962, sent a battalion in support of the US and allies. Australia had also introduced conscription by ballot. Young men whose birthdates coincided with the numbers drawn were sent off to fight in a war they knew nothing about.

Dad was now living in a housing commission flat in Waterloo. David was sharing a house in Belmore with a friend. When I called in to see Dad I brought two bottles of beer. He was delighted.

'Gaol has made a man of you, Johnny,' he said. 'Real men drink beer, not bloody milkshakes.'

It was good to see him again and talk about the good old days. But it was like walking a minefield – so many subjects to be avoided.

We agreed that we couldn't live together. I soon rented a room in Croydon with an old couple and their two attractive teenage daughters.

But Cathy was still the only girl I was interested in. My first priority was to find her. I trudged around Fairfield knocking on doors asking people if they knew the Bishop family. Eventually I hit the jackpot – I met a lady who not only knew them, she was writing to the mother.

Without a lot of confidence, I wrote a long letter to Cathy. Ten days later I received an even lengthier reply. The John and Cathy saga was back in play. I was still her favourite guy but there were others in the running. Millie wrote to me and said a rich guy who owned a Porsche was crazy about Cathy.

At this stage, I had started working for Franklins at Bankstown. My move. Déjà vu! If I don't get to America soon I lose – again. How the hell do you compete against a rich guy who is already there when you have nothing and can't get there? It was no contest. Rich guy wins.

No way was I going to give up now. Cathy encouraged me in her letters – I was the one for her. I rang her every week, a ten-minute phone call cost a quarter of my wages. It would take years of scrimping and saving to finance a move to the US. Anyway, they would never let me in.

She didn't understand. She always knew I would find her again. There was an unbreakable bond between us. I went into a depressed state. Resigning from my job, I bought an old car and began doing break-ins. I stole 500 pounds worth of coins from a coin dealer and sold them to another dealer for half price. He didn't even ask for ID.

I began to gamble heavily on the horses. When a gambler has to win, he rarely does. I caught a train to Victoria and went to the Melbourne Cup where I watched the champion little mare, Light Fingers, beat Ziema in a photo finish. Both gallopers were trained by Bart Cummings. It was the first of his incredible twelve Melbourne Cup wins. I backed Craftsman: he finished tenth. Overall on the day I lost 200 pounds.

Nearly broke, I held up a railway station with a toy pistol. But the day's takings had been collected. I escaped with 20 pounds.

Cathy and America seemed a million miles away.

When I returned to Sydney it was only a matter of time before the inevitable happened. On New Year's Eve, I was arrested at my residence in Croydon. A search of my room gave police enough evidence to charge me with a number of break and enters. As I was led away in handcuffs the law-abiding family who had chosen me from a dozen applicants who had wanted to rent the room, stared at me in shocked silence.

They had chosen me because they trusted me with their daughters. And rightly so.

I spent a night in a cell with a couple of drunks who were complaining loudly about being locked up on New Year's Eve. It was times like this when I wished I had a tin of jam.

At about ten in the morning Harry, the old guy from whom I rented the room, came and bailed me out. It was conditional bail, I had to report to police every night at 8pm.

I hadn't even thought about bail. I had been focusing on making a run from the courthouse – Bathurst style.

As we walked from the police station, Harry said: 'Me, Mum and the girls think you have a lot of potential, John. I put my property at Woy Woy up as security. If you run off on us I will lose faith in human nature.'

'Whatever happens, Harry, I promise you won't lose your property.'

I knew what I had to do. I still had a shot at getting to America and Cathy but the odds were lengthening. Petty crime was out, I would graduate to robbing banks. Get enough money to repay Harry the bail money (400 pounds), buy a false passport and a ticket to Chicago. I figured robbing a bank wouldn't be too difficult. The tellers had guns but I could handle that. In 1966 there weren't many bank robbers on the loose in Australia. Kevin Simmonds and Darcy Dugan were infamous bank robbers and escapees – they were both serving life sentences. But Ryan and Walker, who had escaped on 19 December from

Pentridge Prison in Victoria, were still on the run after robbing a bank a few days later. During the escape, a prison guard had been shot and killed. The intensive manhunt that ensued even surpassed the hunt in 1959 for Simmonds and Newcombe.

On Christmas Eve, Walker and Ryan were at a small party when a truck driver named Henderson recognised Ryan. He had made the fatal mistake of not recognising Walker. When he told Walker that they could share a reward that was on offer for Ryan's capture, Walker played along with it until he got him in a public toilet where he shot and killed him.

Four days after I was bailed, Ryan and Walker were arrested in Concord Sydney after Walker had arranged a double date with a nurse and her friend. He had previously met the nurse in Sydney a few years before he moved to Victoria where he was arrested for bank robbery. Because she had known him under an assumed name he thought she wouldn't know who he was. But she recognised him from photos in the media and notified the police that one of Australia's two most wanted men was going to meet her and he was bringing a friend. The police had a good idea as to who the other guy might be. They had fifty specially trained police waiting for the escapees.

Thirteen months later Ryan was hanged. He became the last man to be executed in Australia. Walker was sentenced to thirty-six years and was released after serving nineteen.

An interesting sidelight to the Ryan and Walker story: during the largest, most intensive manhunt in Australia, another infamous escapee slipped into Australia on New Year's Eve under an assumed name. The next day, always the cheeky one, he went to the races at Randwick. His luck was in and he backed a couple of winners. His name was Ronald Biggs, one of Britain's Great Train Robbers. He would remain a fugitive for thirty-six years.

I didn't tell Cathy about my arrest. She thought everything was hunky dory. We were writing love letters, I was ringing her every week and telling her how good it would be when we were together. I even sent her three three-hour tapes where I sang songs and spoke nonstop for nine hours. No one could say I wasn't serious about her.

I was also serious about robbing a bank. I chose the Commonwealth in Canley Heights. I knew that a good getaway would be the key to success and I knew the area well. I bought a single shot .22 rifle from a gun shop. I wasn't asked for ID. Then I bought a couple of clown masks. Last but not least, I recruited a young guy, Jerry, who had spent a bit of time in gaol. We stole an FJ Holden at Strathfield and drove to Canley Heights.

My plan was to rob the bank, then run down a passageway out to a street that led to a school. Being late January, the schools were still closed. The car would be waiting on the other side of the school. We would soon see if anyone tried to follow.

Jerry's role was to jump the counter and collect the money from the tellers' drawers. Wearing gloves, I pulled the mask over my face as we entered the bank. Inside there were six or seven customers.

'This is a hold up!' I yelled. 'Hands in the air everyone.'

No one argued, all hands were raised. Jerry jumped the counter and began collecting the cash. I ordered the manager to open the vault but he said he only had half the combination and the other guy had gone for lunch. At that moment, I saw one of the tellers reaching under the counter. I didn't want to shoot him so I fired a shot into the floor. In the tense situation the shot, to my ears, sounded like a cannon going off.

The teller jumped back and put his hands in the air. I quickly pretended to reload the rifle, then pointed the empty weapon at the manager. 'Hand me your gun! Hold it by the barrel.'

I glanced around. No one had moved. 'Just keep calm everyone and no one will get hurt.'

The manager handed me the pistol. It had Commonwealth Bank engraved on the side. I dropped the useless rifle on the floor. Jerry jumped back over the counter with the bag of money.

'If anyone tries to follow us they'll get shot,' I said.

We ran outside and through the school to the car without incident. After driving a few miles, I stopped and quickly divided the money. Leaving Jerry with the car I walked away. I never saw him again.

After catching a taxi to Cabramatta railway station, I walked to the taxi rank and hired another taxi to take me to Croydon station. From there I walked home.

I went to my room and counted the money. A bit over 600 pounds. I packed a suitcase, then walked into the lounge room where Harry's wife was watching television.

I handed her 500 pounds. 'This will cover the bail money with a bit extra for expenses.'

She was shocked. 'John, what have you done?' I grinned. 'The right thing.'

As I walked to the railway station I felt as though a weight had been lifted from my shoulders. I could go to America without Harry losing his faith in human nature. I had robbed a bank and had a little over 100 pounds to show for it. But I now had a loaded pistol and I had discovered how easy it was to rob a bank.

No way could they stop me from getting to Chicago now.

I felt invincible...

AUSTRALIA'S FIRST DECIMAL CURRENCY BANK ROBBER

1966

A few hours after the robbery I booked into a small rooming house in Meadowbank. There were only four other lodgers. The lady in charge, Helen, didn't ask for ID or references. All she wanted was two weeks in advance.

That night, thinking it would be too risky, I didn't report on bail.

The next morning, I rang Harry's wife. She told me a team of detectives had been there looking for me – and it had nothing to do with my bail conditions.

'And I think they have tapped the phone.'

I wondered how they had come up with me as a suspect so quickly.

Maybe Jerry had been caught and had told them about me.

I soon learned that in this instance the law and order machine had quickly moved into full flight. A few days after the robbery, when I tried to ring Cathy, her mother answered the phone. She calmly told me that the Chicago police had been to see them and Interpol was on the lookout for me.

'If you ring again I'll contact the police immediately,' she said.

Well, I could forget about Cathy. I had done all I could to get to her but from the start the odds had been stacked against us. My heart went out to her, she would be totally disillusioned. But now for me it was all about survival. If Interpol was looking for me, I would be high on the list of *Australia's Most Wanted.*

I kept a low profile, remaining in my room most of the day reading. At night, I'd go to a small cafe for dinner and sometimes take in a movie at a suburban cinema. Helen, who was curious about my lifestyle, often brought me cups of tea and sandwiches. Eventually we became lovers.

Low on cash, I decided to rob another bank. This time I chose the ANZ in Cabramatta – only a few miles from the Canley Heights bank. It was 14th February 1966 – Valentine's Day and the day after my twenty-fourth birthday. I figured the banks would hold a lot of money because it was C Day – the day Australia changed from pounds, shillings and pence to decimal currency. Stealing a car from Parramatta, I parked across the street from the bank. This time, wearing only sunglasses as a disguise, I strode inside and yelled that this was a hold-up. The inside area was much larger than that in the Canley Heights bank and there were more people inside. Plus, it was on the main street and a lot of people were walking past.

I had to hurry. I couldn't get to the vault without someone watching my back. Again, I would have to settle for what was in the tellers' drawers.

One of the tellers told me there wasn't much money left – customers had cleaned them out, taking most of the new currency.

I exited the bank with $2600 – some of it in the old pounds shillings and pence. I ran across the road and got into the car. As I sped off I noticed a car following me. I didn't know it then, but it was the bank manager and a customer.

He forced me to speed, risking drawing attention to myself from the cops. But luck was on my side and I soon eluded my pursuers. I dumped the vehicle in a no through street. From there I ran across a paddock to Warwick Farm railway station. Soon I was on a train and out of danger. The media made a fuss about it being Australia's first C Day hold up.

The affair with Helen was becoming a problem. She was becoming inquisitive about my secluded lifestyle. I couldn't tell her that I was on the run. I became concerned she may discuss the situation with friends who might call the police.

I would have to leave – go interstate to Melbourne. First, I had to take a risk and visit Dad. It could be the last time I'd see him. I figured it would be too expensive for police to put 24-hour surveillance on his place in the unlikely event I would call on him.

I circled his block of flats three times. There was no sign of someone in a parked vehicle.

When I entered his flat he visibly paled. 'Johnny, the bulls have been watching the place – if they find you here they'll kill you.'

I thought that unlikely, but I didn't stay long. I gave him 500. He didn't want to take it but I told him I had plenty.

It was a pathetic scene: giving my father $500 of stolen money while he urged me to leave before the cops burst in and shot me.

As I left I wondered how on earth my life had reached this point of no return.

A few days later, on a Saturday, I held up an SP bookie and his minder in a carpark in West Ryde. The minder was in two minds as to whether to jump me or not, but when a .32 automatic is pointed at you by a man wearing a clown's mask, discretion usually prevails. After all, the money was only proceeds from the losses of the mug punters, me being one of them. They would lose more next week.

When I told Helen I was leaving, she was upset. I had a habit of hurting the people who cared about me. It wasn't by intention but that doesn't help them.

In late February, I caught a train to Melbourne. By now I was in a depressed state. With the cops and Interpol after me, it was impossible to make plans for the future. I was 24, physically at my peak but psychologically I was a mess. I began gambling heavily and most of the time I lost. I dated quite a few girls and it didn't bother me if they liked me or not as I had no intention of continuing the relationships.

One of the girls, a shapely blond Polish girl named Marie, scratched my face when I made advances towards her. But we hit it off and I began dating her regularly. For a while I hit a lucky streak on the horses. I was also frequenting a baccarat game in the city where I used my old system of doubling up. I had a bank of $2000 and would have to lose ten consecutive bets to lose. As always, I was prepared to go all or nothing.

Although I wore gold-rimmed glasses with plain glass to change my appearance, I was becoming too conspicuous at the baccarat game and decided to change the venues. I began playing two-up at Brewster's in Prahran. He was an old gangster who, I had been told, had offered to hide Ryan and Walker when they were on the run.

I wouldn't have stepped within five miles of the place if I'd have known that Sparrow, one of the three amigos with whom I had robbed the Western Stores in 1960, was a regular player. I had decided I would never trust him again after he had hidden some of our loot in his socks. It was also probable that he had told the police where to find Taffy.

Despite my glasses and the six years that had passed, he recognised me immediately. Within an hour he asked me for 20 dollars.

I knew he was cunning enough to guess I was probably on the run. I didn't mind giving him money if it meant he would keep his mouth shut. It became a regular occurrence – I would give him money when I won. And I always won, because if I didn't it was equal to losing my entire bank.

Eventually I hit a losing streak on the horses. I would have to rob another bank.

While I was deciding on which bank, Sparrow told me he was in trouble. The cops had caught him with housebreaking implements. He had to come up with 200 dollars for the cops and they would drop the charges; otherwise he was facing six months in gaol.

Even if I had the money I would not have given it to him. But I made him an offer:

'Sparrow, I'm going to pull a job and I need a driver. You'll get a third.'

'Will I get at least 200?' he asked.

I grinned. 'I reckon a bank would cover that.'

He paled. 'A bank?'

'Yeah. You know those places that hold a lot of money.'

'I'm in. I'm sick of being pinched on shit blues.'

And so, it was John Killick the fool teamed up again with his old amigo Sparrow the pickpocket, who was prepared to step up to rob a bank.

Of course, it didn't work out that way. I was taking expensive private dancing lessons at the Fred Astaire Dancing Studio in town. Girls love a guy who can tango.

The night before the planned robbery I made arrangements to meet Sparrow outside the studio after my lesson. At this stage, I hadn't told him which bank was our target. I intended to drive him to the area that night and go over the getaway route.

When he didn't come I decided to do the job alone. I had chosen the Commonwealth at Kensington.

The next morning, after stealing an FJ Holden a few miles from Kensington, I drove to where the bank was situated and parked in a nearby side street. Again, wearing only sunglasses as a disguise, I entered the bank and pointed the pistol at a young male teller and ordered him to fill up an overnight bag I handed him. The only other person in the bank was a guy in his thirties who I later learned was the manager. When I ordered him to rip the phone from the wall he merely loosened it.

I pointed the pistol at him. 'Rip it out!'

Glaring at me he tore it from the wall. He wasn't frightened – he was angry.

The young teller handed me the bag. 'That's all there is, sir.'

'Try to do better next time,' I said and ran out the door and across to where the car was parked. As I opened the door I glanced around. The two bank employees, armed with pistols, were only about 20 metres away. The older one fired a shot which hit the rear of the vehicle.

Kneeling behind the door I pointed my pistol in their direction. Both of them took cover behind some parked vehicles. Scrambling into the car I was prevented from driving away by a truck which cut in front of me. Swerving along the footpath I gunned it and managed to get past it. But the truck driver didn't give up – he followed me.

I had timed it to drive to the end of the no through street, then run across a grass field to the railway station in time to catch a train. I had given it a trial run and allowed 30 seconds extra time. Usually during a bank robbery, I keep my cool. But this time emotion and anger took control. A bloody bank teller had tried to shoot me! Now a truck driver, who had seen one guy try to shoot another, was chasing the guy who had been shot at. Why? Did he know I was the bad guy? What the hell was he going to do if he caught me?

At the end of the no through street I came to an abrupt halt, jumped out of the car and ran back to the truck which had stopped a few car lengths behind me. The driver wound up his window. Maybe he thought it was bulletproof.

I tapped on the window. 'Well, you've got me – what are you going to do with me?'

He sat there staring at me, fear in his eyes.

My anger dissipated – he was just a fool who had overplayed his hand. At the top of the street about 200 metres away I could see the two bank employees running towards us. They had something the driver didn't – loaded pistols.

Time to catch my train!

Waving goodbye to my truck driver buddy, I ran as fast as I could across the field. Unlike Sydney, the train was on time. But I hadn't counted on the pedantic railway guard who unwittingly assisted law and order. Although he saw me running towards the platform he closed the barrier when I was about 10 metres away.

'Quick, open the gate!' I said. 'I have to catch this train.'

He gave me a serious look. 'Too late, fella.'

No passengers had alighted. With an air of authority, he blew his whistle. My ride to safety left without me.

Smiling at me he re-opened the barricade, then returned to his office and closed the door.

I jumped onto the railway track and, putting the handle of the overnight bag around my neck, heaved myself up a 3-metre-high wire fence. Scrambling to the ground I took a quick look around. I was inside the car park of what was obviously a factory. I could see two guys sitting in the front seat of a car eating sandwiches.

I opened the rear door and got in. They turned to look at me.

I showed them the pistol. 'Hi guys. I've struck a bit of trouble and I need you to drive me into town.'

The older guy in the driver's seat who looked to be about forty kept his cool. 'I'll do that for you.'

Without any further conversation, he drove out of the exit and headed towards the city.

Police cars with sirens blaring rushed past us. The other passenger who looked to be in his early thirties commented: 'They are after someone.'

'Must be serious,' I said.

We began talking about Aussie Rules. Melbournians were crazy about the game. Both of them were Collingwood supporters.

On the outskirts of the city I told the driver to stop. I gave him forty dollars. 'This is for the petrol.'

He looked surprised. 'It wouldn't come to that.'

'Danger money,' I said.

I gave the other guy forty dollars. 'Put this on the Magpies to win the flag. If they win remember me.'

'I wouldn't forget you, mate. I'll whack it on the Maggies, for sure.'

Neither of them reported the incident to the police. Collingwood made the Grand Final but lost by a point to St Kilda.

I had stolen $3400. It was the lead story on the six o'clock news. The truck driver was being hailed as a hero. In his interview, he said: 'I chased him in my truck. But he jumped out of the car and ran across the paddock and caught a train.'

Sparrow would know it was me who had robbed the bank. He didn't know where I lived but instinct warned me to get out of Melbourne. Maybe go to Western Australia.

I had paid for one more dancing lesson. I decided to learn a few more moves with the tango, then head west.

But a little bird had told the cops they might find me at Fred Astaire's. They set a trap, I walked into it and was quickly handcuffed and waltzed off to a waiting vehicle.

I was taken to an office at Russell Street Police Headquarters where a group of detectives stood around, delighted with the catch of the day.

I knew they had me on the Kensington bank. The tellers and the truck driver would identify me. Plus, they soon found the pistol in my car. It would be used to link me to the Canley Heights robbery. But I would worry about that later.

They questioned me until midnight about other Melbourne robberies but I knew nothing about them and eventually they gave up.

'The police in New South Wales will eventually be down to see you about a couple of banks up there,' the detective in charge said.

'They'll be wasting their time,' I said. We both knew that I would probably be in gaol in Victoria for at least five years. Then I'd have to face the music in Sydney.

I was taken across the road and placed in an unoccupied cell. But a few hours later they brought in a young, dark-haired guy. He was crying. 'Keep an eye on him, he's suicidal,' one of the cops said before locking the door.

'I'm not suicidal,' he said. 'I got drunk and they said I strangled an old lady. I can't remember anything.'

His name was David. He was a good-looking lad who I later learnt was only eighteen. He told me he was worried his wife might leave him. She was nineteen.

I didn't tell him there were no 'mights' about it.

Although, even years later, he insisted he didn't know if he did it or not, the jury told him he did murder the old lady and the judge sentenced him to forty years with a non-parole period of thirty years. Within a few months of his arrest his wife filed for divorce. He turned gay and proved quite popular with some of the older guys who fancied younger men.

I was remanded in custody on the bank robbery and was taken back to the City Watch House which was situated next to the Old Melbourne Gaol – where Ned Kelly and 134 other unfortunates were hanged.

I had come to the conclusion that Sparrow was the one responsible for my arrest. Although I only learnt about it years later, Karma caught up to Sparrow in the late eighties. He was taken to a secluded area in bushland where he was bashed and had both legs broken. His assailants then left him there. It took him hours to drag himself to the roadside where a motorist found him and drove him to hospital. He spent months in traction and told people that the pain was unbearable.

WELCOME TO PENTRIDGE AND H DIVISION

1966

When it was time for me to be taken to Pentridge, they didn't take me in the big prison van with the other prisoners. I was handcuffed to a red-haired guy who was about my age and we were placed in the back of a small police van. I noticed a police car following us.

Redhead didn't want to talk which was fine by me.

At Pentridge we were escorted to a large reception area. After our handcuffs had been removed I was asked my name.

'John Killick.'

'You come with us, Killick.'

As I was led away, three prisoners who had been standing nearby rushed in and began to bash Redhead. He started screaming. I saw him fall to the ground and they began kicking him.

'Keep walking, Killick,' one of the guards said. 'You saw or heard nothing.' The guy on the receiving end of the bashing was Keith Ryrie. He had raped and murdered two little girls. After being bashed by the prisoners he was taken to the notorious H Division, ostensibly for his own protection, but where instead, I had no doubts, he would be regularly flogged by the sadistic guards who worked there.

I was put in a one out cell in D Division on the second tier close to the crosswalk that also served as a gallows. There was a trap in the catwalk and, above it, a beam from which the hangman could suspend his noose. There was little doubt in the minds of most that Ronald Ryan would be the next man to be dropped through the trap with a noose around his neck.

On the Sunday, Marie visited me. She told me that she couldn't believe she had been dating a real bank robber. I signed over my record player and record collection to her. The cops had taken my money and my car all of which, they told me, would be given to the bank.

Even though the visit with Marie was non-contact, it was good to see her. I recalled when, three years earlier I had, out of pride, refused to accept a visit from Cathy before she sailed to the US. I regretted that now. She was still in my blood. Marie never would be.

I wasn't in her blood either. After about a month the visits stopped.

I hoped she thought of me when she played my Elvis records.

The days in the yards were miserable. It was autumn and there was very little shelter. There was only one open shower for about thirty of us.

'You would think they'd put a cubicle around the shower,' I said to one of the prisoners.

'They won't do it' he said. 'They reckon we will have sex orgies.'

I was scheduled for sentencing in June at Hawthorn Court. I wasn't concerned about whatever sentence the judge might impose. I intended to escape. All I needed were the handcuffs off and a split-second start and no one could catch me. Maybe they would try to shoot me, but I had been shot at twice before and believed it was in my destiny to never be shot. No, with a bit of luck I'd soon be free again.

The day of the sentencing I knew I had the element of surprise in my favour. It's a powerful ally.

My two escorting guards held onto me as they brought me handcuffed from the cells to a small waiting area outside the courtroom. As per procedure they uncuffed me at the courtroom door then, with one either side, ushered me into the courtroom.

After a bit of a lecture, the judge sentenced me to seven years with a non-parole period of five years. It was a fair, appropriate penalty.

I intended it to be the shortest served seven year sentence in history. As we stepped outside the courtroom, my two guards held onto me.

One of them, who was about forty and a little overweight, released his grip and held out the handcuffs. 'It was a light sentence,' he said. 'You should have thanked the judge.'

He had probably done this hundreds of times before. He was in charge, and when he brought out the handcuffs, the remorseful prisoner would hold out his hands and allow himself to be manacled.

Instead, I hit him as hard as I could in the solar plexus and he staggered backwards, shock and pain and maybe a little fear registering on his face.

The other guard, younger and more athletic than his partner, grabbed me in a bear hug and began shouting for help.

Desperation gives you strength. I broke from his grip and flung him sideways. The exit door was only metres away. If I could get out the door and onto the lawn, the main street wasn't far away. How could they catch the 1961 Goulburn Gaol 440 champion? Although I managed to open the door, the young guard came rushing towards me demanding I stop!

I leapt to the bottom of the steps but he crash-tackled me from behind and we rolled around in the grass. He was clinging to me and screaming for help.

I punched him a few times and jumped to my feet just in time to be hit with a barrage of punches from a team of angry cops who had arrived in time to catch the baddy.

Oh well. I went close. They half dragged me back to the cell and gave me a bit of a flogging. I expected it, but a few of the kicks hurt. I knew it was nothing to what was coming when I returned to Pentridge. I had guaranteed myself a direct trip to the dreaded H Division.

Within an hour I was on the way back to Pentridge. On arrival, still handcuffed, I was immediately escorted to the entrance of H Division. On the way, I tried to psyche myself for the beating I knew was coming.

The earlier beating by the cops had left me with a few aches and pains. A guard inside, a giant of a man, opened the grille gate. Two others stood beside him. One, the senior, was small and thin with a pinched in face. He reminded me of a monkey. The other guard was near as big as the giant who had opened the gate. I was ordered inside. After removing the handcuffs, the two escorting guards went away.

I was immediately hit across the back of the head by one of the guards with a baton. The pain was excruciating and I fell to the floor.

'Get up!' the senior screamed.

Staggering to my feet I clutched the back of my head.

'Stand to attention, hands by your sides!' he yelled. A detached part of my mind noticed the spittle around the corners of his mouth. His eyes were wide with excitement. I concluded he was quite mad.

He pushed his face centimetres from mine. 'You are here because no one wants you. We own you. Whether you survive or not depends solely on us.'

One of the guards whacked my left arm with his baton. 'Answer the officer!'

My left arm went numb. But I still had my right. It flashed through my mind that in a split second I could smash his jaw into multiple pieces. Wouldn't it be lovely. But sanity prevailed. They would probably kill me with their batons. Justifiable homicide.

'Killick attacked us! Look what he did to the senior.' I swallowed my pride. 'Yes, sir,' I said.

'Strip off.'

I stripped off. Because of my injured left arm, I was slow.

One of the giants poked me in the ribs with his baton. 'Move it!'

'Now bend over and pull your cheeks apart,' the senior said.

Maybe he thought I had a pistol hidden there. I wish I had. I would have killed the three of them.

I stared at the senior. 'No.'

I knew what was coming. As the two giants swung at my head with their batons I tried to raise my arms to protect myself but my injured arm wasn't quick enough. I was felled by a heavy blow to the left side of the head. Probably I was momentarily unconscious. The three of them began kicking me. Strangely, I didn't feel a lot of pain. I bit through my lip to prevent myself from uttering a sound.

After a short time, they stopped. I was bleeding profusely from the mouth. 'Get up!' the senior said.

I got up. I felt dizziness but still had coordination.

'Not so tough for a bank robber, is he?' the senior said. The others laughed. I was marched through a corridor to a block of thirty-nine cells. On the way, I was whacked on the backside a few times with the baton before being shoved into one of the cells.

'This is your home,' the senior said.

It was about 3 metres long by 2 metres wide. It contained a chair, small desk, bed, mattress, sheets, blankets and a pillow. In the corner, there was a toilet and a tap above it. There was a shiny aluminium bowl to wash in. The sheets and blankets were folded with precision into a rectangular pack.

'Make sure they are folded exactly like that in the morning,' one of the giants said, as he undid the bundle and tipped it on the floor. 'And if we can't see our face in the dish in the morning, you'll get another flogging.'

H Division. It was designed to psychologically break down the hardest of men. Violence, fear and sensory deprivation were the chosen tools.

I learnt that some men were so fearful of not meeting the required standards that they put their stack of blankets and sheets on the floor and slept on the mattress – afraid that if they used the linen they wouldn't be able to fold and pack it correctly. Many men debased themselves by using the toilet to wash in to ensure they didn't dull the mirror-like sheen of the washing bowl.

If I wrote about the four and a half years I spent in H (Hell) Division it would take up the entire book. I was taken there on four different occasions and some of the events which occurred and the people I met are worthy of inclusion.

Every day I heard prisoners being yelled at, threatened and on hundreds of occasions I heard them being beaten. No matter how emotionally strong you are, these incidents wear on your nerves. You are always aware that you could be the next victim.

Usually when a prisoner arrived in H Division he was beaten. For a few weeks, perhaps even months, he would be forced to work in one of the small yards called the labour yards. In the morning, he had to use a sledge hammer to break down large rocks to the size of his fist. In the afternoon, he would use a smaller hammer to break the fist-sized rocks down to thumbnail size. When it was time to return to his cell the guards would enter the yard and check the pile of rocks. If they weren't of the required size the prisoner either would be charged with disobeying an order or else he would be beaten. The usual procedure was to bash the prisoner. It saved a lot of paperwork. This process alone broke many men to the point where they became snivelling nervous wrecks.

During my four trips to H Division I spent a total of fifteen months in the labour yards which was virtually solitary confinement. In late December 1966, I was transferred to B Division which housed prisoners who were serving heavy sentences.

In 1967, I was returned to H Division for seven days for possessing a race guide. Surprisingly, probably because of the absurdity of the charge, I wasn't assaulted. A few months later I was involved in a fight and was returned for another fourteen days. This time I was punched five or six times by the guards, but they didn't use their batons. It was about a six out of ten 'biff'.

The senior screamed at me that I was a 'three-time loser' and that anyone who came to H Division three times was insane. His eyes bulged, the omnipresent spittle decorating the thin lips. I concluded probably both of us were insane.

In June 1968, with the aid of two prisoners, I made another desperate escape attempt. This time I hit a guard, John De Boer, on the head with an iron bar and took his pistol only to discover he didn't have the keys and we were trapped in the wing. Barricading upstairs, we threatened to shoot it out. When the cavalry arrived, we were surrounded by sixteen carloads of police armed with a small arsenal. Expert marksmen were strategically placed around the building. I figured the odds were against us in a shootout, best try to hold out for a deal. After six hours of negotiations the gaol Governor, Ian Grindlay, promised on the loud speaker that we would go to H Division but we wouldn't be bashed and the matter would be dealt with by a magistrate, meaning we couldn't be sentenced to more than two years. This is what I had been trying to achieve, fearing that a judge might give us fifteen years or more. Every prisoner in Pentridge heard Grindlay's promise. He was honour bound to keep it and to the chagrin of most of the guards, he did his best to ensure it was honoured. When the three of us were each sentenced to eighteen months the guards threatened to go on strike. But it meant they would have to go without wages and wouldn't be able to bash anyone because outside gaol, people are able to hit back. Fortunately, De Boer was okay after receiving five stitches in his head. About a year later he admitted to me that if he could have he would have shot me – nothing personal but it was his job. It made me feel better about what I had done. Since that time, I have never hit anyone on the head with anything other than fists. Governor Ian Grindlay later wrote about the incident in his book, Pentridge Papers.

When the senior was ordered by the governor to ensure the three of us weren't bashed it just about broke him. I was a record four-time loser. I had hit an officer on the head with an iron bar and I couldn't be touched!

A few months after the incident he was transferred to another gaol.

Unable to physically harm me, the guards focussed on mind games with the intention of maximising the stress to break me. Sometimes, despite being covered in sweat and grime after breaking rocks, I would miss out on a shower for nearly a week. I was often the last one brought out for a shave and by then the electric razor was usually hot and close to being ineffective. The guards would wait until I was half finished, then order me to return to my cell. My image in the mirror shocked me, much of my jet black hair had turned white and my features were taut and drawn. The guards could always find a reason to scream abuse at me. The cell was dirty; the rocks I smashed were not the correct size; letters I wrote were destroyed because of their offensive content; my hat was never on straight; I always saluted incorrectly; why had I only half shaved? Why didn't I shower properly? I stank! The toilet was dirty; my dish didn't resemble a mirror. Sometimes the guards would bang my door in the early hours of the morning demanding I stop snoring.

Every morning I'd psyche myself to get through the day and just focus on surviving.

I did a few writing courses by correspondence in 1969 and 1970. My tutor, the well-known South Australian poet and author Ian Mudie, taught me well and assured me I would be a published writer on release. Often when I returned to my cell I would find my paperwork strewn all over the floor, trodden on and sometimes ripped. Without Ian's encouragement, I would not have persevered with the writing.

Early in 1970 Cathy wrote to me and included a studio photo of herself. She looked beautiful, as I knew she would, and the letter and the photo shattered the barricade I had built between myself and thoughts of her. We corresponded for about fourteen months, with her planning to visit Australia when I was released in 1972 – ten years after our first meeting.

But our love affair was not meant to be. On the day of my release police intended to extradite me to Sydney for two bank robberies. When I gave her the news she once again became disillusioned with this crazy Australian who couldn't stay out of trouble. After that the letters stopped. The gaol authorities also told me her parents had contacted them and any letters I wrote to her wouldn't be sent. I never give up on anything, but this time I knew I was beaten. It was the end of a disastrous love affair – and the pain I experienced was physical in its intensity.

SERIOUS CRIMINALS

1966–72

During my six years in Pentridge I met some of the most infamous criminals in Australian history. Although Ronald Ryan wasn't one of them, while I was in H Division until late December 1966, every day I went past his observation cell. The front of the cell consisted of steel bars, including a steel bar door. At all times, he was in sight. His light was always on and the guards were rostered to ensure he was observed twenty-four hours a day. Each day he had a leather security belt strapped around his waist with his hands cuffed to the front section. He was then taken by a guard to an exercise yard for an hour's exercise. It was a terrible existence.

The day before the scheduled hanging he was taken to the condemned cell in D Division. The morning of the execution, 3 February 1967, I was in B Division. Thousands of protestors had been outside the gaol all night. The atmosphere in the gaol was one that I had never experienced before or since. B Division was literally a powder keg. The slightest incident would have set it off. The guards, who normally walked around by themselves, walked in threes. We all knew that precisely at 8.00 am Ronald Ryan, with a noose around his neck and a cloth covering his face, would be dropped through a trapdoor and have his neck snapped. We all hoped it would be quick.

A few minutes after 8.00am it was announced on the radio that Ronald Ryan was dead. No-one was asked to go to work that day. As was the custom with executed criminals, Ryan was buried face down in an unmarked grave in the prison grounds. It took another forty years before his family were able to have his remains exhumed from the closed Pentridge site and he was laid to rest beside his former wife at Portland cemetery in south-west Victoria.

Peter Walker, the man who escaped with Ryan, had been fortunate to avoid the hangman's noose. Apart from being found guilty of manslaughter for the crime which Ryan was hanged for, he had received twelve years for the manslaughter of the tow truck driver, Henderson, whom Walker had shot in the head in a toilet block at Middle Park.

The jury accepted Walker's version of the facts: that the pair had struggled and the gun went off.

When I wasn't confined in the labour yards breaking rocks, I spent the time in a security workshop threading broom heads – attached to a steel vice – with coarse fibre and horsehair.

There were two security workshops. I was always assigned to No. 2 with eleven others including Peter Walker, William John O'Mealley and Stanley Brian Taylor.

Walker and I had remarkably similar backgrounds: The same age. Both born midway through World War II, although his birthplace was England. Both our mothers had committed suicide. At the age of twenty-four both of us had robbed a bank. And both of us had been involved in assaulting a prison guard and taking his weapon during escape attempts. From there the similarities ceased. But now we both found ourselves sitting beside each other in the workshop in H Division. Over the years I had many conversations with him. I found him to be well read and intelligent. I also considered him to be more dangerous than Ronald Ryan.

He spent nineteen years in prison before being released in 1984. In 2014, he was arrested in Perth and extradited to Victoria for drug trafficking, possession of firearms and other offences. He is due for parole in late 2018.

• • •

William John O'Mealley was a short, solidly built man with a bald patch that he tried to cover by combing his wavy, grey side hair straight across it.

In May 1952, he had been sentenced to death for the shooting murder of police officer Constable George Howell. But in 1953 the newly elected Labor government commuted the sentence to life.

In March 1957, O'Mealley and another prisoner, John Henry Taylor, who was armed with a .38 pistol, ran through the main gates of Pentridge after shooting a guard in the thigh, breaking his femur. Shortly afterward they were recaptured.

In April 1958, as a reprisal for the escape and the shooting, they were each strapped to a steel triangle and flogged with twelve strokes of a water-soaked cat o'nine tails wielded by a masked man. Both men were left with permanent scars, as was the prison officer who had been shot.

This was the last time corporal punishment was administered in an Australian gaol.

When I met O'Mealley in 1968 he had been confined in H Division for ten years. When he smiled, it was a grimace. Everyone knew that during those ten years Bill had experienced tough times.

The first thing he said to me was: 'You know you done the wrong thing by trying to escape, don't you? I was due to get out of here but what you did will set me back two years.'

His illogicality stunned me. I was tempted to ask him if I should have sent him a letter first:

'Dear Bill, would it be all right if me and a couple of mates assault a prison officer, take his gun and escape over the wall? Or do you think we should wait until they decide to let you out of H Division – if they ever do?'

Instead, aware I was dealing with a tough, frustrated, possibly insane cop killer, I said:

'I didn't know you were due to get out of here, Bill, but it wouldn't have made any difference. I was desperate. It was an all or nothing go. You've had two goes, so surely you understand that.'

He glared at me, the grimace more pronounced. Instinctively I felt my body go into a fight mode – he looked ready to attack.

'When I escaped there was no Bill O'Mealley in H Division. I've been here for ten years. Ten years of living hell.'

For a few seconds we stared at each other.

'I'm sorry about that, but it's not my concern. I've got plenty of problems of my own.'

'You should have waited,' he mumbled, and walked away.

I knew it would only be a matter of time before he attacked me. I tried to be on my guard every minute we were in the same enclosure.

But he waited seven months. When it happened, in early July 1969, I was playing cards with three others during the lunchtime recess in the exercise yard.

O'Mealley rushed over and threw a punch at me. 'You aren't king of the yard!' he yelled.

At the last second, I saw it coming and tilted my head back. The punch caught me on the mouth, pushing the only gold tooth I had through my bottom lip. My top lip remained numb for three months. Dazed, I jumped up and grabbed hold of him. He was forty-nine but fit and strong. He broke free from my grip and began throwing wild punches at me. Fighting more from instinct than strategy I retaliated. For a while it was evenly balanced. Both of us took heavy blows to the head and body. But I was only twenty-seven and the older man began to wilt. He went down. I stepped back and let him get up. That's the way we fought in those days. He had a big heart. He came at me again. I backed him into a corner and hit him with a barrage of punches.

Suddenly I was hit with such force I was flung across the yard. A guard had turned the fire hose on me.

The fight was over. The door opened and guards came rushing in, grabbing hold of both of us. I was pushed and pulled to my cell, on the way collecting some heavy baton whacks on the backside and a sneaky little punch in the head.

Both O'Mealley and I were sent to the labour yards to break rocks again. While I was there a man named Armstrong walked on the moon. I learnt about it months later.

When both of us returned to the workshop O'Mealley came up and shook hands. It was the end of the drama. He knew fighting me would only earn him extra time in H Division.

Nevertheless, a decade later O'Mealley and I would play out one more drama. This time he would lose badly. I will come to that later on.

Stanley Brian Taylor, a solidly built guy of medium height who was balding, was another who shared our workshop for a number of years. After receiving a sentence of nine years for the armed robbery of a TAB, he escaped with another prisoner, Martin Nagle, from Ararat Gaol. The two of them went on a rampage holding up three service stations. They received a lot of publicity which in turn always ensures a heavy sentence – especially for armed robberies and escapes.

The judge added twelve and a half years to Taylor's sentence, leaving him with a crushing twenty-one and a half years. I once heard Walker saying to him: 'You're only doing a little one – I'm doing thirty-six years.' Walker was joking, but Stan didn't see it that way. In his eyes, he had been literally crucified by the justice system. His hatred of police increased to the point where he said: 'When I get out I'm going to strap a vest of gelly around me and walk into Russell Street Headquarters and take all the dogs with me.'

But Taylor was no suicide bomber. He did it the coward's way. On 27 March 1986, with the aid of three accomplices, he placed a Holden Commodore loaded with fifty sticks of gelignite outside the Russell Street Police Complex. At about 1.00 pm the car exploded, sending shrapnel from the car and rubble from the police building as far away as three blocks. Twenty-two people were injured. One of them, a policewoman, Angela Taylor, suffered massive injuries and died in hospital four weeks later.

On 31 July 1988, Taylor, aged fifty-one, was convicted of murder and sentenced to life. His accomplice, Craig Minogue, twenty-six, was also sentenced to life with a thirty-year non-parole period. A few weeks after he was sentenced he killed another prisoner, multiple murderer Alex Tsakmakis, by smashing his head in with a pillowcase filled with gym weights. He received another life sentence for that to run concurrent with the other. At the time of writing he is eligible for parole.

The third man proven to be connected to the crime was Peter Reed who, during his arrest, shot and wounded a police officer and was also shot and wounded by police. He was later acquitted of the bombing but was convicted of a number of other charges including the attempted murder of a police officer.

A fourth accused, Rodney Minogue, brother of Craig, was later acquitted of involvement in the bombing.

Stan Taylor, aged seventy-nine, died while still in custody in St Vincent's hospital in Melbourne in October 2016. He had been ill for some time with failing lung and heart problems.

There are no excuses for his actions. But it is worth noting that he was another serious criminal who had suffered traumatic abuses as a child during his time in juvenile detention. He described some of those abuses to me and I was shocked. I didn't believe a lot of it. But history has revealed that much of what he told me was systemic in many institutions.

Another memorable prisoner in our workshop was Joe Tognolini. Joe was in H Division for escaping from a prison van despite being handcuffed. In 1980, while I was there, he escaped from Yatala, the maximum security prison in South Australia which resulted in a Royal Commission. There is a bit of humour in the story which I will reveal later.

Although he never came to our workshop, Christopher Dale Flannery was in H Division part of the time I was there. For a while he went on a hunger strike and gave a lot of cheek to the outraged thugs in uniform. Flannery eventually went to Sydney and became known as 'Mr Rentakill' – hitman for hire. On 9 May 1985, he vanished. There are numerous theories as to what happened to him. The only certainty is that he is dead.

Of the numerous notorious criminals whom I met in Pentridge, dozens met violent deaths.

A CHANGE OF LUCK

1971–73

The riots in H Division in 1971–72 were a result of years of unofficially sanctioned, unlawful brutality inflicted by guards on prisoners. Regardless of what act the prisoner committed, be it assaulting a guard, as in my case, or for possession of a race guide, again as in my case, there was no provision in law for physical violence to be used. The law provided other forms of punishment, including solitary confinement on bread and water, breaking rocks in segregation, loss of remissions and extra gaol time. One morning, before the riots in H Division began in earnest, we were ordered to work on a public holiday. Despite being threatened, Taylor, Walker and I refused. We knew that if we complied, working on public holidays would become a regular occurrence.

The other prisoners looked at O'Mealley to see what he'd do. He walked over to the sink and began washing his hands. Why would you wash your hands before you started working? After about a minute of scrubbing and then drying his hands he walked to the table and placed a broom in the vice. 'You can't win,' he mumbled. 'I've been fighting them for eleven years, you can't win.'

The other prisoners quickly sat down and began working. If the self-proclaimed Iron Man of Pentridge was prepared to work on a public holiday, so were they.

The guard in the tower again ordered Taylor, Walker and I to sit down and work. We each refused. We began walking up and down the yard.

When I caught O'Mealley's eye, I gave him a wink. He shook his head. I didn't blame him for capitulating. He had fought them for over a decade – and lost. Now it was up to the new generation to take up the fight.

About five minutes later the door opened. A group of guards stood outside. One of them barked: 'Taylor, step outside!'

After they took him away they came for me. I figured that if they had bashed him it had been quick.

When I stepped into the passageway I was marched upstairs to where the chief was waiting.

He told me that from that day on, don't ask him for any favours. I wanted to ask him if he could write on the back of a postage stamp all the favours I had received. But I said nothing.

I was locked away and that was the end of it. No one was asked to work again on a public holiday.

It had been a test. To my knowledge it was the first time anyone had refused to work in H Division and came away unscathed.

The next test came when a new form of work was introduced to H Division. It consisted of putting metal pins in small, plastic electrical components. Some of the men in the labour yards were given the choice of breaking rocks or 'doing buttons' as the chore became known. Most chose the buttons.

But then pressure was applied for the prisoners to take trays of the work to their cells and finish them before lights out at 9.00 pm. Most of the men did it.

Taylor Walker and I refused. Soon our meals became half rations. Undeterred, we persuaded other men in our workshop to refrain from working at night.

I had no doubt there was some incentive for the gaol authorities to return as much completed work as they could to the supplier.

The retaliation by the authorities was swift: the three of us were taken to the labour yards and remained there for three months while most of the other prisoners occupied themselves by doing buttons in their cells at night.

When we challenged the validity of being put in the labour yards we were told a conspiracy had been uncovered. They had received 'information' from another prisoner, Geoffrey Gair, that Taylor, Walker and I were going to have a gun smuggled in and hold up the guards, take three of their uniforms, gag and lock them in a cell, and walk to the front gate dressed as guards. From there we would force the guards to unlock the entrance so we could escape.

Gair was rewarded with a trip out of H Division to a country gaol where he later climbed over the wall and escaped. There's humour there. But the guards couldn't see it. When he was recaptured and returned to H Division, Gair wasn't laughing either.

Taylor, Walker and I were never given the opportunity to share a joke with him.

Occasionally in H Division there was a lone rebel, someone who refused to obey orders. The rebellion never lasted for long. Floggings and isolation on bread and water soon forced their capitulation.

Taylor, Walker and I had, by refusing to work on public holidays, and again in our cells at night, put a slight chink in the armour of the tyrannical regime in H Division. Then Steven Sellars and Christopher Dale Flannery went on hunger strikes, refused to break rocks and abused the guards. After that five prisoners, drunk on a home brew, were brought down and rebelled from the start. Soon the entire division rebelled. Cells were flooded, furniture destroyed, the sledgehammers in the yards used to smash down the adjoining walls. Instead of breaking rocks, men stripped to their jocks and sun-baked.

Taylor yelled from his cell he would put an ice pick in the heart of any guard who bashed him. (I wondered where he would get an ice pick from). Robert 'Bertie' Kidd, who had a top barrister visiting him regularly, dared the guards to bash him. The guards didn't know what to do.

B Division and C Division began to protest in support of H Division.

With support from outside the gaol, including the powerful anti-war movement, the riots continued. Lawyers became involved.

The government succumbed to the pressure and launched a Royal Commission headed by Kenneth Jenkinson QC to investigate Allegations of Brutality and Ill Treatment at HM Prison Pentridge.

When the terms of the Jenkinson Enquiry revealed that only allegations of events having taken place since 22 May 1970 would be considered, I figured it would be a whitewash. It prevented testimony from the man who had the most to tell: William John O'Mealley who had been transferred from H Division on 4 May 1970. It also precluded me from detailing the savage beating I had received in June 1966.

But when Walker declined to give evidence I felt obligated to reveal what I could about the abuses of power which virtually forced the prisoners to rebel. On 19 September 1972, I testified before the Enquiry.

The media picked up on it and ran with the headline: 'Man's Inhumanity to Man'.

Despite over 100 prisoners giving evidence, not one prison guard was sent to gaol.

The authorities hadn't learnt a thing: they went hi-tech and in 1980 opened Jika Jika – nicknamed 'The Electronic Zoo'. It had electronic doors, closed circuit TV and remote locking. In 1983, four prisoners escaped from the reputed 'escape proof' unit.

In 1987 the unit was permanently shut down after prisoners stacked mattresses and other bedding against the doors and set them on fire. The electronic mechanism failed and five prisoners died. But by then I was long gone.

Shortly after testifying at the Royal Commission I was released into the custody of two New South Wales detectives and flown to Sydney to face charges on the two bank robberies.

When I arrived at Long Bay Gaol I was immediately placed in segregation. The governor told me he had received a report from the head of security at Pentridge that I was the most dangerous man he had ever met.

I commented that maybe from his ivory tower he hadn't met many prisoners.

Everyone, including myself, expected me to receive another hefty sentence. But a wise old judge, Judge Hicks, decided I had paid a heavy price for my crimes. He sentenced me to two years and six months with a recommendation for parole after six months. Freedom was in sight. I thanked the judge and assured him I would stay out of trouble.

After the authorities had recovered from their shock and realisation that the most dangerous man the head of security at Pentridge had ever met was close to release, they grudgingly let me out of segregation and gave me a job in the bookbinding store.

A week later I was involved in a fight with another prisoner. He attacked me, but it made no difference. Both of us were charged.

Being in a different section of the gaol, I was taken before the residing governor. Last time I had seen him he was a two-striper at Goulburn Gaol in 1962.

He had the report of the fight on his desk. He knew I hadn't thrown the first blow.

'Killick, this could cost you your parole. I'm going to give you a chance.

I'm recording no conviction – stay out of trouble.'

My luck had changed. First Judge Hicks, now this governor.

Over the remaining months I went to debating classes and spoke with female visitors for the first time in seven years. I participated in organising a gaol magazine, Inside Out, of which I became the editor.

The publisher at Angus and Robertson, Richard Walsh, wrote informing me that Ian Mudie had spoken highly to him about my work and he would be interested to see anything I considered worthwhile.

Good old Ian, he always said I would become a published writer and he was doing his best to ensure it happened.

I became friends with one of the prisoners, Bobby Merrit. He was an indigenous guy with a prison record rivalling mine.

Both of us rejoiced when the Labor Party under Gough Whitlam won the Election for the first time since 1949.

'Gough will do good things for the Aboriginal people,' Bob said. He was right about that.

Bob went on to write a play The Cake Man which was successful both here and in the US.

On 22 June 1973, I was released on parole. I was far from rehabilitated, whatever that means. I was filled with resentment at the seven years I had lost. I had lost the girl I loved, my hair had turned white, my credibility and respect were gone. I knew within me that I was responsible by my actions for all of this, but it was hard to accept that those thugs in uniforms, who had consistently broken the law in administering their own brand of justice, had gone unpunished. My mind was scarred. The rational, decent part of me reminded myself that Judge Hicks had given me a chance that bank robbers don't deserve; even the governor had turned a blind eye to my last fight. I had been given an opportunity to come good. I owed it to Dad and to myself. I had to suppress the anger and give it a try. When I looked back at some of the major events that had occurred in the past seven years I realised that what had happened to me was of no significance: I didn't matter.

More than a million Biafrans had starved to death after a disastrous war against the Nigerian government; the just as disastrous Vietnam War was coming to an end, with the US and its allies looking for an 'honourable' retreat. How many lives lost? Terrorism struck the Munich Olympics with the massacre of eleven Israeli athletes by Arab gunmen; the Soviet Union had moved into Czechoslovakia with tanks and killed 150 Czechs in a ruthless suppression of Alexander Dubcek's effort to liberalise his country; Robert Kennedy had been assassinated; Martin Luther King had been assassinated; the Watergate scandal was hotting up with Nixon blaming everyone but himself and, of course, man had walked on the moon.

By comparison my experiences weren't even a fly speck on a page of a ten-volume book about events worthy of mention.

I was only thirty-one. I could still do good things from here. I would give it a try.

LUCY DUDKO

1958–76

In Russia, in 1973, a fifteen-year-old girl had no idea that twenty-six years later she would make world headlines by staging one of the most daring and outrageous prison escapes in Australian history.

Was there anything in her childhood behaviour to even hint that she would be capable of such an act?

Looking back there were numerous indicators.

Better known now as Lucy Dudko, she was born Lioudmila Zhdanove on 28 April 1958 in the industrial city of Kuibyshev on the Volga river. Today this city is known as Samara. It has now a large (population 1.2 million) important political, economic, industrial and cultural centre which hosted the European Union – Russia Summit in 2007.

Her father, Vitali, was an Air Force officer who commanded a helicopter squadron. Military rules were strict. Lucy was never given the opportunity to get inside a chopper. Her mother, Tonia, was a building manager. Lucy's brother, Gennardi, was ten years younger than her. They were a cultured family. As a military officer, Vitali was posted to various distant areas including Mongolia and Siberia. As a result, Lucy went to a lot of different schools.

As a child, she was independent and secretive. In her own words, she was a 'tomboy.' She climbed trees and often fell out of them. She got into fights, often with boys, and gave as good as she got.

She often wandered miles from home alone exploring the countryside. She never got lost because her father had taught her how to use the position of the sun as a compass. In winter, when trekking through the snow she used her footprints to backtrack.

One winter's day, when she was nine, she trekked along a frozen snow-covered river. Usually the ice was thick and safe to traverse. But sometimes fishermen came and hacked an opening in the ice to enable them to catch fish. Although it didn't take long for a covering of ice to reform, initially it was very thin. Lucy stepped on to one of those sections and fell through the ice into the freezing water. Spreading her elbows as wide as possible she anchored herself against the thick ice surrounding the opening. She began to feel her body go numb and she knew that if she didn't manage to quickly get out she would die. Without panicking, she grasped the jagged edges and, twisting from side to side, heaved herself waist high and got one leg on to the surface before dragging herself out. Although exhausted, she knew that if she stopped to rest in her soaking wet clothes she would freeze to death. She walked, jogged and even ran the long journey home, with the exercise warming her body enough to counter the cold. When she arrived home, no-one was there. Changing clothes, she dried the others by the heater.

When her mother came home and asked her how was her day she simply replied: 'Boring.'

When she was ten years old she was with a group of friends listening to a boy telling them ghost stories. One particular story was about the dead getting out of their graves at night and haunting the living.

Lucy told them categorically that the dead are dead and stay in their graves. After a lengthy argument, she was challenged to go to the local cemetery at midnight to prove her point.

Lucy took the challenge. She would meet her friends outside the cemetery from where she would enter the graveyard and walk around for a while, defying the dead to do anything about it.

A few minutes before midnight she tiptoed out of the house and met up with three of her friends. Apart from them there wasn't a sign of activity anywhere. Every house was in darkness.

When the four of them came to the gates of the cemetery, the others, already wide-eyed with fear, tried to dissuade Lucy from going inside. But she was unafraid and told them she would return in half an hour.

'The dead will grab you and take you to their graves!' one girl said despairingly.

The town was hundreds of years old and the cemetery was large and overcrowded.

Even at that age Lucy was interested in history. She wandered around reading the inscriptions on tombstones and large vaults. Some of the older ones with Polish surnames dated back to the 17th century.

Suddenly Lucy saw a dark figure emerging from a nearby large white marble vault. Crouching behind the vault from where she'd been reading the inscription, she watched as the dark male figure squeezed through a narrow gap between the door and the vault wall. After dusting himself off he walked away.

She waited about five minutes before returning to the entrance. Her friends were nowhere to be seen.

The next day she told a large gathering of curious kids about what she had seen.

Some of them insisted she had seen the walking dead. How lucky had she been that he hadn't smelled her!

But others concluded that she had seen a grave robber. Apparently, there was a gang of gypsies who wandered around robbing graves.

These two incidents at the ages of nine and ten were an indication of her proclivity for adventure, her daring and her coolness under pressure.

For a while after she started university she was also employed, part-time, in a racing stable working horses. She loved horses and became an adept rider.

Early one winter morning a friend who drove trotters warned her about a pack of wild dogs that had chased his sulky for quite a distance. They didn't bark, simply came after him silently. It is probable that with the winter and the snow they were starving.

Lucy loved to ride at night when the riding tracks were mostly deserted. Ignoring the warning about the wild dogs, she took her favourite galloper, Podgon, for a ride in the snow. The stars and distant lights provided adequate vision for night riding.

Suddenly Podgon, usually a calm, confident animal, began to snort. His taut body demanded more rein to enable him to increase his speed.

Then Lucy saw them – five huge feral dogs racing silently towards them. It is not in Lucy's nature to panic – she kept her cool. She knew that feral dogs couldn't catch a fit, trained galloper. But one slip from a panicking horse in the snow could result in an horrific death for both of them. She rode him as though they were in a championship race and Podgon responded magnificently. They reached the stable with just enough distance between them and the dogs to enable Lucy to jump down, open the door, get inside and close it again.

They were safe. After she spent some time soothing and cooling down Podgon, she left the stable and walked to the local bus stop.

Years later she told me that this experience was one of the most exciting and unforgettable moments in her life. The combination of extreme danger and galloping at full speed in the snow at night gave her an incredible high.

It was clear that Lucy was not averse to risk taking.

WHAT HAPPENED TO THE RUSSIAN?

1973

A lot has been written about the difficulties long-term prisoners have in coping during the first few months of their return to the community.

However, serving more than seven years in maximum security to walking the streets as an ordinary citizen seemed a natural process to me.

The conditions of my parole required that I live at Dad's place in Waterloo. They had found a job for me working at the magazine distribution centre in Alexandria, Gordon and Gotch. My job was to pack magazines and comics and have them ready to be delivered to shops and newsagencies around Australia.

The foreman, a wiry little guy who was about forty years old, was aware of my background and made it obvious from the start that he didn't like me. I resolved to not allow him to bait me into behaviour that could result in my parole being revoked.

After two weeks of living at Dad's I told him I had found a room to rent in Mascot. We had been arguing over trivial matters and when he'd had a few drinks he was still his old belligerent self. Anyway, I needed my own space. My parole officer was sympathetic to my situation and agreed to the move.

I applied for a Commonwealth Literary Grant. Although I wasn't overly optimistic, my ex-tutor, Ian Mudie, and his friend, the well-known writer Judah Waten, who was a hard-line Communist Party member, gave me good references. Ian told me that Gough Whitlam's government was handing out grants to anyone who could write an application and even a few who could not.

I also went to see Anne Brooksbank, an attractive blond lady of about thirty whom I'd met in Long Bay during the debating classes. She was an accomplished scriptwriter who wrote scripts for the popular crime shows at the time: *Homicide, Division 4* and *Matlock*. She had asked me to drop by her place when I was released and to bring my best stories with me. I gave her three: *The Perfect Alibi, Larry the Lair* and *Number One Power Puss.*

'I have a few friends in the industry,' she said. 'I'll see if we can do something with these.'

I thanked her and left. (Anne, who married the firebrand writer, the late Bob Ellis, is still writing good scripts four decades later).

Surprisingly I hadn't gone out of my way to find a girlfriend. The wounds from the disastrous affair with Cathy still hurt. Although I rarely thought about her now, I knew that I wasn't psychologically ready for another serious relationship. I had subconsciously put her on a pedestal and no woman could, at this stage, replace her.

A few weeks after I'd moved into the Mascot rooming house, a Russian guy with whom I'd played a few games of chess came banging on my door at about eight o'clock at night. He was so drunk he couldn't stand up straight. 'Time for a game of chess, you bastard,' he said, slurring his words and grinning like the village idiot.

I stared at him. He was a big, lean guy of about forty. When he was sober he was a likeable guy and a good chess player, but at the moment he reminded me of Dad at his worst. 'Go away, you're drunk,' I said. He stank of vodka.

'You are my chess friend,' he said and tried to push past me. I shoved him away. He staggered back, lurched sideways and somehow stayed on his feet.

He gave me a sad look. 'What's the problem, my friend?' I slammed the door. He banged on it.

'Fuck off!' I said.

I heard him stagger away and start banging on someone else's door asking for a game of chess. From what I'd seen of the other tenants they would be hard pressed to play a good game of draughts.

There was a bit of shouting and abuse as he wandered around banging on a few other doors and then it was quiet again.

The next day while I was at work the manager called me to his office. I could see he was upset.

'There's some woman on the phone and she insists on talking to you,' he said. He handed me the phone. 'Tell her this is not a social club and don't call again.'

It was Lisa, a lady I had met during debating classes at Long Bay. She also had conducted a class called 'Crime and the Criminals'. She had helped quite a few prisoners after their release.

'I'm at the pub near the Chinese takeaway in Mascot,' she said. 'Come immediately.'

'I can't,' I said. 'I'll see you when I get off at four.'

'It'll be too late,' she said. 'Get here now!' She hung up. I told the manager an emergency occurred and I had to go.

'What emergency?' he asked.

'I won't know until I get there,' I said, and rushed out the door.

When I arrived at the hotel, Lisa was waiting outside. She took me to a nearby lane where a guy of about thirty approached us. He was of medium build, had brown dishevelled hair and I noticed he was wearing prison trousers. I'd met him in Long Bay earlier that year. (I forget his name; I'll call him Paul).

'He's just escaped from Emu Plains,' Lisa said. 'He'll need to stay at your place until we can move him over to Glebe tonight.'

'Why would you escape from Emu Plains?' I said. 'It's a holiday camp.

How long did you have to go?'

'Six months, but I was getting a hard time.'

'Well this is going to cost me my job, which could cost me my parole.'

'Bullshit,' Lisa said. 'We can't just stand around here – better take us to your place.'

We walked a few hundred metres to my rooming house. Inside, Paul began to relax. 'If I can get to Melbourne I've got connections,' he said.

'Just catch a train,' I said. 'There's hardly going to be a manhunt over you walking off a prison farm.'

'You never know,' Paul said.

'I do know,' I said. 'You're not the Ryan and Walker type.'

'We won't take the risk, anyway,' Lisa said. 'I've already arranged for the people at Glebe to look after him until they can get him down to Victoria.'

A few minutes later there was a knock on the door. 'Who is it?'

'Police.'

Lisa looked at me, disbelief on her face. I noticed Paul's hands were trembling. 'Get under the bed,' I whispered to Paul. I walked over and opened the door. Two uniform cops stood there. One was a big, overweight guy of about thirty with a red complexion; the other, a younger, fitter looking guy, held a pen and notebook in his hand.

'What's the problem, officers?'

'Mind if we come in for a moment?' the big cop asked.

'Well, I was spending a bit of time with my girlfriend before I go back to work,' I said. 'Is it serious?'

'Very,' he said and pushed past me into the room.

My mind was racing. If they knew Paul was here there would be more than two uniform cops here. Had my parole been revoked? Had the manager rung the cops when I left work?

'Mind if I sit down?' the big cop said and immediately sat down on the bed. I figured his backside was about eight inches above the escaped crim's head. The other cop closed the door and stood by it. Lisa was seated on the only chair in the room.

The big cop nodded at her. 'Sorry to interrupt, Miss. We won't be too long.' He turned to me. 'This Russian bloke down the hall, when did you last see him?'

'Last night. He came to my door wanting to play chess but he was drunk so I sent him away.'

'We have information that you were arguing with him.'

'Well, I think everyone was arguing with him. He was drunk and belligerent and banging on other people's doors after he left me.'

'Well, he banged on the wrong door,' the big cop said. 'Now he's in the hospital on life support. Someone bashed him black and blue.' He paused, and gave me a hard look. 'You must have heard something.'

'Nothing like that,' I said, shocked.

He eased himself off the bed. 'Well, you'd better give us your name and where you work in case we need to talk to you again.'

Lisa was staring at me. I knew what she was thinking. If I gave my correct name and date of birth and they checked me out they would soon be back with an arrest warrant. A guy on parole for armed robbery would be a perfect patsy. An escaped crim under the bed would be a bonus.

I walked over to the cop with the notebook. 'My name is Reginald Killick, date of birth 7 July 1941. I work for Gordon and Gotch at Mascot.'

'Okay, Mr Killick. Thanks for your help.'

The big cop nodded. 'Don't leave town, will you.'

After they had gone, Paul scrambled out from under the bed. 'Was it you?'

I was angry. 'Of course, it wasn't me. Why would I bash him? He went away after I told him to.'

'Let's focus on getting Paul out of here,' Lisa said. 'I don't think we should wait until night now.'

'In case they come back and arrest me for attempted murder, you mean?'

'No. But they'll probably come back when the other tenants come home.'

'Somebody's home. Who told them I was arguing with the Russian?'

She nodded. 'We'll have to be careful. They might have Paul's picture on the news.'

'Not a chance,' I said. 'He can use public transport without a worry.' Eventually I convinced them that there would be no manhunt for Paul.

After I supplied him with a clean change of clothes the three of us walked to the shopping centre where he and Lisa caught a taxi to Glebe. A few days later he went to Victoria. After about six months he returned to Sydney where he was re-arrested.

A PASTA FOR CHECKMATE

1973

When I returned to work I knew it was only a matter of time before I was sacked. The foreman's attitude towards me was one of open hostility; I had an urge to punch him in the mouth but that would be the end of my parole. I was already one of the suspects for the Russian who was on life support.

There were plenty of jobs available for labourers so I resigned and took a job with Australian Tin Smelters (ATS) in Mascot. They taught me how to use a small crane and I moved and stacked packs of tin bars.

About a week after I started at ATS I received a letter from Richard Walsh inviting me to visit him at his office in Cremorne to discuss my book. I showed the letter to the foreman, a big blond bear of a man named George, who was also our union rep. I asked him for a day off.

'I'd have never taken you for a writer,' he said. 'What's the book about?' I met his gaze. 'Prison, among other things. I did a long stint in Pentridge.' For a few moments, he stared at me in stunned silence. Then he said:

'What were you in gaol for?'

'Bank robberies.'

'Bloody hell...' He called one of the men over. 'You'll never believe this Frank – John here is an ex-bank robber.' He looked at me. 'You are an ex, aren't you?'

I nodded. 'Definitely.'

'And now,' George said, 'they want him to write a book about it all.

We've got another Darcy Dugan here.'

'Well, there's no certainty they want the book. That's what the appointment's about.'

'What do you reckon, Frank? Do we give him the day off?'

'Have to,' Frank, a little nuggetty guy, said. 'We don't get too many writers here – or bloody bank robbers.'

We all laughed – probably for different reasons.

A few days later I took the first three chapters of my book to Richard Walsh. He was a small, brown-haired man in his thirties with a friendly manner that immediately put me at ease. He invited me to sit down. There was a pile of paperwork on his desk.

'I've spoken again to Ian Mudie,' he said. 'He said your book will be a cut above the usual prison literature.'

Good old Ian – always trying to help – even from South Australia. I leaned forward to hand the manuscript to Richard then pulled back. He gave me a surprised, quizzical look.

My three opening chapters were nothing short of a vindictive diatribe against the prison system – dominated by my experiences in H Division. It would hardly qualify as a 'cut above the usual prison literature.' I owed it to Ian, and myself, to write a more balanced account of my experiences. 'I've wasted your valuable time, Mr Walsh. I apologise. What I've written isn't up to scratch.'

He leaned back in his chair, appraising me. Then he nodded. 'That is your decision and I respect it.' He paused. 'I also publish *Nation Review* – have you heard of it?'

I nodded. *Nation Review* was a weekly news magazine that wasn't afraid to be critical of the establishment. 'I've read a few issues. I like its style.'

He smiled. 'Not everyone does. George Munster is the editor and I feel certain that if you go and see him he will commission you to write a few articles about the prison system. How do you feel about that?'

'I feel I could do a good job. I'd give a balanced account.'

'I'm sure you will. I'll give you the address and I'll let him know you are coming.'

I shook his hand. 'I appreciate that.'

'We always welcome new writers.' I picked up my manuscript and was about to leave when he said: 'And don't forget, when you feel ready to write your book, I'm interested.'

I nodded. 'I'll do it. I just need time.' One of the great understatements – it would take me forty years to finish it.

George Munster had an office in Haymarket. He looked to be about fifty; he had brown wavy greying hair, was of medium build and had a slight German accent.

After we had a long chat over a cup of coffee, he told me: 'This is what we are going to do: you will write me a lengthy article, six or 7000 words, about H Division and why you were there four times. After that, we'll see. If you do well, I'll give you more work.'

I left his office feeling elated. It was only a step, but a step in the right direction to becoming a published writer.

A few days later I received notification from the Commonwealth Literary Grants Department that I had been awarded a $750 Literary Grant. Then, that same week, I got the trifecta: the editor of *Man Magazine*, Don Hogg, wrote informing me that Anne Brooksbank had given him some of my short stories to read and that he felt some of them were worthy of publication. He wanted me to call into his office in Clarence Street.

When I asked George for another day off, he wasn't happy. 'We all work hard here, mate,' he said. 'Some of these blokes couldn't write a letter. But I can count on them to turn up every day.'

'Fair enough. When do you want me to finish up?'

'I don't. I like you – we all like you. It's good to see a bloke turn things around like you have. When you're here, you do a good job. But we can't go on like this.' He paused and ran his fingers through his blond locks. 'I'll tell you what...how do you feel about a three day a week job?'

'It'd be perfect. Can you arrange it?'

'I'm the union rep – I can arrange anything. I'll fix it up today. Naturally you'll be taking a forty per cent pay reduction, but you'll more than pick that up with your writing.'

I shook his hand. 'Thanks, George.'

'You can repay us all by writing a bestseller. You said they've given you a $750 grant?'

'Yes.'

'Can you spare me a hundred?' I wouldn't ask but I'm in a bit of a bind.

Won't be able to repay it for about a month.'

'Sure, George. I'll give it to you when I get to the bank.' George liked a beer and a few bets. I knew there was a good chance I'd never be repaid but I figured it was a good investment. Three days a week fitted into my schedule perfectly.

That day George arranged for me to work Wednesdays to Fridays.

Don Hogg was a dark-haired, slightly built New Zealander who wore thick-rimmed glasses. He was about thirty-five. He made me feel at home by having his secretary serve coffee and cakes in his office.

'I'm going to publish a couple of your stories,' he said. 'But first I want you to give me a rundown on your time in H Division. Were you there when they hanged Ronald Ryan?'

'They hanged him in D Division,' I said. 'But I was in H Division in 1966 when Ryan was there. I didn't get to talk to him – they had him in the condemned cell.'

'What about his mate, Walker?'

'I spent a couple of years with him.'

'Great stuff! What about O'Mealley – the Iron Man of Pentridge?'

I grinned. 'I call him the Paper Tiger of Pentridge. I was with him for a few years. I actually fought him.'

'What, in H Division?'

'Yes.'

'You and O'Mealley had a fist fight in H Division. This is great stuff!

How did you go?'

'Broke about even.'

'Broke about even – I love it!' He paused and took a sip of coffee. 'Ryan, Walker, the Paper Tiger of Pentridge...we've got some great stuff here. I'll do a one-on-one interview with you and we'll lead with it in next month's edition.'

'What about my stories?'

'We'll do them afterwards. I love *The Perfect Alibi* and we'll also publish Number One Power Puss. Both brilliant.'

And that is how it panned out. We did a lengthy interview about H Division and some of the infamous prisoners who had been incarcerated there. My two short stories were published in issues following the H Division article. *Nation Review* also published my 6,000-word article about H Division as well as four other short articles.

George and some of my other workmates were fascinated with the details about H Division and continually pestered me with questions about it and prisons in general.

Although busy, I was also lonely. I decided to enter a chess competition held at the Sydney Chess Centre in the old Anthony Hordern building in George Street.

The lady who was in charge of the proceedings, Gloria, was a tall, attractive brunette about my age. On the second night of the tournament I won my game in quick time and had a discussion with her about movies.

The rapport between us was good and I asked her to have dinner with me. Without offering a reason why, she declined.

'I'll tell you what,' I said, 'if I win the tournament, then will you have dinner with me?'

She smiled. 'If you win the tournament I'll cook you dinner.'

She later admitted she had underestimated me as a chess player. I went through the tournament unbeaten. After the final game, she came over to congratulate me.

'Never mind the congratulations,' I said. 'I want a T-bone steak, medium–rare, with French fries, onions, peas and gravy. Baked rice pudding served with Blue Ribbon ice cream would be nice for dessert.'

'I didn't say you could choose,' she said. 'If I cook you dinner, it will be pasta.'

But we clicked and it soon became serious.

WALKING IN THE RAIN FOR A DOLLAR A DAY

1973–74

Gloria worked in the city at a secretarial service. After a while I told her about my criminal background. I gave her a totally unabridged account. She was upset and I feared it would be the end of our relationship, but after she discussed it with her sister, Eve, she decided I had paid a huge price for my crimes and was doing everything I could to redeem myself. Not long afterwards I moved in with her at her unit in Louisa Road, Birchgrove.

Getting to work on time became a problem. I explained the situation to George. 'I run down Louisa Road,' I said, 'and up a steep hill to Darling Street where I scramble on to a bus that takes me to the back of Central. The sweat is pouring off me. Then I run full speed through the tunnel, dodging and weaving between people, to catch another bus to get me near here. Then I run to work.'

'What are you training for – the Olympics?' George asked.

I grinned. 'It's the way the bus timetables work. I'm going to have to leave George.'

He nodded. 'Yeah, I knew it was coming. What are you going to do?'

'I don't know. I'll find a job closer to home.'

'What about the writing?'

'It sounds impressive but it doesn't pay much. There are a lot of good writers in Australia driving taxis. I can't live on what I get from writing.'

We shook hands. 'If you ever want to come back, I'll fix it. Okay?'

'Three days a week?

'Get out of here.'

Gloria and I pooled together to buy a second-hand blue Volkswagen Beetle. This enabled me to get a position with Bernies Studio in the city. They specialised in child portraits.

My job was to go door to door trying to persuade people to allow a photographer to come to their home and take twelve photos of their children. The sitting was free. The photographs were in black and white and later a saleslady would call around with the proofs. If the parents liked the photos they could order their favourites which would be enlarged to a portrait size (5x7, 6x8, 10x8 inches) and hand-coloured by an artist. The average order was over $200, but I didn't tell them about that. Bernies knew that most mothers, after viewing the proofs of their children, would buy them. Although I had no proven experience as a salesman, my having transport clinched the position. The manager, a glib Irishman in his forties, gave me a map of streets in the Pennant Hills area to work. I had to take a girl, Miriam, with me. She was a twenty-year-old, dark-haired beauty who had no transport.

'You can work the area together,' Irish said. 'Mark the streets off as you do them. You can do Epping next.' He paused. 'If you only work a few hours you'll get nowhere. We expect you to average six appointments a day. That's 30 a week. For every appointment after that you'll get a $2 bonus – so if you put in the hours you can make good money. And if it rains, you'll get $1 rain money.'

I had to bite my tongue. I looked at Miriam. She was nodding as though trudging in the rain all day for an extra dollar was a good deal.

'What about petrol expenses?' I asked.

'Can't do it. If you are any good at the game you won't need it – you'll make plenty.'

I was good at it. My days as a raffle ticket seller had taught me how to persuade people into buying.

'It's a win/win situation,' I would tell the mothers. 'A professional photographer comes to your place, and free of charge, takes twelve photos of your beautiful children. If you don't like any of the photos, you simply don't buy any.'

I was averaging twelve appointments a day. Miriam was a hopeless salesperson. After the first day, she had only one appointment. The next day she doubled it to two. I felt sorry for her. I began to give her a couple of my appointments each day.

'It's really nice of you, John,' she said. 'I guess if it wasn't for you I would be out of a job.'

'This is not much of a job,' I said. 'Your income is uncertain. You might be better off getting a job with Coles or Woolworths.'

I could see she was upset. 'I'll get better.' But she didn't. A few times she was propositioned when she knocked on the doors of guys home alone. I could understand it. She was one of those girls who were sexy without trying to be sexy. If I hadn't been deeply involved with Gloria at the time, I would have made a move on her. Instead, I was a perfect gentleman and I knew she respected me.

After a few weeks, she left. She told me she had a boyfriend in Israel and would go there soon.

• • •

I received a letter from Don Hogg with a cheque for $50. 'Congratulations,

John. A Norwegian publication saw your story *The Perfect Alibi* in our magazine and asked if they could print it. I gave them the okay and they paid you $50. You are now a published writer overseas.'

I should have been excited but my career as a writer had almost come to a standstill. The financial reward was lousy and my discipline had waned. I didn't have much spare time. I still played chess one night a week and every Saturday I went to the races, sometimes taking Gloria. Although she enjoyed it, she expressed concern that I had been outlaying hundreds of dollars. I didn't tell her that less than eight years ago I had been outlaying thousands. To me, a few hundred dollars risked at the racetrack was nothing. For a man earning less than a hundred dollars a week, it was flawed thinking...

In October, Australia issued $50 notes. For the first time on an Australian bank-note, it had the word 'Australia' on it instead of the usual 'Commonwealth of Australia.' But we were still bound by British tradition. Later that month the Queen arrived to open the Sydney Opera House.

Just before Christmas my brother, David, who had lived in New Zealand for the past seven years, returned to Australia with his wife Colleen and their two sons. I took Dad to the airport to meet them and it was an emotional time.

David's friend, John, had found him a house in Newport to rent.

Bernies paid the bonuses for the extra appointments monthly. The first month I didn't get much. Irish explained that it took a while for the orders to be finalised. The second month I again received a cheque well short of my expectations.

When I confronted Irish about it, he said: 'We only pay a bonus when someone buys some photos.'

'That's not what you told me. You said a bonus is paid for every appointment after the first 30 each week.'

'No, John, you misunderstood. We aren't a charity here. Why would we pay if someone cancelled an appointment or chooses not to buy because they don't like the photos?'

'Because it's not my job to convince them to buy the photos. It's my job to persuade them to have the sitting. Then it's up to your saleslady to persuade them to buy the photos.'

'If we paid for no sales we'd go broke.'

'What, at $2 a time? You get hundreds of dollars for successful sales.' I was getting angry. 'What about your farcical $1 a day rain money and no petrol expenses?'

'Well, John, if you don't like it, you know what you can do.'

'Well I know if I want to do slave labour I can go to Pentridge and break rocks – and not have to work in the rain.'

'Don't talk nonsense. You are doing well here. You've still got bonuses to come.'

'Either I get paid for every appointment I've made over the 30 a week or I'm leaving.'

'Can't do it. You need to think about this.'

'I'm finished, Irish. You'll get a lot of Miriams before you find another John Killick.' I walked out.

I had been toying for a while with the idea of starting my own photographic business. David, who hadn't found a job yet, had once worked in New Zealand as a photographer. During my door-knocking to get appointments, I had met a lady in Epping who had worked for Bernies for a few years colouring photographs. I mentioned that I was considering starting my own business and asked her if she might be tempted to come out of retirement. She told me she would discuss it with her family, but if she took up the offer she would need to work from home. That was fine by me.

I ran the idea by Gloria after telling her I had left Bernies. She was supportive of it and offered to help finance the venture.

David was all for it. The three of us got together and structured a plan: it would all be contingent on my being able to persuade the lady in Epping, Ruth, to work for us. If I could, I would get the appointments, David would take the photos and develop them at night; Gloria and I would take the proofs around on weekends and take orders. We would print business cards under the name 'Home Portrait Studios' and Colleen would play secretary at home and take messages.

Full of enthusiasm and confidence, I went to see Ruth. 'Bernies rip people off,' I said. 'Most people can't afford the prices they charge. We will cut them by fifty per cent and instead of a wage, I'll pay you a percentage of each portrait you do.'

'I have three children,' she said, 'and I do miss the extra income. I'll do it for twelve months, but that will be it.'

I agreed to that. Twelve months gave me ample time to find another artist, or two or three if the business went as well as I anticipated.

On the way home, I was grinning. Wait until Irish discovered he had a rival who was undercutting him by fifty per cent!

Home Portrait Studios became a serious rival to Bernies Studios. It cost us about $1200 for an expensive Mamiya camera, lighting equipment and 500 business cards. When I explained to people that our prices were half of those charged by Bernies, I got more appointments than David could handle. At one stage, there was a serious petrol shortage and you could only buy it every second day, depending on whether your number plate ended in an odd or even number.

My Volkswagen was easy on petrol but David's Monaro was a gas guzzler and when we learnt that, for some reason, there were no restrictions on the amount of petrol you could buy in the country, Gloria drove to Wyong and brought back a load of four gallon drums.

It took about five weeks before the money started to come in. After showing the proofs to the mothers, Gloria and I had about a ninety per cent success rate of sales. Ruth was a true professional; after she had hand-coloured the photos they looked like portrait paintings. All of us were under a heavy workload and the strain began to get to David. He had to develop the photos at night in his bathroom and it was interfering with the family routine. A few times he gave me photos that were streaked and because we used a white background I had to insist on him doing them again. A couple of times we had arguments that descended into shouting matches. But we persevered.

On Sunday afternoon, 3 February 1974, Bathurst Gaol experienced the worst prison riot in Australian history. I remember the date because it was seven years to the day that Ronald Ryan had been hanged. When I heard the news on the radio I was concerned for my friend, Bobby Merrit, who had been transferred there to finish his sentence. Reports came through that up to twenty prisoners had been shot and wounded. Bob wasn't one of them. The prison chapel, textile workshops and three of the four cell blocks had been set alight with petrol soaked mattresses, furniture and anything else that would burn. Guards had been pelted with fire bombs, fluorescent light tubes and pipes forcing them to retreat to the perimeter wall. The police riot squad was rushed in. Nearly 70 per cent of the prison complex had been razed in the flames. Although no one was killed in the riot, one of the wounded prisoners became a paraplegic. The NSW government launched a Royal Commission headed by Justice Nagle which would result in a scathing assessment of treatment of prisoners and conditions at both Bathurst and Grafton Gaols.

Although the riot resulted in Bathurst being closed down for over a decade, and the cost of repairing more than $10 million, this didn't discourage the NSW government from its plan to build a new, more secure punishment gaol. In 1975 Katingal – later described by Justice Nagle, in his Royal Commission report as an 'electronic zoo' – was opened at Long Bay. After damning reports by Nagle on its austere nature, including sensory deprivations, it would be closed in June 1978. There are parallels here with H Division and its replacement Jika Jika, another 'electronic zoo' – also forcibly closed down.

A week after the riot, I came close to breaking my parole. After viewing the proofs of photos of her three sons, a woman in the West Ryde area had ordered a few hundred dollars' worth of hand-coloured photos. She wanted to give some of the photos to relatives. It was our biggest order to date.

But when I delivered them to her, she complained that 'Geoffrey in the middle' wasn't smiling. 'The other two are perfect,' she said, 'but Geoffrey has a serious look about him – it spoils the whole thing.'

'But Madam, you knew that when you made the orders. You had twelve photos to choose from, and this is the one you chose.'

She gave an embarrassed smile. 'I know, but the proofs were so small – I didn't pick up on it.'

'It's a beautiful portrait,' I said. 'Twenty years from now you'll look back on this with pride.'

'I'm more concerned about now – I want to send one of them to the grandparents. Can we do the sitting again?'

'Well we could. A free sitting. But you'll have to pay for these – all the work has been done.'

She gave me a stern look. 'I'm not paying for a product that is not satisfactory. The more I look at this photo, the more I realise it is not what I wanted.'

Sometimes you can talk people around. But I knew, instinctively, that this woman couldn't be swayed. I was bitterly disappointed that our biggest sale had fallen through. The time involved, the expenses, Ruth would still have to be paid – it was frustrating. I tried to be professional about it, and managed a resolute smile.

'Okay, Madam, I'm sorry it didn't work out.' I picked up the photos. 'You might as well leave me the big one,' she said. 'It's no use to you, is it?'

'I can't do that.'

'Well what are you going to do with the photos?'

I tried not to smile, but failed miserably. 'Destroy them,' I said, delighting at the look of shocked disbelief on her face.

'Why on earth would you do that?'

'As you said, Madam – they are no use to us.'

'I'm asking you as a mother to at least leave me the large one.'

'If you, as a mother, really wanted that beautiful photo of your boys, you'd pay for it – instead of trying to get it for nothing.'

She was enraged. 'I'll tell everyone to boycott your company. Your attitude is disgraceful. In fact, I'll make a complaint to Consumer Affairs about your rude and insulting manner.'

I snapped. 'You want the photos? You can have them!' With that, I walked out onto the lawn and ripped all of the photos into shreds, dropping the pieces onto the grass.

She shrieked, and ran down the stairs towards me. Thinking she was going to attack me, I ran for the car. As I drove off, I saw her picking up the pieces, mumbling to herself.

I knew it wouldn't end there – a few hours later, Colleen got a phone call from the woman's husband. He told her that his wife had suffered a nervous breakdown due to my outrageous behaviour, and to tell me that if I had any guts, to come over and fight him like a man.

Half an hour later I was knocking on their door. The husband answered. He was a tall guy, of about forty, of medium build. I noticed he had a bit of a paunch.

'Do you want to come outside and settle this like a man?' I said.

He paled, not moving. I knew my manner was intimidating and immediately sensed that this man had no stomach for a physical encounter. Probably, when he phoned Colleen and threw out the challenge, he had been putting on a show for the benefit of his wife and kids. He hadn't expected me to front up.

'You were rude to my wife,' he said, a slight quiver in his voice.

Suddenly, sanity prevailed. What the hell was I doing here? Did I want to go back to gaol? Okay, I'd lost a sale – get over it. The woman's attitude had been outrageous, but attitudes can be a lot worse in prison.

'We were rude to each other,' I said. 'But I shouldn't have ripped the photos up in front of her. I apologise.'

He became confident. 'Too right you shouldn't have ripped them up.

You broke her heart, mate.'

'Well she could have bought them.'

'You'd better leave, mate,' he said loudly, no doubt for the benefit of any eavesdroppers. 'We won't be dealing with your mob again.'

I began to walk away.

'Think yourself fortunate that we didn't have you charged!' he yelled.

He had come to the top of the steps.

I turned and grinned at him. 'Thanks. But it's only a $5 fine for littering.' Fuck him. That's all it had been – littering....

A few weeks after the ripped photos incident, David pulled out of the venture. He taught me a few techniques about studio photography and I became the professional photographer for Home Portrait Studios. For a small fee Colleen remained my 'secretary'. Pacific Studios, a photo processing giant, developed the photographs for me at a discount rate due to the amount of work I provided. I hired a couple of girls to trudge around the suburbs to get bookings for me. But they had a similar strike rate to what Miriam had managed for Bernies. I suspected that they were only working a few hours each day and after a while I sacked them. This necessitated my arranging for the appointments to take place on only three days a week to enable me to spend two days trying to persuade mothers to take a free sitting. Before Ruth could colour the photographs, I had to sepia them in a bathtub. Sepia is a dark brown ink, deriving from various cuttlefish. You sometimes see the process in a movie when they do flashbacks.

Eventually, I was forced to shut down Home Portrait Studios. Apart from the excessive workload, it became farcical when mothers with whom I had made appointments, recognised me when I arrived to do the sitting. And more often than not it was me who came to show them the proofs and take the orders.

Ironically, I had a few super sales before calling it a day.

• • •

The week I did my last appointment Dad went into hospital. After visiting him I had a talk to his lady specialist. She told me he had 'about twelve months left'. I was shocked. 'What's wrong with him?'

She sighed. 'What isn't wrong with him: heart, liver, kidneys, lungs – all damaged by excessive drinking and smoking. He's also got chronic back pain resulting from an old injury that is now irreparable.'

'What if he stops drinking and smoking?'

'He might survive another two or three years. But you should know your father – he won't give these things up.'

To everyone's surprise he did cut down. Dad was a survivor and he wasn't going out without a fight. Over the next six months his health considerably improved.

'Your old man will outlive all those bloody doctors,' he told me.

Then the normal, law-abiding life I had managed to adapt to was blown out of the water when Lisa gave my address to the madman, Steven Sellars...

MADNESS IN MELBOURNE

1974

The night Steven Sellars knocked on our door I was undecided about the future and thus susceptible to the proposition he was to put to me that night.

Unsuspecting Lisa had given him my address when he told her I was an old friend. In fact, he was little more than an acquaintance whom I had last seen in H Division.

He was a dark-haired, medium-built man of about my age. For a while we talked about the 'old days' in Pentridge – particularly H Division. Steve had been one of the first to rebel, going on a hunger-strike and abusing guards, resulting in quite a few bashings.

After Gloria went to bed he opened his bag and handed me a .32 Beretta automatic pistol. 'What do you think of that?'

I examined it. It was loaded and appeared to be in working order. 'You're taking a risk carrying this around.'

'I don't usually. It's a gift for you.'

'You're kidding.'

'Nope. I brought it for you. I've got others.'

A man like me should never have a gun – there were too many banks around.

'Okay, Steve, what's the catch?'

'You're a pro. I need a pro to help me knock over a bank in Melbourne.

Big money.'

'I'm getting married. I can't risk it.'

'How much have you got in the bank?'

'That's not the point.'

'It is the point. Easy money doing something you're good at. They'll never know you were in Melbourne. You'll have a kick-start for your marriage.'

'How many people involved?'

'You, me and Laurie Prendergast.'

Prendergast was another ex H Division prisoner who had been involved in the riots while I was there.

'Why this particular bank?'

'I was there one day and saw about $200,000 stacked on the far counter. I checked it same day, same time a week later – same deal. One of us just has to jump the counter and grab the money. It'll take twenty seconds.'

'What about a getaway vehicle?'

'No problem – I'll steal one.'

I doubted there would be that much money on the counter. But even if he had over-estimated the amount of money he had seen, I figured it would have been at least $100,000. We could also clean out the tellers' drawers, pushing the take to maybe $150,000. With a $50,000 split, I could buy a small supermarket.

'Okay, I'm in. And the Beretta is mine.'

He shook my hand. 'If you do the job it's yours.'

I lied to Gloria about my reason for going to Melbourne – telling her I was going with Steve to see some old friends.

The drive to Melbourne was a disaster. Steve pushed his old Falcon beyond its limits, resulting in the radiator overheating and cracking. We had no choice other than to leave it on the side of the road about 300 kilometres from Melbourne. Eventually we managed to hitch a ride to Melbourne with a truck driver.

On arrival, we caught a taxi to his girlfriend's place. She was an attractive brunette in her late twenties. After a few hours' sleep, we met up with Laurie Prendergast. He was a little younger than me, more ginger-haired than blond, of medium height and build. I had never liked the guy. He was brash, cocky, walked with a swagger and liked to talk the talk. His brother, Billy, whom I had met and liked, was a top-class boxer.

He drove us around in the suburbs until Steve found a car he knew he would have no difficulty stealing. Within a minute he was inside the vehicle, started it and began driving it away. We followed him to a block of units where he parked it inside the carpark which wasn't visible from the street.

We went for a walk, discussing the intended robbery.

'I need to see the bank,' I said. Where the tellers are, what security there might be and the getaway route.'

'I've done all that,' Steve said. 'I can fill you in on all the details. We park near the bank, run in and stick it up and grab the big stuff.'

'Who's driving?' I asked.

'I will,' Steve said. 'I've spent a lot of time setting this up. A lot of people have seen me in the bank and outside the bank. If they pick my photo out, I'm gone.'

'While we're in the bank we'll be wearing masks,' I said.

'Aw, fuck this! Steve can drive,' Laurie said. 'What's it matter?' I shrugged. 'Doesn't bother me. I usually rob banks by myself.'

'We do it tomorrow,' Steve said. 'Two pm. I've got balaclavas and gloves.'

The next morning Steve was sick. 'Been smoking too much pot,' he said. I stared at him. 'Are you up to driving or not?'

'No. I'm deadest crook. I'd be a liability. You two can do it – just park outside the bank.' He paused. 'Or we can put it off until next week.'

I shook my head. 'If we don't do it today, I won't be doing it.'

'Yeah,' Laurie said. 'We can do it ourselves. You stay here, Steve.'

I realised that Steve never had any intention of doing it. That's why he had brought me down – it was a two-man job. It wasn't that he didn't have the courage – he had shown plenty of that in H Division. But Steve now saw himself in the role of 'organiser' – a mastermind who recruited guys like me to take the risks. I was tempted to walk away, but I wanted the money and I wanted the Beretta.

I turned to Laurie. 'Do you want to jump the counter or hold the fort.' He gave me his tough guy look. 'I'll jump the counter.'

Steve gave each of us a balaclava and gloves. I had the Beretta, Laurie had a revolver.

We drove to where the stolen car was parked. Leaving the weapons and balaclavas with Laurie I drove the vehicle, with Laurie following, to a side street about a kilometre from the bank. We left Laurie's car there and I drove us to where the bank was situated, parking about 30 metres away.

As always before a robbery – and it had been eight years since my last one – my heart was pounding, my senses on high alert. But my hands were steady.

We got out and walked to a wooden bench near the bank.

As we sat down I said: 'Act casually. Put the 'bala' on your head and as we enter the bank pull it over your face. I'll hold everyone at bay while you jump the counter.'

I began to put the balaclava on when he said: 'We're sprung.'

'What are you talking about?'

'That woman over there is watching us.'

I saw a woman standing outside a shop about 30 metres away. She was looking in our direction.

'So, what's she going to do?' I said. 'She's too far away to give a good description. We could be anybody. We can run into the bank, get the money and be back in the car in 60 seconds.'

'No way, mate. She's watching every move we make. We have to call it off until next week.'

'Fuck it, we do it now or never!'

'I'm not doing it now. We've been sprung.'

I thought about doing it myself but immediately rejected the idea. Too many things could go wrong now. The whole thing had been a stuff up from start to finish. I'd go home and get married.

'All right,' I said. 'If she is watching us and sees us go to the car she'll take the number. Let's casually walk away and go to your car. She'll soon forget about us.'

As we walked away the lady turned and went into the shop. We jogged to Laurie's vehicle without incident.

On the way to Steve's place we hardly spoke.

When we arrived, Steve had the audacity to reproach us. 'You should have gone ahead,' he said.

'The bird made us,' Laurie said. 'She was staring straight at us, wasn't she John.'

'Yes. She was about to arrest the both of us.' He glared at me, colour rushing to his face. We were close to exchanging blows.

'How about we do it next week?' Steve said. 'No, I'm out,' I said. 'I'm going home.'

'We won't get another go like this,' Steve said. 'You and Laurie can do it.'

'Yeah, we don't need him,' Laurie said.

'The only problem is I've been seen around the bank too often,' Steve said.

'We've all been seen now,' I said. 'It's been awhile since you were there.

Anyway, whatever, I'm out.'

'If I'm going to do it, I'll need the Beretta,' Steve said. 'The deal was I keep it.'

'If the job got done. That didn't happen. But I'll make another deal with you.'

'I'm not rushing into some other job. I came here to do the one you targeted, it didn't work out. Now I'm going home.'

'You don't have to do a job – just go with Laurie and pick up the hottie and bring it here. Then the Beretta's yours.'

I figured the odds: the proximity of the vehicle to the bank increased the risk. But nothing had happened to draw attention to the car. The woman hadn't seen us get out of the vehicle. She had probably forgotten all about us. I was a risk taker and the Beretta was worth the risk.

'All right, you've got a deal.'

Leaving the Beretta with Steve I set off with Laurie to retrieve the vehicle. First, we drove past where it was parked, reconnoitring the area to see if it was under surveillance. There were no signs of anyone or anything suspicious.

'It looks okay,' I said. 'Drive up to the car and let me out. I'll follow you to Steve's.'

Wearing gloves, I got into the stolen car. Steve had hot-wired it and the engine kicked over at my first attempt. I then proceeded to follow Laurie.

After a few kilometres, I noticed a vehicle three or four cars back. A few minutes later I was certain it was following us. Laurie, directly ahead of me appeared to be unaware of the situation.

As we approached a set of traffic lights they turned to amber. Laurie went through. I slowed down then accelerated as they changed to red. The vehicle following me, siren blaring, came through the red light after me, forcing vehicles which had the green light to jam on their brakes.

The traffic was heavy. They must have staked the entire area out. Police vehicles had come from everywhere. Swerving into a side street I was suddenly blocked by a police car. Another drove up behind. Déjà vu! During my last bank robbery – also in Melbourne – a truck driver had blocked my path. But on that occasion, I had eluded capture. Not this time. As they grabbed hold of me I was thankful I'd left the Beretta with Steve. All I was guilty of was driving a stolen car. I might have to postpone the wedding, but not for long.

I was taken to a nearby police station and placed in a cell. My request to ring a lawyer was denied. After about half-an-hour I was driven to Russell Street Police Headquarters. They don't take you to Russell Street for a stolen car. I silently cursed Prendergast. If we had have gone ahead with the robbery we wouldn't have come back for the vehicle.

Eventually a couple of detectives took me to an interview room. One of them, a gangling, balding guy of about forty, did all the talking.

'I've looked at your record, John,' he said. 'So, don't try to tell me you didn't come here to rob that bank.'

'All I did was drive a stolen car. I want to talk to a lawyer.'

'Forget the lawyer. A woman has given a very good description of you and Prendergast.'

I wondered how he knew about Prendergast. They must have arrested him in the other car.

'I don't know anything about a bank.'

He stared at me. I could see he was agitated. In fact, to me, he looked unstable. 'Listen, I don't give a stuff about the bank. Your mad mate jumped out of the window from two floors up and he's badly smashed up. He told the ambulance people that we threw him out.'

I was shocked. 'Who, Prendergast?'

'No. We've got him. Steven Sellars is the bloke who jumped out. There's going to be a big stink over this.'

Whether Steve jumped or was thrown from the window was never legally decided. Police had followed Prendergast to Steve's place. Minutes later Steve was lying on the pavement, severely injured.

Deals were done to hush up the incident. I was charged with theft of a motor vehicle, given bail and told to get out of the state and never return. Neither Sellars nor Prendergast did a day in gaol, although I did hear that Prendergast received a bit of a touch up by the cops which gladdened my heart.

Apart from a few broken bones, Steve was okay. Years later he admitted to me that he had jumped – not wanting to be caught with the weapons in his unit. He had hoped to land on his feet like a cat and run away. Crazy, really. But he always had been a little bit mad.

Overall, the three of us were fortunate to have avoided a prison sentence.

The entire episode had been a farce from start to finish.

In October 1978, Laurie Prendergast, Raymond 'Chuck' Bennett and one other went to notorious criminal Les Kane's place, locked his wife in another room, killed Kane and took his body away. The body was never found. In November 1979, Bennett was gunned down outside Melbourne's Magistrate Court in Russell Street. In 1985, Laurie Prendergast disappeared, believed murdered.

The last time I saw Steve Sellars was at Parklea Prison in 1988. He hadn't aged well and was quite thin. At first, I didn't recognise him. His right shoulder was crippled. He told me Graham 'The Munster' Kinniburgh had shot him with a shotgun after Steve had tried to persuade Kinniburgh to give him a cut from the 1978 Murwillumbah bank robbery that netted millions. Sellars was convinced that 'The Munster' – one of the best tankmen (safe breakers) in Australia – was the mastermind behind the job. Less than six months after I spoke to him at Parklea, Steve Sellars was killed in a car accident. Fifteen years later, Graham 'The Munster' Kinniburgh was shot dead outside his house in Melbourne.

It was 1982 before I again set foot in Melbourne.

TROUBLE AT THE ORANGE SPOT

1974–75

After the Melbourne debacle, Gloria and I decided to buy a milk bar/delicatessen in Elanora Heights. A friend of David's wanted a quick sale to enable him to take over a Minit Market in Willoughby. Consequently, we negotiated a good deal.

Gloria arranged to let her unit at Birchgrove and, after our wedding in late July, we would move into rented premises in Warriewood, close to Elanora Heights. There would be no time for a honeymoon.

Gloria's parents paid for a great reception at the Carlton Rex Hotel where Gloria and I stayed the night. We had twenty friends and relatives at the table. Lisa brought her latest lover, Joe Owens, who at the time was the right-hand man to the firebrand union leader, Jack Mundey. He and David spent a good part of the time arguing about politics. But Dad was the star of the show. He had everyone laughing as he told a few off-coloured jokes. He was at his drunken best when it was time to leave. As the guests got up, ready to depart, Dad holding up an empty glass yelled: 'Waiter, the tide's gone out – do your job!'

The waiter, a slight scowl on his face, walked over to Dad. 'I'm sorry, sir, drinks are off!'

'This is my son's wedding night. I'm declaring drinks are back on!

Johnny, straighten this man out before I call the manager.'

Everyone was staring at us. Gloria looked at me and shook her head. I went to the waiter and took him aside. 'Look, I know what it's like to be serving people and taking orders from them. You've done your job and want to go home.'

'That's correct, sir.'

'This is a special night for me. Don't let my father spoil it. Get him another drink and there's $10 for you. That way we all win.'

'Very well, sir. One drink.'

Dad had a new story for his repertoire. He often told those willing to listen about the night of 'Johnny's Wedding' when he refused to leave the party without being served one more drink and how he offered to fight the waiter in a phonebox if he didn't get it.

Every day I opened the shop at 7:30 am and closed at 8:30 pm. When I went to Campbell's warehouse to buy stock or I had to leave the shop for some reason, Gloria took control.

I went to some of the work sites and car yards and took orders for sandwiches, pies and drinks from the workers. Compared to most of our stock, these were high profit items. After a while I had to employ a girl two hours a day to help us prepare all the lunches.

Business was good. We had a shop and storeroom crammed with stock and a surplus bank balance.

Instead of going to the races I had been placing bets with the local bookmaker, Jack, who was a regular customer. I had an understanding with him to limit me to $200 credit.

For a few months, the arrangement worked well until the Saturday prior to Christmas. Alone in the shop, I lost $200. I rang Jack and told him to increase the limit to $500.

'Are you sure?' he said. 'Of course, I'm sure.'

'Okay. What are your bets?' They all lost.

I rang him again. 'Make it a thousand.'

'Okay. You know what you're doing.'

I rang him a few more times. After the last race, I was down $6000. A few of my bets were beaten by the proverbial inch.

I was back in 1966 where, for me, it had been all or nothing. I disregarded history and the fact that 'nothing' had won that day...

I rang Jack. 'I'm going to place a few bets on the dogs tonight.

We'll make $10,000 the limit.'

'How are you going to pay $10,000?'

'The same way I'll pay six – I'll borrow it.'

'I think we should leave it at six – you're in enough trouble.'

'Listen, Jack – it's too late to tell me I'm in trouble. We had an agreement that $200 was my limit – I'm a fucking shopkeeper not Hollywood George!'

'You said you could pay thousands, so I took your word. Are you going to try to renege?'

'I'm going to $10,000. If I lose, you'll get your money. I'll arrange a mortgage on my shop and we've got a property in Birchgrove.'

'All right. But I'm warning you I've got an arrangement with a high-ranking police officer at Collaroy. You'll be dealing with him, not me.'

He shouldn't have said that. I immediately decided that if I couldn't recoup my losses, I wouldn't pay this bastard.

'I understand. I've picked two dogs. I want $2000 to win on each.'

Both were about 4 to 1. If one of them won, I'd be square. If both won he would owe me ten thousand. Both were beaten.

In a state of deep depression, I stayed at the shop until about 10:00 pm. In 1966, I wouldn't have hesitated – I would have robbed a bank. Things were different now. Gloria was eight months pregnant. As much as I enjoyed successfully owning and operating a shop, I knew we couldn't stay. I had no doubts Jack wasn't bluffing when he said he had a Collaroy cop on side. Once they checked my background and discovered I was on parole for armed robberies, I'd be a shot duck. The incident in Melbourne might also resurface to bite me.

We had no choices: we had to cut and run.

I went home and told Gloria. It was one of the hardest things I've ever had to do. Although she took it well, I could see the disappointment and disillusionment in her eyes.

After the initial shock, she said: 'What are we going to do?'

'We'll move out. I'll stall Jack, sign the shop over to David and that will be the end of it.'

'But Jack will get the police onto you.'

'For what? An illegal SP bet? Legally he doesn't have a leg to stand on.

But once the cops find out who I am they could make life difficult for us. Maybe even get me extradited to Victoria.'

'But if we leave they'll still be after you.'

'Maybe. But they'll be trying to get the ten grand and first they have to find me.'

'Do you think David will want the shop?'

'He's out of work. He'll jump at the chance.'

Early the next morning Jack was on our doorstep. Inviting him in for coffee I explained that it would take a week to arrange the loan of $10,000 which, by today's standards would be the equivalent of more than $80,000. 'Just so you know,' he said, 'I've informed my contact, Sergeant Keenan [not his real name] at Collaroy. He will be around to see you to explain why it will be in your interests to pay the money.'

Gloria was fired up. 'Don't you dare threaten my husband!'

Jack's face reddened. 'I'm not threatening anyone, but a debt's a debt.'

I smiled. 'Of course it is. But tell the cop not to bother – I don't want to see him. I understand the situation perfectly.'

Jack nodded. 'One week.' He got up and walked out.

Although David was enthusiastic about taking over the shop, Colleen, as always, was resistant to anything that involved me. But David prevailed and a few days later signed all the legal documents, taking ownership and responsibility for monthly repayments. Gloria and I suffered about a $3000 loss – but the way I figured it, we were $7000 ahead.

Until we could find suitable lodgings we stored most of our belongings and moved into a motel.

A few days later an agitated Jack called into the shop demanding to know where I was.

David truthfully told him he didn't know. Jack became aggressive and pulled a house brick from his bag and threatened to bash David's brains out unless he told him where I was.

'I own the police!' Jack yelled. 'Tell your no-good brother that we'll track him down and we'll get the money with interest.'

David refused to be intimidated. 'Get out before I call the police!'

Gloria and I spent Christmas day at the motel watching on TV the terrible aftermath of Cyclone Tracey which virtually destroyed Darwin – flattening 90 per cent of the houses and taking 65 lives.

We lived in motels until after the New Year then I rented a house in Summer Hill.

John Junior was born on Sunday night, 19 January 1975 at Paddington Women's Hospital [now closed]. Undoubtedly one of the more important events in my life. But I didn't realise it at the time.

About a week later I applied for a job at the Orange Spot in George Street at the top end of Wynyard Ramp. Impressed by the fact I had recently owned a milk bar/deli, the proprietor, Tommy, a short plump man of about forty, told me the guy who managed the shop for him, Eddie, would soon be returning to Lebanon and if I proved suitable I could manage the shop. It was open seven days a week selling sandwiches, drinks, milkshakes, pies, cakes, ice creams, fruit salads, yoghurts – all high profit items.

When Eddie left, I began working fourteen hours a day, seven days a week. One of my duties was to clean the shop and empty the garbage every night before locking up. Then I would catch a train and jog home from the station. Although I had female assistants until 6:00 pm Monday to Friday and Saturday mornings, I operated the shop solely on Saturday afternoons and all-day Sunday. Even on weekends I was rarely home before 11:00 pm. Sometimes the baby would start crying in the early hours of the morning and after a while I was suffering from sleep deprivation. I told Tom that I couldn't keep going at fourteen hours a day, particularly when he was deducting a large amount of tax from my wages. There were no tax file numbers in those days and he offered to pay me two sets of wages, one under a false name to offset the crippling tax. It was an offer I couldn't refuse.

Saturday afternoons were usually quiet. Bored, I developed the routine of closing the shop for fifteen to twenty minutes while I rushed down to the nearby TAB and placed a few bets on the races. I brought in a transistor to listen to the races.

On Easter Saturday, I won $700 on Dalrello when he flashed home to win the Doncaster. Then a huge thunderstorm struck and the remainder of the Randwick races were called off. I closed the shop and went to the TAB to collect my winnings.

The next morning Tom came in. 'I've been told you're closing the shop to duck down to the TAB.'

I shrugged. 'I close to go to the toilet. Then, sometimes on a Saturday I slip in and put a bet on. It takes two minutes.'

'I won't have a gambler running my business.'

'What's that mean?'

'It means you stay away from the TAB or you don't work here.'

'I'm here fourteen hours a day – I have to go to the toilet.'

'If you must, you shut down and go to the toilet. Be back in five minutes.' He paused and gave me a hard stare. 'I've got spies all over the place, so I'll know if you go to the TAB.'

I was tempted to tell him to give the job to one of his spies and see how they go working fourteen hours a day, seven days a week. But I'd never earn this type of money in another job.

'Okay,' I said. 'I won't put any more bets on at the TAB.'

'I notice you bring a radio in – that will stop. If you don't listen to the races you'll lose interest.'

On Friday night, I gave Gloria $300 to place on the champion mare Leilani to win the Queen Elizabeth Stakes at Randwick the next day. I couldn't imagine her being beaten.

When Tom came in on Saturday morning he checked to see if I had a radio. 'Good to see you've got the message,' he said. That afternoon business was almost non-existent. Closing the shop, I walked down to the railway toilet. There were only a few shops open – I figured Tom's 'spies' would be inside one or more of them. It was about twenty minutes before Leilani's race was due to be run. I resisted the temptation to go to the TAB and check the latest odds.

Back in the shop, as the time for the race approached, I wondered whom I could ring to get the result. Gloria wasn't on the phone; David would be in the shop at Elanora Heights. I decided to give a stranger a go. I dialled a random number. A male answered.

'Hi,' I said. 'You have a chance to win $50. Do you have a radio handy?' For a few seconds there was silence, then: 'Well, yes, but what station are you from?'

'Get the radio and tune it to 2KY. Hurry.'

After about 30 seconds he said excitedly: 'I've got it. I'm putting it on 2KY now. What's this all about?'

I could hear the race caller. The race was already in progress! 'Turn the volume up. If a horse named Leilani wins you'll win $50.'

'But what's this all about?'

'Just listen my friend and pray for Leilani.'

Leilani was fighting it out with another horse Jandell, all the way down the straight. They were well clear of the rest of the field. Surely the little champion mare would prevail?

They went across the line locked together. The announcer screamed that Jandell had won by an inch.

'Aaaagghhh!' I yelled. 'Did it lose?'

I slammed down the receiver. A guy at the counter ordered a chocolate milkshake – with ice cream.

'I noticed that last time I bought a milkshake you didn't put any ice cream in it,' he said.

Normally, I'd be sympathetic to the guy. I had already argued with Tom about his mean-spirited insistence on making milkshakes minus the ice cream. It was outrageous. Twice I had been abused by disgruntled milkshake connoisseurs. But at that moment I was ready to explode: I was sleep-deprived, overworked and forced to gamble surreptitiously and ring strangers to get the results. Now, after just losing $300 in a photo finish, I was in a dispute about what ingredients should be put into a milkshake.

I stared at the guy. He was solidly built, about thirty years old. He looked angry. I spoke slowly. 'We don't put ice cream in the milkshakes.'

He became aggressive. 'A milkshake is not a milkshake without ice cream. You already charge more than most places.'

Tom told me that if the customer insisted on ice cream, to give it to them and charge them 20 cents surcharge. 'If you want ice cream it will cost you an extra twenty cents,' I said.

He looked as though he was ready to jump the counter. 'I'm not paying extra for something I'm entitled to!'

I shrugged. 'Well go elsewhere. It's your choice.'

He tried to stare me down but I was just as angry as he was. If he didn't back off I was prepared to fight him.

'I'm reporting you to consumer affairs. What's your name?'

I nearly burst out laughing. 'My name is John Reardon,' I said, giving him the second name I was employed under. 'Spelt with an 'o' not an 'e'.'

'You'll be hearing more about this Reardon,' he said, and stormed off.

I made myself a double chocolate malted with three scoops of ice cream – on the house...

ADELAIDE AND THE FRUIT AND VEGETABLE MANAGER

1975–76

One Saturday morning in June when I opened the shop I discovered that somehow rats had managed to get into the premises overnight and had eaten pieces of most of the tomatoes. When I rang Tom requesting more tomatoes he insisted I cut out the bite marks and dice the remainder to use on the hamburgers and sandwiches. Hanging up I threw the tomatoes into the garbage bin.

Later, when Tom came around he asked me where the tomatoes were. 'In the garbage,' I said.

'I'll make your pay up – you're finished.'

'Great. I'll just have time to get to Randwick for the first.'

'That's another thing – I just don't trust gamblers.'

The insinuation was obvious.

Ironically, a few months later he begged me to return. He had employed a married couple to run the shop and they had robbed him shamelessly.

'I realise now that you were totally honest,' he confessed.

Well, not totally but compared to the crooked couple, I was a choir boy. I delighted in telling Tom that although I appreciated the offer, I had another good job, nine to five, which enabled me to spend plenty of time with my wife and son.

Dad was responsible for my new 'job.' One day when I called in to see him I noticed someone had installed a 'peephole' in his door.

'All he had was an electric drill and a bag full of peepholes,' Dad said. He charged me five dollars and I'll bet he only paid a dollar each for the peepholes.'

I decided to give it a try. After buying an electric drill and fifty peepholes (security door viewers) at 95 cents each, I drove to Burwood and concentrated on the blocks of units in the area. Charging five dollars to install one, I had plenty of takers. When I occasionally came across a block of units where no peepholes had been installed, I found that if I could persuade one person to get one, he or she would urge the other residents to follow suit.

During the day, a lot of the people were out and if I thought it would be worthwhile I'd return at night. After a while I was averaging $120 a day tax-free – good money in 1975.

For a while my life was incident free. Gloria and I were enjoying married life and young John was a delight. We both thought he was the best-looking boy in Sydney.

November 11 is a date I always remember. Apart from it being the day in 1918 when the Allies signed the Armistice with Germany, effectively ending World War I, Ned Kelly, Australia's most infamous outlaw, was hanged on this day in 1880. And, on 11 November 1975, a constitutional crisis occurred in Australia that is still hotly debated today: Gough Whitlam was sacked by the Governor General, Sir John Kerr, who represented the Queen. Seemed to me at the time the Poms were still running our country. Although insignificant by comparison, another incident occurred on this day in 1975 that impacted heavily on me. I was working in the Randwick area. An Asian lady, who couldn't understand what I was talking about when I showed her a peephole and my electric drill and pointed to her door, called the police after I had gone. At least she knew enough English to be able to do that.

As I came out of a block of units, two uniformed cops stopped me and asked me what I had in my bag. I handed it to one of them. 'See for yourself. There are about twenty security-door viewers and an electric drill.'

'What would you be carrying an electric drill around in your bag for?' the other one said.

I looked at him, then at the other one. They were both big, but overweight. I guessed they would both be in their mid-twenties.

'I'm a professional peephole installer,' I said. 'Do you have a security licence?'

'I don't know if I need one.'

'You are entering people's homes – you need a security licence,' he said. He grabbed me by the arm. 'We've had a complaint about you. We'll take you in and if your story checks out we'll let you go.'

I wasn't worried about my story checking out. My concern was with being held in a police station while they checked me out. Was there a warrant out for me from Victoria? I was confident that these two baby elephants wouldn't be able to catch me if I could get a start on them.

'All of those security-door viewers have my initials on them,' I said. 'Would I do that if I was committing criminal acts?'

As the cop with the bag let go of my arm and took out a few of the peepholes to check I simply ran away. After I had gone a few hundred metres I glanced around. They hadn't even bothered chasing me! I assessed the situation: they could get my fingerprints from the bag or the drill. But what criminal act had I committed? I ran away but I wasn't under arrest at the time.

I went to a shop and bought a new, different coloured shirt to the one I was wearing. Then, keeping an eye out for a police vehicle, I walked to the street where I had parked my car.

After driving home, I told Gloria the police had hassled me and I was giving up installing peepholes. I felt it best that she didn't have the additional stress of worrying if the police would come looking for me yet again.

Aware that if I was arrested in Sydney it could result in a gaol sentence, I discussed with Gloria the pros and cons of moving to Adelaide. She felt it could be a positive move if I could first arrange employment and a place to live.

In early January, I drove alone to South Australia.

As soon as I arrived in Adelaide I fell in love with the place. The streets were wide, traffic rarely congested, trees and parks everywhere. Accommodation was much cheaper.

I rented a half-furnished house in Netley, not far from West Beach, for $50 per week, but the landlord deducted $5 per week if I mowed the lawns.

Even though I used the alias of John Reardon and had no identification in that name, I was able to talk my way into a job with Coles as a relieving fruit and vegetable manager. I told them that what I didn't know about fruit and vegetables wasn't worth knowing. They were looking for someone to replace the permanent managers while they were on leave. I would spend two to four weeks in each store. If I did a good job I would be given a permanent position. I was scheduled to start in early February at West Lakes. I also visited Globe Derby to watch the 1976 Interdominion Pacing and Trotting Championships. My favourite horse the champion, Paleface Adios, starting from a 15-metre handicap, unluckily missed qualifying for the Final after a few poorly judged drives in the heats.

On the night of the Final, I backed him at the generous odds of 6 to 1 to win the Consolation Final. The champ quickly made up his handicap then raced around the field to win brilliantly – running near a second faster than they recorded in the Final. That night I won about $500 and it couldn't have come at a more opportune time. I was on a high for the entire drive home.

Before leaving Sydney, we called in to see Dad. He looked well. He loved young John and I knew he'd miss him.

'I'll be sad to see you go,' he said. 'But I think it's best. How many jobs have you had? I worked at Yellow Express for twenty years.'

'Yeah and they tried to palm you off without a cent.'

'You've got another chance, Johnny. If you stuff this one up you deserve what you get.'

He was right. 'We have to go, Dad. We'll be back for Christmas.'

'If the bulls come looking for you, I know nothing,' were his parting words.

• • •

Gloria liked the house and the area. Somehow, we had managed to put everything behind us and make a fresh start – a thousand miles from Sydney!

I told myself that from here on, I wouldn't put a foot wrong. We were in Adelaide which, compared to Sydney, was like a big country town. We had a nice house and suburb to live in, no debts – and I had a job! I had a loving wife and a beautiful son. We had a car.

Comparisons prove the point. Rather than compare my situation with others of my age, I compared it to mine a decade ago. It was exactly ten years ago to the week when I had robbed my first bank. Not only destroying my relationship with Cathy, but putting myself on the list of *Australia's Most Wanted*, as well as being sought by Interpol. Yes, ten years ago I had been an outlaw.

I had to smile to myself. I had a come a long way: Now I only had the Victorian police, and an angry SP bookmaker looking for me.

I had no problems adapting to fruit and vegetables. Taking the order book home, I studied the trends for the past twelve months. The fruit and vegetable section of Coles made about twenty-two per cent profit overall. This was huge compared to the grocery section which, I was informed, ran at about two per cent profit. I realised that my job was an important one. The management would expect me to run at a profit of at least twenty per cent. There were three imperatives: do not run out of stock; do not order too much and have to write some of it off as shrinkage; keep the counter full and the products attractively displayed.

I had three girls to help me. Their job was to cut, weigh, price and wrap in cling-wrap most of the items.

Although it wasn't a difficult job, I was constantly on the go. I had no doubt I was underpaid for the work I did. I learned that Coles management ordered stock from farmers up to eighteen months in advance at an agreed price. The farmer was obligated to supply at that price regardless of flood, drought and market prices at the time of provision.

Overall, I increased the profit margin in every store in which I worked. I had the knack – or maybe it was luck – of ordering stock so that we didn't run short or lose too much through shrinkage. If I had a surplus of one item and it was close to its use by date I'd reduce its price and announce it on the loudspeaker. But having to reduce the price of perfectly good stock to try to force the little guys out of business troubled me.

Although I had to work on Saturday mornings, I usually drove to the races on Saturday afternoons at either Cheltenham, Morphettville or Victoria Park. At this stage, the lure was more the thrill of the racetrack rather than the gambling because I rarely had more than $20 to risk.

The main setback for us in 1976 was when John was diagnosed with febrile convulsions. He would become feverish and lapse into a near unconscious state. Twice he lost consciousness and we had to rush him to hospital. The only positive prognosis was that he would grow out of it in two or three years.

Basically, in 1976, we were just a normal working class family. I worked without a problem in about a dozen stores. Sometimes Gloria would bring John to where I was working and do her shopping while I'd show off John to the girls who all made a fuss of him.

It all changed when I was rostered to the Modbury branch for two weeks. The assistant manager, a tall thin guy of 31 who had a pock marked face, took an instant dislike to me. He resented my intervening when about five of them were manhandling an old Russian guy who had stolen some garlic.

'He stole it from right under your nose and you didn't even notice it,' he accused.

'You could have left him some dignity,' I said. 'The way he was being pushed and dragged he probably thought the KGB had him.'

'He should have thought about that before he came into our shop and stole from us.'

A few days later I snapped. We were just closing up for the day when I heard the assistant manager admonishing one of the boys who worked every afternoon for a few hours after school stacking shelves.

'If you aren't happy about working twenty minutes overtime without wanting to be paid for it, you can leave. I have another twenty boys waiting for a job!'

I walked over and confronted him. 'You pompous hypocrite! What you're asking him to do is slave labour – working for no pay!'

'It's all right, sir,' the boy said.

'It's not all right,' I countered. 'If you work an extra twenty minutes you should be paid for it. Stacking shelves is hard work.'

The assistant manager took a step back. He was staring at me, obviously shocked by my manner. 'We have a budget for casuals,' he said.

'Stuff the budget. Pay the kid.' I walked out, got into my car and drove home.

The next morning the manager asked me to come to his office. After a brief discussion, we both agreed I wasn't suited to be a fruit and vegetable manager. I was able to leave without giving the required week's notice.

As I drove out of the car-park I felt as though a weight had been lifted from my shoulders. My time in H Division had made me incapable of working with people like the assistant manager. He reminded me of some of the guards.

BACK INTO THE LION'S DEN

1976–78

Although Gloria was disappointed that I was now a permanent absentee from the fruit and vegetable sections of Coles, I was relieved. I simply bought another electric drill, fifty security door viewers and I was again ready for business.

Compared to Sydney, the high-rise blocks of units in Adelaide were sparse. And a lot of those units had been fitted with peepholes. After a few weeks, I began trekking around the suburbs going from house to house. My success ratio was lower than it had been in Sydney, but my profit each week was always more than the wages Coles had been paying me.

In November, I hit the jackpot at the races. I had $100 to win at 6 to 1 on the New Zealander, Van Der Hum, in the Melbourne Cup. The track was rain affected and I knew the horse was a 'swimmer' (loved wet, heavy tracks). Just before the race was scheduled to start, the dark clouds hovering over Flemington unleashed torrential rain so heavy it was difficult to see the horses. During the race, the course announcer couldn't distinguish the colours worn by the jockeys. Loving it, Van Der Hum ploughed through the conditions to beat the favourite, the Bart Cummings trained Gold and Black (who went on to win it in 1977).

I also backed a few other good winners. On the day, I won more than $1000. At the time, it was a fortune for us.

Financially stable we drove to Sydney and spent Christmas with Gloria's family.

In Sydney, everyone made a fuss of John and he received a lot of presents. For me there is something absurd about Christmas. You spend a lot of money on presents for people which they don't need or want. In return, they give you presents that you don't need or want. But the kids love it. So do the shops.

After visiting David and his family, we drove over to see Dad. He was upset I had left Coles. 'You can't put peepholes in people's doors for the rest of your life,' he said.

'Don't worry, Dad – I do a bit of shoplifting on the side.'

He turned to Gloria. 'Johnny's still the mug lair. He's always got the smart-arse answer.'

He was pissing me off. 'Just telling you where your presents came from, Dad.'

'Take them back! I don't want them!'

Gloria intervened. 'He's only joking, Reg. I bought those presents myself.'

He calmed down and played around with John for a while. It was good to see.

Overall it was a pleasant, uneventful trip.

In January 1977, Gloria began working part-time for a town planner.

Financially we were going well and we moved into a fully furnished house in Parkside, near Unley. It had a spacious backyard with dozens of tomato plants. The front lawn was surrounded by rose bushes.

One day at the races I ran into Allan Scott – nicknamed 'Scotty.' He had been the driver in the disastrous Hotel London robbery in Melbourne in 1966 where an off-duty cop was shot five times but survived. Scotty spent five years in Pentridge while I was there and he never stopped complaining about it. He had been totally out of his depth driving a getaway car in an armed robbery: his forte was shoplifting and picking pockets at the races. Occasionally, he came to visit us, bringing expensive clothes for John.

He told Gloria that he'd had a few big wins at the races, but I suspected that he had shoplifted the items. It didn't bother me.

After a while I went on a few shoplifting sprees with him. 'Adelaide is a big country town,' he said. 'The security in the shops is piss weak.'

While I kept lookout, he would walk into a department store with one of those canvas-covered two-wheeled trolleys, stuff it full of cardigans and pullovers and stroll out unchallenged. In smaller shops, he'd place his suit coat on one shoulder and put items under his armpit and walk out. Sometimes, if he went into a department store, filled the trolley and exited without arousing suspicion, I would take the trolley and go and fill up in a different section.

Scotty had no problem selling the items to his friends and at some of the hotels he frequented. He often had a list of items which people had ordered. I was reminded of the days in 1959 when Jim and I – on a much smaller scale – stole from stores and sold the goods to hotel patrons.

After a few weeks, I pulled out of the venture. Scotty couldn't understand it.

'By the time you sell the stuff and we split the money it's not worth the risk,' I said.

'Come off it, mate. Even if they catch you, you'll probably get a fine.'

I didn't tell him that an arrest in Adelaide could activate a warrant for my arrest in Victoria.

'I don't care,' I said. 'I make enough installing peepholes.' Scotty still came around from time to time.

Disregarding my disastrous history with gambling, I made a decision to become a professional gambler. I kept meticulous records of all racehorses and assessed what price I thought a horse should be. If a bookmaker bet what I considered 'over the odds' on a horse I fancied I'd put my money on it to win.

I enjoyed the challenge and the lifestyle. Sometimes I would take John with me to a country race-meeting, give him a little bag and, keeping a close eye on him, tell him to pick up all the discarded tickets. If he found one that was 'good' I'd collect it for him. After every race, I collected 50 cents for him. He couldn't wait to get home and tell his mother. A successful businessman at two and a half.

Overall, as a professional punter in 1977, after expenses I broke about even. Gloria continued to work for the town planner. I had given up installing peepholes. On a few occasions after I lost at the races I'd team up with Scotty for a few days of shoplifting. I knew I was pushing my luck.

In August 1977 Elvis Presley died. Not since the assassination of John F. Kennedy had the death of a person created such attention. Radio stations began playing his records all day; the newspapers and television stations gave it huge coverage. Everyone I spoke to wanted to talk about it.

That same week I received a phone call that would change the entire course of our lives. John, the guy from whom I had bought the milk bar delicatessen, wanted me to run his minit market for him during the weekends. We could reside there three nights a week.

'You are the only person I can trust to not rip me off,' he said.

I talked it over with Gloria. Both of us missed Sydney and the regular contact with family and friends. We knew that the bookie would still have his policeman friend looking for me who, if he found me, could cause problems for me in Victoria.

'Jack and his copper mate will never know I am back in Sydney,' I said. 'I'm old news. It happened three years ago.'

'Then Sydney it is,' Gloria said.

We rented a unit in Cavendish Street, Stanmore. But from Friday evening until Monday morning we lived at the shop premises.

Gloria and I enjoyed running the mini-market on the weekends. A two-bedroom residence was attached to the shop. Although John and his wife resided there Monday to Friday, we stayed there on weekends.

Sometimes, at night, I would unlock the door into the shop and tell John to go and get some food for us. He always returned with an armful of potato chips, chocolates and lollies.

During weekdays, I returned to trudging the suburbs installing peepholes. But after a few weeks I gave it away. It seemed that during my near two years in Adelaide most of Sydney had been 'peepholed'.

Without even realising it I returned to my old cycle of pushing my luck gambling and inevitably had some heavy losses.

In February, just before my thirty-sixth birthday, I began systematically shoplifting Monday to Friday. I'd turn my suit coat inside out, push the sleeves into the pockets and, carrying it on my shoulder, slip expensive toiletry items, razor blades or even fillet steak down the sleeve. A few shopkeepers I knew always bought the items for half price. Occasionally, I'd go to another store and get a refund. It was petty stuff, but I was averaging more than a $1000 a week – tax free.

In March, I was arrested at Coles in Merrylands. As they grabbed hold of me I was reminded of the old Russian at Modbury. Sooner or later, Coles always get their man.

I was taken to Fairfield Police Station where they also charged me with an old break and enter warrant on a Flemings grocery store. Although I had never been arrested over it, the vehicle used to take the stolen items away in had been identified as mine.

I pleaded guilty to the shoplifting but not guilty to the alleged break and enter.

The magistrate fined me $250 for the stealing from Coles and remanded me for trial on the other.

Gloria bailed me out. The way I looked at it, being arrested had been a positive thing. It brought to a halt my shoplifting spree and there had been not a whiff of interest from Victoria. A lawyer advised me that if I stayed out of trouble and we prolonged the matter for another year, I could take a plea and get a bond.

The money Gloria and I received for working at the mini-market on weekends wasn't enough to live on. Gloria began working part-time for a lawyer. When she was at work I looked after John. I enjoyed my time with him. Regardless of where I went, I always took him with me.

Dad loved him and I usually brought John at least twice a week to see him.

As part of my bail conditions I had to report every night at 8:00 pm to Chatswood Police Station and sign a register. Chatswood was the designated police station because I had given the Willoughby mini-market as my address.

I was always punctual until one Saturday night after closing the shop at 7.00 pm we drove to Newport for dinner and a few drinks at David's place. 'I'll drop in and sign the sorry book on the way home,' I told Gloria.

'It's the first time I've been late and they'll cut me a bit of slack.'

It was a good night. I even managed to have Colleen laughing at one of my jokes. John enjoyed seeing his cousins, particularly Andrew who was the same age.

We stayed until about 11:00 pm, then drove straight home.

On Sunday afternoon, leaving Gloria to run the shop, I drove to Chatswood

Police Station. An old sergeant was at the desk. I gave him a friendly smile. 'Hi, Sarge. I've got a problem.'

'Oh, and what might that be?'

'I have to sign the register every night and last night I had too much to drink and my wife wouldn't let me come.'

He laughed. 'Don't worry, son, we've all been there. You're the bloke who works at the mini-market, aren't you?'

'Yep. I've just come from there during a quiet period. The wife is looking after it.'

'You've been clocking in on the dot every night,' he said with an approving tone. 'Tell you what, how about we sign you in for 8:00 pm last night and 8:00 pm again today. Save you coming back tonight. Keep the missus happy.'

'I appreciate that, Sarge. Drop into the shop sometime.'

He gave me a stern look. 'My missus does the shopping. Now, give me two signatures and make sure you don't stuff up again.'

Without either of us realising it at the time, the sergeant had just involved himself in a controversial case that would go all the way to the High Court of Australia and become known as the Perfect Alibi case.

IMPENDING DISASTER

1978

After a while I applied to the magistrate to reduce my bail reporting conditions from every night to any time on Monday, Wednesday and Fridays. Although he agreed to the reduction to three days a week, the 8:00 pm reporting time remained.

The racetrack is a great place to run into people with 'colourful' backgrounds. In May, at Canterbury races, I was having a bad day when Greg Eyles came up and said hello. I'd met him at Long Bay in 1973. He was a small, slightly built guy, boyish-faced, in his mid-twenties.

He told me he had lost all his money.

'I'm not doing much better,' I said. 'Today we should throw the form guide in the rubbish bin and go home.'

He didn't have transport and I drove him to his place at Summer Hill which wasn't far from Stanmore.

He invited me inside where I met his wife, Patricia, a thin pretty girl about the same age as Greg. They had a son, aged about fifteen months. He knew I had been inside for bank robberies and as he walked with me to the car he said: 'If you ever want to hit a bank again, count me in.'

I laughed. 'Those days are gone.'

In early June, I decided those days were here again.

I called in to see him. 'Let's go for a walk,' I said. I had been experiencing a bad run on the horses and had been forced to pawn some of our valuables.

'I'm going to rob a bank,' I told him as we began our walk. 'Are you still interested?'

'I told you I would, John. I need money desperately – we've got nothing and I'm in debt.'

'The bank I've got in mind is interstate,' I said. 'To do it professionally we'll need a driver.'

'Pat will do it.'

'No. If something goes wrong your boy is an orphan. Leave it to me – I'll get a driver. Then we'll get together and make final plans.'

I contacted an ex-prisoner whom I knew was still active and an expert car thief. He also had a pistol. When I asked him if he was interested in being the getaway driver for an interstate bank robbery he was enthusiastic. The three of us had a meeting.

'Greg, this is Bill. He's our getaway driver – he'll also hotwire a car for us.' Bill was an alias. 'The bank is in Adelaide. I've seen a lot of business owners deposit large amounts of money there late on Friday afternoons. Our take should be well over a hundred grand. Even split three ways it's a good day's work.' I paused. 'Bill, you'll wait outside in the hot car, I'll control the tellers and customers while you, Greg, jump the counter and clean out all the tellers' drawers. We need to be in and out in ninety seconds so you'll have about twenty seconds for each teller.'

'As long as you've got me covered I can do that,' Greg replied.

'One of the tellers will probably set off a silent alarm to the police,' I said. 'So, remember, count to twenty as you do each drawer. We'll both need face masks – I'll get them.'

We spent the next hour going over our respective roles, the best place to steal a car and the available getaway routes. I used an Adelaide street directory to familiarise them with the areas.

'My car is too old to drive over,' I said. 'We can't risk a breakdown. Greg, can you get Patricia to hire a car?'

'I haven't got the money.'

'I'll get it for you. Bill, you'll also need to kick in with a few hundred for petrol and other expenses.'

We planned the robbery for Friday, 16th June – exactly ten years to the day when I had made the unsuccessful bid to break out of Pentridge. It was a date permanently etched into my mind. While at H Division I had read James Joyce's Ulysses which focused on one day: Bloomsday – 16 June. The irony hadn't escaped me. Now a decade later I intended to rob a bank on that day.

Although I wasn't superstitious, I was aware that, in the past, June had been an inauspicious month for me. My mother had died in June; I had been arrested in June 1963, resulting in it being the last time I saw Cathy; I had been sent to the dreaded H Division three times in June (1966, 1967, 1968). In June 1974, I had been arrested in Victoria.

The date worried me but I shrugged it off. I didn't believe in such nonsense.

The plan was for the three of us to drive to Adelaide after I checked in at Chatswood on Wednesday night. I estimated that if we rotated the driving we could do the trip in seventeen to eighteen hours. We could steal a vehicle on Thursday night and conceal it in a block of units near the bank. After the robbery, we could exchange vehicles and they could drive me to the airport where I'd catch a flight to Sydney – arriving at 8:00 pm. If I could get to Chatswood before 9:00 pm to sign the register I'd be in the clear. Greg and Bill could drive to Sydney at their leisure.

Bill and I gave Greg the money to enable Patricia to hire a late model

Kingswood for a week. Bill also bought two novelty masks. On the Tuesday, I drove over to Greg's place. I found him and Patricia in the kitchen – arguing. On the table, there was an empty syringe. I realised they were arguing about who had had the biggest 'shot' of heroin. They were unaware that I was there.

I could hear the baby crying in another room. I went and picked him up and brought him to the kitchen.

The knowledge that I was planning to rob a bank with a junkie alarmed me. At that stage, I didn't know a lot about drugs. But I knew that heroin was addictive and destroyed people. Before I was released from Long Bay in 1973, my friend Harry, who had lost most of his liver due to injecting heroin and contracting Hepatitis C via a contaminated needle, told me: 'Never trust a junkie. They'll give up their own mother for a shot.'

My instinct for danger was on high alert. I was a gambler and I'd never been afraid to take risks. But now I felt the odds were against me and I had too much to lose. Not just my freedom, but my wife and child.

Outside, I said to Greg: 'Does Patricia know what we're doing?'

'Mate, I'd trust Patricia with my life.'

'Why did you tell her?'

'She hired the car. She's not stupid. Don't worry about Patricia.'

'You didn't have to tell her. I told you to tell no-one. Anyway, it's done now. I'm out.'

'Out? What do you mean you're out?'

'The job's off. You'll have to find another way to buy your drugs.'

'John, I'm not a junkie.'

'You should have told me you and Patricia are into this shit. Even if we pull this job, how long do you think the money will last? You two will shoot it up your arms.'

'You said we'll get at least thirty grand each. I'm going to buy a little business.'

'What, supplying drugs?'

'What about you. You told me you lost a shop gambling.'

'Right. Maybe I'll lose my share too. So, I'm out. I'll go and tell Bill.'

'I'll come with you. I can do it with him.'

'Forget it. You guys don't know the area, you won't have a getaway driver.' But Bill couldn't be dissuaded from going ahead. My estimate of at least $100,000 take was the deciding factor.

On Wednesday, 14 June they set off with Patricia for Adelaide.

On Friday afternoon, 16 June 1978, two bandits, one of them armed with a pistol, robbed a bank in Plympton South Australia of approximately $16,000. After collecting the money, they ran out to a waiting, stolen car where a third person drove them away.

After driving to a laneway about a kilometre away, the three occupants got out and ran to a yellow Kingswood with NSW number plates.

A boy, Nicholas Bambacas, who was feeding chooks in his backyard, heard the stolen car swerve to a halt. Looking through a gap in the fence he saw the three people running to the Kingswood. Suspicious of their manner he made a mental note of the letters AXM on the number plate.

When he saw a report on the news about the robbery he rang the police. They immediately issued an all points alert for a yellow Kingswood bearing NSW number plates beginning with AXM.

Unaware of what had eventuated in South Australia, I drove to Chatswood Police Station and signed the register at 8:00 pm.

At about the same time, Greg and Patricia, driving a yellow Kingswood with number plates beginning with AXM booked into a motel in Barmera, South Australia.

On Saturday morning police surrounded the motel and arrested them. During a search of the room police found a large sum of money and an unlicensed .32 Beretta pistol.

During interrogation by the police Greg confessed to the bank robbery. He made a signed statement claiming he and a man named 'Bill' had robbed the bank. There was no getaway driver.

The police knew there had been a getaway driver. They believed Patricia had driven the stolen vehicle. To add to his problems Greg couldn't provide them with any information about Bill.

Confronted with the prospect of both he and Patricia going to gaol, Greg made a second signed statement contradicting the original. This time he claimed he and I had robbed the bank while Bill had stolen and driven the car.

While Greg was telling tall tales to the police, Bill came to the shop to see me. There was an air of desperation about him as he looked around to see who might be listening.

'We're in trouble,' he said.

I could feel my heart begin to race. Greg must have stuffed up. If he talks to the police I could be charged with conspiracy.

Leaving Gloria to mind the shop, I took Bill into the lounge room. He handed me an Adelaide newspaper. 'Read the Stop Press.'

It was short but ominous: Two bandits had robbed the National Bank in Plympton on Friday afternoon. Police were looking for a late model yellow Kingswood with NSW number plates beginning with AXM...

'Did you fly back?' I asked.

He nodded. 'Last night. Greg and his missus are in the car. They'll get them.'

My mind was racing. 'No doubt,' I said. 'There's no way we can warn them.

Did you tell him anymore about yourself – where you live or who your friends are?'

'Nothing. Listen, John, if the worst comes to the worst and he involves you, you have to keep me out of this. I can't afford to go to gaol.'

'What, you think I can? I didn't even do the fucking thing. You guys stuffed up, not me!'

'You planned it, mate. You told us there'd be a hundred grand there – we got sixteen.'

'Well, you didn't do it right. Anyway, I urged you not to go ahead with it. But they can't get you unless I talk. You know I won't do that. You did it, but I'm the one in danger. I need two grand so I can give Greg's mother some money to get him a lawyer if he's pinched. It could save me from being implicated.'

'Two grand?'

'At least. Then go to ground for a while. I'll deal with everything.' Reluctantly, he gave me $2000.

Looking back, it is difficult to now argue I wasn't guilty of robbing the National Bank in Plympton on 16 June 1978. I had planned it, organised the participants and then received some of the proceeds of the crime which was given to Greg's mother. But in my heart, I was innocent. I had withdrawn from the venture and remained in Sydney during the committing of the crime. There had been no arrangement for me to receive a cent from the proceeds. It was my belief that once I had advised them to abandon the entire venture, I had washed my hands of any involvement.

The reality was that the moment nosey little Nicholas Bambacas saw and remembered the letters AXM on the number plate of the yellow Kingswood, I was involved up to my neck in legal quicksand...

VERBALLED

1978

On Saturday afternoon, I rang the car rental company stating that my niece had rented a car from them and I hadn't heard from her for four days. Had she returned the car? The receptionist, in a hushed tone, confided that Patricia and her husband had been arrested that morning in South Australia.

Even when you are expecting bad news, when it comes it stuns you. Instinctively, I knew Greg would involve me. It would be a 1966 re-run: John Killick: Wanted for bank robbery. This time I had a wife and child to worry about...

With heavy heart, I told Gloria that I might have to go away for a while.

We closed the shop early and took John with us to a nearby park. After explaining the situation to her I admitted that I had intended to go ahead with the robbery but had pulled out of it. From that point on I was totally uninvolved.

Although she was upset that I had even contemplated robbing a bank, she was relieved that I hadn't gone ahead with it.

'A lot of people saw you here yesterday,' she said. 'It doesn't matter what Greg tells them, you can prove that you weren't involved.'

'They might be able to get me for conspiracy. In the eyes of the law that's just as bad as doing it.'

We looked at each other. I felt like a schoolboy – in trouble again. 'What are you going to do?' she asked.

'I'll give you some money to take to Greg's mother so she can get him and Patricia a lawyer. A lawyer will advise them to say nothing. But it's a long shot. By the time we arrange it, Greg or Patricia will probably have told the cops everything.'

Gloria was angry: 'In that case they'll tell them you weren't involved.'

I nodded. 'We may be worrying over nothing. I'll book into a motel for a couple of nights and we'll see what eventuates. We'll need to make a decision by Monday night when I'm due to appear on bail.'

We arranged to meet again the next morning in the park at Milson's Point.

'Be careful you aren't being followed,' I warned her.

After leaving me, Gloria visited Greg's mother, Bessie. Instead of thanking her for the money, she snatched it from her and abused her.

'Your husband got my son into this,' she said, 'and you tell him that he'd better get him out of it!'

Apparently, Greg had told his mother everything.

Using an alias, I booked a room for two nights at the Camperdown Travelodge.

Some people when they are stressed and need a diversion from their problems, enjoy a few drinks, others take drugs, some look for sex. I like to gamble. That night the great Paleface Adios was scheduled to have his last race at Albion Park Queensland. Tulloch had gone out a winner, and so, too, I reasoned, would the 'Temora Tornado.' I placed most of my money on him to win.

While people lined Oxford Street to watch the gays and lesbians march in Australia's first Mardi Gras, I listened on the radio as the baldy-faced Paleface Adios hung on to win his supposedly last race. The announcer became emotional as he described it and I, too, became emotional – and not just for the champion pacer.

(After 'retiring' to stud, Paleface Adios made a comeback in early 1979 and went on to win many more races – 108 in total).

On Sunday morning, I played with John in the park and discussed with Gloria the options available to us. There weren't many: either I return home and wait and see what eventuated or I go into hiding, ensuring that a warrant would be issued for my arrest for failing to report on bail.

The fact that the police hadn't come looking for me at either the Stanmore flat or the shop was a positive sign that Greg hadn't mentioned me to police.

I decided to stay at the Travelodge for another night. If by Monday night there was no sign of the police, I'd enter the lions' den and sign the bail register. If they set a trap for me that's where it would be. At least they couldn't accuse me of flight if I walked into the police station. I reasoned that if they did charge me they would have to give me bail – especially when I proved I was in Sydney at the time of the robbery.

Gloria agreed to bring John to the Travelodge and stay with me that night.

They arrived at about 6:00 pm. A few hours later I left the room to go and buy some snacks. As soon as I walked from the lift into the lobby I knew I was in trouble. A couple of guys were sitting near the exit door pretending to be reading newspapers. They may as well have had 'cop' tattooed on their foreheads.

Although they gave me a hard stare they made no attempt to apprehend me. I figured they must have followed Gloria and at this stage didn't have a photo of me. I hurried outside. Greg must have implicated me in the robbery! What do I do now? Do I run?

Suddenly I was surrounded by police who emerged from the shadows. 'John Killick?' someone asked.

I knew I couldn't bluff my way out of this one. 'That's right. What's the problem?'

'You're under arrest!'

I was grabbed and handcuffed behind my back. They had a car waiting nearby and bundled me into the back seat.

I needed a lawyer. I had arranged with Gloria that, if I was arrested, she would ring solicitor, Bruce Miles. I had met him through Bobby Merritt. On occasions, I had accompanied both of them to court when Bob was working with the Aboriginal Legal Service. Bruce was overworked and sometimes I helped him prepare statements for indigenous clients. Grateful, he told me that if I ever needed him, I could ring him – day or night.

'My wife and son are in my room,' I said. 'At least let her know where I am.'

'That's taken care of,' one of the cops said.

I was driven to the CIB headquarters at Remington House in Liverpool Street. A thickset, dark-haired detective who looked to be in his forties greeted me. 'G'day, Johnny. I'm Detective Sergeant John Walton of the Armed Hold Up Squad. You're in a lot of trouble.'

'If you're talking about those banks in sixty-six, I've already been sentenced on them.'

'I'm talking about the National Bank in Plympton South Australia that you knocked off on Friday afternoon.'

'I don't know who told you that garbage, but I was in Sydney all day on Friday and I can prove it.'

'It won't wash, John. Your mate is singing like a canary.' He turned to one of the arresting cops who was still holding on to me. 'Take the cuffs off and bring him to the interview room.'

The interview room was small and sparse, consisting of a table with a typewriter on it and four chairs.

'Sit down, John,' Walton said. He indicated two detectives who were also in the room. 'These are detectives Louis and Phillips. They'll be assisting with the interview.'

Louis was a tall, solid guy with light brown hair who looked to be in his mid-thirties; Phillips, who looked a bit younger, was slim with gingerish hair.

I sat down. 'There'll be no interview until you get my solicitor here.'

'It's Sunday night, no lawyer will be coming,' Louis said.

'Mine will. This is a set-up and I want him here.'

'You haven't been charged with anything yet,' Walton said. 'Nor has Gloria.'

I glared at him. 'Leave her out of it.'

'She was with you in the hotel room. She's an accessory.' He paused, a slight smirk on his face. 'She's upstairs with John.'

A combination of rage and despair almost caused me to lose control. I suppressed it and spoke calmly. 'You have to sink pretty low to hold a three-year-old in police custody. 'What are you charging him with?'

He reddened. 'You put him in danger. We were getting ready to bust into your room. You endangered your son by having him with you after robbing a bank.'

'The last time I robbed a bank my son wasn't born. I'll make sure you get charged with illegal detainment of a child.'

'You were hiding in the hotel. That's an indication of guilt,' Walton said. 'Gloria was with you; she's an accessory.'

I knew they couldn't detain her for long. They were holding her to prevent her from contacting a lawyer. 'There's no law preventing us from staying in a hotel for a night,' I said. 'No one told me you guys were looking for me.'

'You had $1600 in your possession,' Louis said. 'Where did that come from?'

'My name is John Killick. I live at unit 1, 29 Cavendish Street, Stanmore. I work part-time at a Minit Market in Willoughby. I know nothing about any robbery in South Australia on Friday. Dozens of people saw me in Sydney that day. I reported for bail at Chatswood police station on Friday night at exactly 8:00 pm. That's all I have to say until I see my solicitor.'

Phillips was writing in a notebook.

'Why don't you type what I just told you and I'll sign it?'

'I'll tell you what we know, John,' Walton said. 'Greg has told the South Australian police everything.'

'Greg who?'

Louis laughed. 'You're not a very good actor. You just turned white.'

'Greg Eyles,' Walton said. 'He and his missus drove over to Adelaide in a hire car. You flew over, stole a car and you and Greg knocked the bank over. You flew back on Friday night. You got one of your mates to go to Chatswood and sign the bail book for you. You found out Greg and his missus had been arrested when you rang the hire car company. You knew he'd give you up so you booked into the Travelodge under an assumed name using money you stole from the bank. The money we found in your possession tonight also belongs to the bank.' He paused and stared at me with a 'See, I'm Sherlock Holmes' look.

'You should be writing short stories,' I said. 'You're good at fiction.'

He didn't like it. Leaning forward, his face close to mine, he tried intimidation. 'Listen, smart arse, you did it and you're going to wear it. Either you make a statement and sign it, or we'll charge Gloria as an accessory and young John will become a ward of the state.'

'I didn't do it. Do what you want.'

'He doesn't give a stuff about his wife and kid,' Louis said. 'Let's take him to the biff room and see how tough he really is.'

'Go ahead – mark me up. I'll add assault to the illegal detainment charge.'

Walton nodded, more to himself than to me. 'We don't bash people anymore, John. We have more sophisticated methods.'

Louis handcuffed me to the chair. 'If you try to escape you'll be shot,' he said.

I sensed that he meant it. They left the room. I told myself that the situation wasn't as grim as it looked. Although it was outrageous that Gloria was being detained, John would probably see it as an adventure. Hopefully by now he would be asleep. I knew that if they dared to charge Gloria with anything, they would have to present her to the court in the morning. As soon as she spoke to a lawyer the court would be obliged to release her.

After about an hour Phillips came in. 'Would you like a coffee, John?'

'No thanks. Where's Gloria and my son?'

'They're still upstairs.'

'You guys are supposed to be the good guys. Why keep an innocent woman and a little boy prisoners?'

'Are you admitting you aren't innocent?'

'You've got a fool in South Australia saying I committed a crime. So, okay, check it out. But no one could possibly be implicating Gloria in anything. Let her go.'

'Tell us the truth and we'll let her go immediately.'

'I told you, I had nothing to do with it. That's the truth. Now let her go.' He laughed and walked out.

They had taken my watch and I lost track of time. It was after midnight when the three of them returned. Walton was surprisingly cheerful. 'We typed up an interview from the notes Detective Phillips took,' he said. 'Read it and sign it. Then we'll let Gloria and the boy go.'

As I read it I became outraged at the audacity and corruption needed for three senior police officers to prepare and sign such a document. Under the heading: 'Record of Interview,' it was a confession. Although unsigned by me, the fact that all three detectives had signed it to confirm its 'veracity,' made it a legal document to be used against me in court.

It began with authenticity: My stating my name, address and where I worked. The names of my wife and child. Even dates of birth which they must have obtained from Gloria who would see no reason to not give them those details. Then, the fiction began. In essence, I was supposed to have said: I flew to Adelaide where I met up with a mate whom I wouldn't name. We stole a car, robbed a bank and I flew back to Sydney that night. The $1600 was part of the proceeds from the robbery. I had lost the rest of my cut at the TAB on Saturday.

It was a classic case of 'verballing' which, in those days before the introduction of electronically recorded interviews, were rife. But it was the first time I had been 'verballed.'

After reading it I realised that for a 'confession' that had taken over six hours to prepare, it was overwhelmingly lightweight. I was confident a good lawyer could tear it apart in court.

I reasoned that if I was a cop and I had a suspect confessing to a robbery that had occurred 1600 kilometres away, I'd ascertain details that only he would know. For example, anyone could say he flew over, met his mate, stole a car, robbed the bank and flew back. Surely a conscientious cop, determined to secure the conviction of a guilty man, would ask: 'Which airline did you use? What time did you arrive in Adelaide? What time did you fly back? What names did you book under? Where did you meet up with your co-offender? Where did you steal the car? What make was it? How did you steal it? How many tellers were in the bank? Male or female? Describe the interior and exterior of the bank. How many customers were in the bank? In which TAB did you lose the money? What are the names of some of the horses you backed? What was your biggest bet and on which horse?'

Why weren't at least some of these questions asked? Simply because the three amigos didn't have the answers. It was late on Sunday night and they had no way of obtaining that information.

The so-called confession was clearly a clumsy fabrication.

I stared at Walton and smiled at him. 'If you think I'm signing this masterpiece, you know nothing about me.'

He shrugged. 'Makes no difference. It's enough to hold you. By the time it gets to trial we'll have plenty of evidence.'

They let Gloria and John go. I was charged with 'Possession of Property stolen outside the state'.

Strange, when I was alleged to have confessed to robbing a bank.

I was taken to the dingy, dirty cells at Central Police Station where I managed to get a few hours' sleep.

Detective Sergeant John Walton would never manage to get the extra evidence needed to convict me. Tragically, a few weeks after my arrest he was killed in a car accident.

Before I was taken into court, Bruce Miles came to the cell to see me. He was a small man of about sixty who always wore a suit and a bow tie. He once told me that he had been a fighter pilot in the Second World War. 'Gloria gave me a rundown of events,' he said. 'I've also spoken to the prosecutor. He claims you made a confession.'

'It's verbal – no detail. You can rip it to shreds in court.'

'We won't be able to contest it today. But you are only charged with goods in custody so we'll try for bail. If we don't get it we'll go to the Supreme Court.'

Gloria was in the public gallery. When the magistrate, citing the fact I had been in the Travelodge as an indication that I was a flight risk, refused bail, I could see she was stressed.

I asked Bruce to tell her that everything was fine – they had no case and I'd be out soon.

I was taken to a relatively new section at Long Bay, the MRC (Metropolitan Remand Centre), and placed in 13 Wing. It was one of two wings consisting of three tiers of cells, most of them holding two prisoners. Each tier had about 34 cells.

My cellmate, Gary, had recently been deported from Haiti after serving seven years for drug offences. Now he was awaiting sentence on old drug charges. He was about my age and we got along well.

Being unconvicted prisoners, we could stay out of our cells until 9:00 pm. Each tier was locked, preventing access to the other tiers. There was a television in the common room resulting in numerous arguments – and the occasional fight – about which programmes would be shown. The majority of us insisted on watching the six o'clock news. Otherwise I didn't care what they put on. Each tier had a block of six showers. Apart from the showers and the 9:00 pm lock-in, conditions were similar to when I had first arrived at Long Bay in January 1960. We had no access to phones and we were locked into an overcrowded yard for six hours a day.

Some of the now notorious inmates who were on remand at the time included men whom I had already met: Arthur 'Neddy' Smith, at Long Bay in 1963; Edward James 'Jockey' Smith, Robert 'Bertie' Kidd and Michael 'Mick' Sayers, all of whom I knew well from my Pentridge days.

Bertie introduced me to the ex-detective, Murray Riley, who had been arrested for importation of 6 tonnes of Buddha sticks at the time the largest drug bust in Australian history.

Murray and I were housed on the same tier and we had a lot of conversations. When the police had swooped on his associates at Forster Tuncurry, he managed to get away. He told me he had been tipped off by his friend the Police Commissioner, Merv Woods, with whom he had won a bronze medal in the double sculls at the 1956 Melbourne Olympics. After the tip-off, he had fled to Adelaide where police tracked him down via phone calls to his girlfriend, Carol.

Murray, notoriously corrupt, was now disillusioned with police. 'They are nothing but gangsters with badges,' he told me.

One night I was having a shower when I heard someone in the adjacent shower sobbing. It was Paul Alister, one of the Ananda Marga guys who, with Tim Anderson and Ross Dunn, were charged with conspiring over the bombing on 13 February 1978 (my thirty-sixth birthday) outside the Hilton Hotel where a police officer and two council workers were killed. The bombing was believed to be political, with the target being the Indian Prime Minister who was at the Hilton to attend the CHOGM meeting.

'Hey, next door,' I yelled. 'What's the matter?'

'We went to the committal today and the police lied,' Alister said.

I was stunned by his ingenuousness. 'Listen, Paul, if the cops think you're guilty, they will lie. That's the name of the game.'

'But we are innocent!' he yelled.

In gaol, you regularly hear protestations of innocence. Usually, you nod your head and forget about it, knowing it is nonsense. But I sensed that this man spoke the truth and it occurred to me that on this night at Long Bay, two accused men, showering in adjacent cubicles, were both innocent of their charges.

'Would you believe me if I told you,' I said, 'that I'm also innocent? The only evidence keeping me in gaol is a fabricated record of interview?'

'I believe you,' he said.

A few weeks later, Anderson, Alister and Dunn, protesting their innocence, went on a hunger strike. It became the talking point of Long Bay. They were a strange sight, the three bearded 'Ananda Marga boys,' sitting cross-legged every day in the yard, refusing to pick up their meals. Their only concession was oranges. In those days, a decade before Corrective Services banned oranges, prisoners, a few times a week, were each given an orange. A lot of us gave the Ananda Marga boys our oranges and they subsisted solely on these for a while. But they began losing weight and eventually two of them were taken to the prison hospital. Shortly afterwards they called off the hunger strike. In those days, the law permitted people to starve themselves to death. Now, after a High Court ruling, the authorities will force feed a person to keep him/her alive.

Anderson, Alister and Dunn were found guilty of the conspiracy and spent seven years in prison before being exonerated after a special enquiry. Each of them was awarded $100,000 in compensation. Less than five years after his release Anderson was charged with the Hilton bombing and, in 1990, found guilty. In 1991 the NSW Court of Criminal Appeal quashed the conviction.

When I applied to the Supreme Court for bail, pointing out that the only evidence against me was a suspect 'Record of Interview,' the judge refused the application. He made it clear that he believed every word in the alleged confession. I knew then that I was in for the fight of my life.

In August, Pope Paul VI died. In September, Pope John Paul I died. A few of the Catholics at the MRC were visibly upset – particularly when some of the inmates made jokes about the Popes 'going down like ninepins'. I simply didn't care. I was reminded of the day in June 1963 when Cathy and I had heard on the radio that Pope John XXII had died. Fifteen years ago – but it seemed like fifty.

In late August at the CIP (Central Industrial Prison), 150 sentenced prisoners, protesting about conditions, set fire to their cells. From where we were in the yards we could see the billowing black smoke. Eventually tear gas was used to quell the riot.

Gloria visited me every week. On the first few occasions she brought John but it was a harrowing experience for the three of us when he wanted to come to me but was prevented by a wire mesh partition. Although he was too young to realise where I was, we decided it would be best if she didn't bring him.

My situation became a classic case of legal limbo. Although the South Australian police wanted to extradite me to face trial for bank robbery, the Flemings' break-in had to be dealt with first.

After a few months, the police came with a warrant to take me to the CIB for questioning. Afraid of again being 'verballed', I asked one of the chief prison officers who was a JP to swear a statutory declaration in which I wrote that I had received legal advice to refuse to speak to police about any matter and I therefore would not answer any questions unless I had a solicitor present.

This didn't prevent the two South Australian detectives, Roberts and Fredericks – accompanied by Phillips – from handcuffing me and driving me to the CIB. On arrival, I was asked if I would supply some sample hairs – if I was innocent they could help prove it. I willingly allowed them to extract with tweezers three hairs from my head.

When Gloria visited me a few days after my trip to the CIB she told me that when the officer at Long Bay rang her and informed her of what had happened, she rang Bruce Miles's office and spoke to another solicitor. He had contacted the CIB where a police officer told him I wasn't in the building. An hour later he rang again, only to be given the same misinformation.

In September, I was taken to the District Court before Judge Goran to get a date for trial for the Flemings matter. Bruce Miles told me the Crown would recommend a 'light' sentence of twelve months if I pleaded guilty. I instructed Bruce to ask the judge if I could speak to him.

In court the judge, who had a reputation for a quick wit and a sense of humour, told me to go ahead.

'Your Honour,' I said, 'I'm in a legal limbo. I'm refused bail on this matter because I'm alleged to have committed a crime in South Australia. I can prove I didn't commit that crime, but I can't do that while this matter lingers on. If I go to trial I'll spend months in custody waiting for it, with the South Australian matter still hanging over my head. If I plead guilty, I'll be in gaol for I don't know how long, with this serious South Australian allegation constantly on my mind. It's a Kafkaresque situation.'

The judge met my gaze, a twinkle in his eyes. 'Are you certain you can prove you are innocent of these interstate charges?'

'I am, Your Honour.'

'Well, I'll tell you what we'll do. How long do you think it will take you to go to South Australia and clear these matters up?'

'I'd estimate six to nine months, Your Honour.'

'That could be a little optimistic, Mr Killick. I'll hold this matter over for twelve months while you duck off to South Australia and beat this bank robbery allegation. When you do that you come back and see me.'

Bruce Miles, the prosecutor and everyone else I glanced at were smiling. 'Thank you, Your Honour, I'll duck off as soon as I can.'

Before they could extradite me to South Australia the police had to take me before a magistrate and obtain an extradition order. The hearing was scheduled for mid-October.

On 6 October, the dynamic Johnny O'Keefe died. In gaol, deprived of the good things in life, you tend to reminisce. I recalled the days just after I'd left school when I went to a few of his concerts and had been inspired by his on-stage charisma. Now, aged 43, he was gone. When, the previous year, Elvis Presley had died, aged 42, I had actually grieved for him as though I'd known him. This time I simply felt a sadness that another great performer was prematurely gone.

For the extradition hearing we were allocated a small courtroom at Central. We fought the extradition on the grounds that I had been in Sydney at the time the bank robbery had been committed. To support this, Bruce called Gloria and David as witnesses. He also supplied an affidavit from Dad who was too ill to attend court. Finally, he called Mrs Sheppard who testified I had come into her shop that afternoon. Despite aggressive cross-examination from the prosecutor, my witnesses remained resolute with their testimony.

When Bruce pointed out that I had signed the bail register at 8:00 pm that night and the only flight out of Adelaide after the robbery had arrived at Mascot at 8:03 pm the magistrate indicated he was about to dismiss the charges.

After a hurried, whispered conversation with Ryan, the prosecutor said: 'Your Worship, the officer who was on duty the night Killick reported for bail is on sick leave and can't be here today. But I'm informed that he started his shift that night at 8:00 pm and he recalls making a cup of coffee and Killick arriving about half an hour later.'

The magistrate pounced on this misinformation. 'That makes it possible for him to have rushed to a waiting vehicle and, driving fast, get to the police station by 8:30 or thereabouts.'

'Your Worship,' Bruce Miles said, 'the bail register has him signing it at 8:00 pm – not 8.30.'

'The policy, Your Worship,' the prosecutor said, 'is to give a little leeway when someone who is normally punctual arrives a little late.'

I couldn't help myself. 'Your Worship, if the officer started his shift at 8:00 pm, does that mean the next shift starts at 4.00 am!' (It later eventuated that the officer had started his shift at 3:00 pm).

Ignoring me, the magistrate focused his attention on Bruce. 'I'm not implying for one moment that your client is guilty, Mr Miles. But there is sufficient evidence to send it to trial. I order he be placed in the custody of the South Australian police for extradition.'

Gloria and I looked at each other. The nightmare was set to continue – 1,600 kilometres away.

While the cops were organising everything, Bruce came to the cell to see me. I was angry. 'What's he talking about – enough evidence? I had four witnesses who saw me in Sydney at crucial times. I signed the bail register at 8:00 pm and the cop witnessed it. Why didn't you ask for an adjournment and subpoena his worksheet? He didn't start his shift at eight o'clock. They have done nothing but lie and now I'm being extradited to South Australia.'

'Calm down, John. They've made a mess of the case. You told Judge Goran you'll win it and you will.'

'What, in twelve or eighteen months' time? They won't give me bail! What will Gloria and John do? Appeal to the Supreme Court, Bruce. Subpoena this cop who was supposed to have started at 8.00 pm.'

'John, it won't change anything. Go to Adelaide. I'll be a witness at your trial and testify how the police told my office you weren't at the CIB the day the Adelaide police took you there. I guarantee you will beat this. But it will have to go to trial.' He paused. 'I've arranged for you to see Gloria for ten minutes.'

I did my best to cheer up Gloria. Ten minutes isn't much time to discuss the things we needed to talk about.

When it was time for her to leave I told her: 'I wasn't happy with the way Bruce handled this case. We should have nailed them. I want you to go to Chris Murphy, he's an up-and-coming lawyer who Murray Riley recommended. Get him to send a letter immediately to the South Australian Police Commissioner advising that he has instructed me to say nothing to police on the journey to Adelaide or after arrival, unless I have a solicitor present.'

Chris Murphy did as Gloria instructed and sent the letter. He charged a fee of $400 – a substantial amount for a letter when you consider the average weekly wage at the time was $220.

I felt that whatever the cost, it would be worth it to ensure I didn't get 'verballed' again.

ADELAIDE GAOL

1978

The flight to Adelaide with Roberts and Fredericks was uneventful. I ignored any attempt at conversation by either of them.

At the Adelaide Magistrate's Court, knowing that the Crown case was flawed, I made an impassioned plea for bail.

'Your Worship, I'm being held in custody despite numerous witnesses having testified under oath that I was in Sydney at the time the robbery occurred.'

The prosecutor interposed: 'Your Worship, it is the Crown's submission that the accused has committed four armed robberies – two TABs in 1977 and a TAB and the Plympton National Bank in 1978. The accused has made three separate Records of Interview admitting to the offences.'

'Under the circumstances,' the magistrate said, 'bail is out of the question. The prisoner is remanded in custody.'

Four armed robberies? Three Records of Interview? In a state of shock and disbelief, I was taken to Adelaide Gaol which had been built in 1841. (It closed in 1988).

In 1978 the cells' sanitation system had improved from metal buckets to Porta Potties. I was told the National Trust wouldn't allow flush toilets to be installed because it wanted to preserve the gaol in its natural state. Even the scaffold remained where twenty-one-year-old Glen Valance became the penultimate person to be executed in Australia when they dropped him through the trapdoor on 24 November 1964.

Gloria arranged for Derrence Stevenson, regarded by many as the best criminal lawyer in the state, to come and see me.

On meeting him I was a little nonplussed. He was about forty, had dark wavy hair, and was wearing slacks with an open-necked flowery sports shirt and a thick gold chain around his neck. I immediately sensed he was gay.

After introductions, he said: 'I've spoken to the Crown about your case. They claim you made three Records of Interview admitting to the four armed robberies. Did you sign any of them?'

'Until I arrived here I didn't know of the existence of two of them. I certainly haven't signed any of them. It's all fiction.'

He was watching me closely. 'Gloria said the South Australian police took you to the CIB and told your lawyer you weren't there. They'll allege that is where you made the statements.'

'I signed a document giving them permission to take hair samples that day. Why would I sign it and not two so-called confessions? They've been verballing me from day one.'

I told him about the witnesses who saw me in Sydney on 16 June. 'They've got no case without the verbal,' I said. 'I signed a bail book at Chatswood Police Station at 8:00 pm and the only plane out of Adelaide after the robbery touched down at Mascot at three minutes past eight.'

'You have a strong case,' he said. 'I'll get a copy of the brief and see what they've got. Then I'll come and see you again. How much can you afford to pay?'

'Not much. I was hoping to get Legal Aid.'

'You'll need to come up with some cash. We'll discuss it next time.

By then I'll know if we can beat these charges.'

I had no chance of raising the thousands of dollars I knew he would be accustomed to receiving. I would have to apply for Legal Aid and then convince him to accept the reduced fee. Any lawyer who could get his client acquitted on four armed robberies would have his reputation considerably enhanced.

About a week later he returned. He had copies of the alleged Records of Interview. I was supposed to have confessed to robbing a TAB in May 1977, another in June 1977, another in May 1978 and the bank in June.

'There's not a lot of substance in these statements,' he said. 'I think we can get them thrown out. But if we don't, you'll go down.'

'What about Eyles, are they going to call him?'

He gave a dismissive wave of the hand. 'Forget Eyles. He made contradictory statements. I'd love to get him in the box. The Crown won't risk it.' He paused. 'They're out to get you, though. They think you are some sort of John Dillinger. They believe you robbed two other TABs on the same day and conned the old desk sergeant at Chatswood to give you an alibi.'

'You can see what they're doing, can't you?' I said. 'They're going over all the armed robberies in Adelaide and checking to see where I was. Those two I'm charged with in 1977, they knew I was living in Adelaide at the time. They want to clear their books with me as the scapegoat.'

'There aren't a lot of armed robberies committed here,' he said. 'If they believe you were one of the culprits who robbed the National Bank, it's reasonable they would target you for the others. Now, let's talk business. I see you've applied for Legal Aid and nominated me as your choice. I'll do it but you will have to get Gloria to pay another $5000 – that will cover everything from the committal to the trial, if it gets to trial. I believe we can get these charges thrown out at the committal. But I'll need to put other cases aside to do this one justice.'

'Gloria can't get it. You said we can win this at the committal. That would be a huge boost for your reputation.'

'My reputation doesn't need a boost – my bank account does.' He stood up and shook my hand: his hand was soft, his grip weak. 'See what you can do, I'll give you a month. You can win this, but you need someone who is not afraid to take on the police. I'm the best.'

I didn't ask Gloria to borrow the money. She had to provide for herself and John without any assistance from me. There were other good lawyers who would do the case for Legal Aid rates. I'd spend all my time going over documents looking for flaws in the Crown case, of which there were many. I could do most of the preparation. All I needed was an eloquent mouthpiece willing to tell the judge and jury the police had verballed me. I had no doubts we could prove it. I also had no doubts that the case would proceed to trial. No magistrate would be prepared to allow me to walk away at the committal on four charges of armed robbery.

Eight months later, in July 1979, Derrence Stevenson was murdered in a jealous rage by his teenage lover, David Szach, who hid his body in their freezer.

In early December, Gloria and John moved to Adelaide, residing with friends we had known while living in Parkside.

Legal Aid refused my application for representation at the committal. I spent most of my time going over the brief, studying witnesses' statements and preparing a defence.

Apart from the three Records of Interview, they appeared to have no evidence. The four robberies were committed by bandits disguised with either face masks or motorcycle helmets. The only weapon recovered was found in Eyles's possession.

Magistrate Clark presided over the committal. Although he permitted me to sit at the bar table, he warned me that he wouldn't tolerate any attempt to bully or intimidate the witnesses.

'Your Worship,' I said, 'I have no intentions of intimidating anyone. If I was one of the bandits who held up some of these witnesses do you think I'd be prepared to question them so they can hear my voice?'

'Good point, Mr Killick. But keep in mind what I said.'

I looked at Gloria who was sitting at the front of the court. We both knew that without a lawyer I was up against it.

My chance came when Detective Fredericks took the stand. He testified that I made the two Records of Interview at the Sydney CIB, admitting to the four robberies. When the time came to cross-examine him, I knew I had a chance of trapping him. 'Detective Fredericks, you said two Records of Interview were taken that day?'

'That's correct. One by myself and the other by Detective Roberts.'

'Was anyone else present?'

'Detective Phillips.'

'Why didn't I have a lawyer present?'

'You didn't ask for one.'

I stared at him. 'When you typed up the Record of Interview where was everyone positioned?'

For a moment he hesitated, then said: 'You were seated at the middle of the table, I was seated at your left, Detective Roberts sat on your right.'

'And Detective Phillips?'

'He was standing by the door. It was a small room.'

'And when Detective Roberts made his Record of Interview what were the positions in the room?'

'The positions were the same.'

I had him! 'So, you were on my left, I was in the middle, Detective Ryan was on my right. Is that correct?

'Yes.'

'What did Detective Roberts use for a typewriter?' His face flushed noticeably. 'Pardon?'

I glanced at the magistrate and perceived a slight smile before it disappeared.

'I asked you, Detective,' I said politely, 'what did Detective Roberts use to type this alleged statement with?'

'I handed him the typewriter so he could record your confession.'

'They're big, heavy typewriters – why would you pick it up and hand it across the table? Wouldn't it be easier to simply change seats?'

He was glaring at me, the muscles in his jawline tightening. 'As I said, I handed the typewriter to Detective Roberts.'

'This alleged, unsigned by me, Record of Interview never took place, did it, Detective?'

'Yes it did.'

'Why didn't I sign it?'

'This is what criminals do. They make a confession then have second thoughts and decline to sign it.'

'But you're alleging I made two unsigned Records of Interview that day.

Why didn't I sign the first one while I was in a confessing mood?'

The magistrate intervened. 'Mister Killick, you can't ask the detective why you did or didn't do things. Keep to the facts.'

I nodded. 'Is it correct that when Detective Roberts extracted hairs from my head I signed a document giving permission?'

'Yes.'

'But I wouldn't sign two Records of Interview made on the same day?'

'That's correct.'

We stared at each other, then I smiled and looked at the magistrate. 'Your Worship, I'm finished with this witness. Could you now call Detective Roberts?'

He glanced at his watch. 'It's almost two o'clock. I have to finish proceedings early today. We will resume tomorrow at 9.30 am.'

'Your Worship, I only need to ask Detective Roberts a few questions. It will take five minutes.'

'Mr Killick, I told you proceedings are finished today. You can ask him the questions tomorrow.'

I wondered if he would have taken the same approach if Derrence Stevenson had requested five minutes.

'I need to ask these questions now,' I said.

'This session is closed. We will resume tomorrow at 9.30 am.' Gloria got up and walked out – slamming the door.

Everyone in that courtroom knew Fredericks would now have time to detail the alleged seating arrangements and handing the typewriter across the table to Ryan. If I could have questioned Roberts immediately he may have given a different version, discrediting the entire Crown case.

The next morning when Roberts took the stand I asked him a few questions, avoiding the main issues that I knew he would have been well prepared for. Overnight I had concluded that I had at least managed to dent the Crown case. Now it would be up to a barrister to break it apart at trial.

As expected, Magistrate Clark sent the matter to trial.

The trial was scheduled for January. A week before it began Gloria arranged for John to live in Sydney with her sister's family, all of whom loved him and spoilt him.

My Legal Aid appointed barrister, Erikson, told me: 'Justice Mitchell is the trial judge and she's tough. The prosecutor, Rice, has a high conviction rate at trials. The Crown want to win this one. They want to send a message to criminals who come from interstate to commit armed robberies here.'

I stared at him. He was about forty years old, with light brown hair, a moustache and rugged features. He spoke well, loud and precise. Perfect for courtroom assertion.

'Well, they've picked the wrong man to make an example of. I'm not guilty.'

I gave him copies of all the work I had done on the case. 'I've dissected the testimony of all the witnesses,' I said. 'The police have nothing. They're relying on the unsigned Records of Interview which are clearly flawed.'

He gave me a grave look. 'They have more than that. The sample they took of your hair match those found on one of the masks they found.'

December 1942, a newly adopted and unaware 'war baby.'

Mum, with David (left and) me outside Central Railway in 1948. We were poor but she always had us neatly dressed.

Mum and Dad at the front of our family home in Fairfield, shortly before they lost the house.

Cathy looking good in Chicago, 1970.

Newly released from Long Bay … feeling and looking like a new man, November 1973.

Gloria and I at our wedding reception at the Carlton-Rex Hotel, July 1974.

Gloria showing off a happy baby John at Cremorne, 1975.

Me and John at Willoughby in January 1978, getting ready for a trip to the shops.

Lucy, the centre of attention in Russia, circa 1965.

Lucy and Alex signing the marriage register in Russia, 1983.

The former Yatala Prison tennis champion, feeling good at Taree, 1982.

Jackie and me enjoying dinner and a drink in Adelaide, May 1983.

With Faye in happier times at Queanbeyan, July 1996.

Gloria visiting me at Long Bay, January 1986.

Father and son enjoying a bike ride at Waverton, 1983.

Gloria with John the cricketer at Waverton, January 1982.

John wants the present my Dad Reg has for him, Christmas 1977.

John and Gloria at a picnic, missing Dad, 1981.

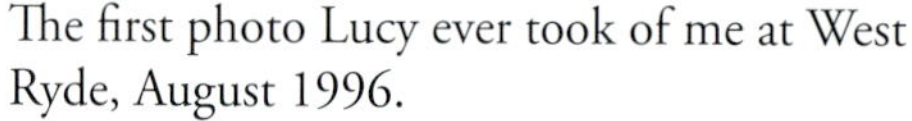
The first photo Lucy ever took of me at West Ryde, August 1996.

Posing for Faye at Eastwood, December 1995.

Posing for Jackie at Taree, 1982.

The first photo I ever took of Lucy at West Ryde, August 1996.

Lucy and me at Rosehill Races in 1998.

Gloria and Lucy, 1998... an unusual friendship.

Ready for action at Canberra Casino, 1996.

Queanbeyan, June 1996.

My escape from Silverwater in a helicopter dominated the news (courtesy Channel 9).

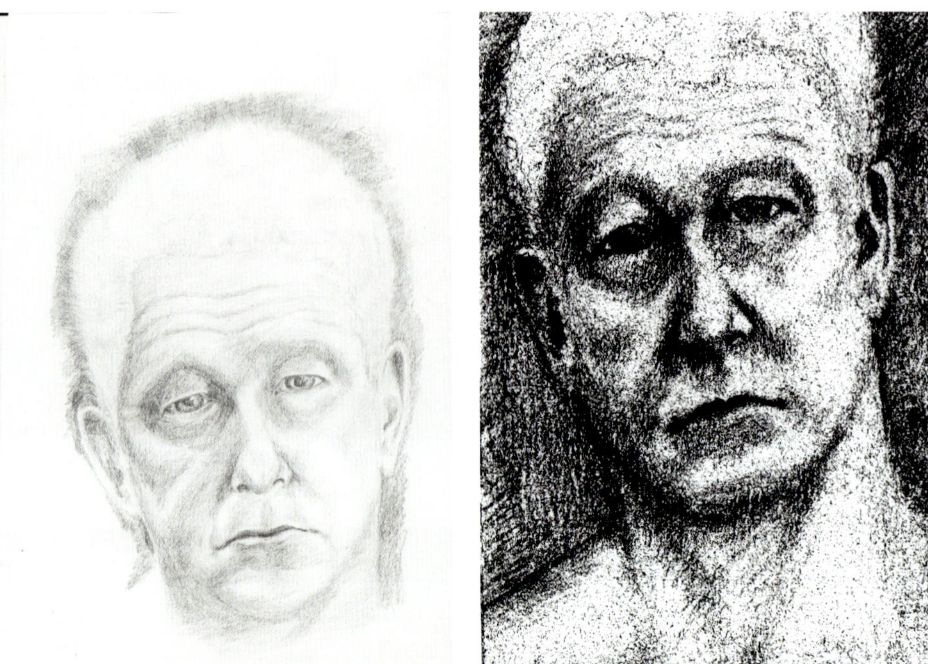

Above and opposite: drawings of me by Lucy when she was in Silverwater's Mulawa Women's Prison, 2000.

Lucy in Mulawa … talented, beautiful and determined.

Reunited with my son John after doing time in Yatala, December 1981 … still the apple of my eye.

Me in the warehouse at Yatala, 1979 … looking back at my time in prison, I regret the wasted years, especially the three years in Yatala for a crime I didn't commit.

With the staff at ICS Artarmon, 1995 …working two jobs, trying to go straight. It didn't last.

Gloria visiting me at Lithgow in 2006 … throughout everything she has remained a loyal and supportive friend.

I had become inured to bad news. But this allegation sent a cold rage coursing through me. 'What mask?'

'Eyles took police to a place in Gawler where he had thrown away the masks used in the robbery.'

'If they say they found my hairs on a mask they planted them,' I said. He shrugged. 'It won't be easy to convince a jury of that.'

'Look, if they are prepared to fabricate three Records of Interview against me, do you really believe they wouldn't plant hairs on a mask?'

'It's not what I believe. It's what the jury will believe.' He paused. 'They also found one of your fingerprints on the rental car.'

I felt like a boxer being mercilessly pummelled in a corner. 'So, I was smart enough to set up a perfect alibi, but then I made three separate confessions, left some hairs on a mask and a fingerprint on a car? No intelligent person will believe it.'

'Our problem will be to convince a jury that the police would go to those lengths to convict you. When they give evidence, if we accuse them of lying the Crown can reveal your criminal record to the jury as a counter attack on credibility.'

I knew that a jury might well convict me solely on my criminal past. I was an ex-bank robber and an escapee. They would be more inclined to believe the police than anything I said. I was playing against a stacked deck. But I was still confident. 'They've thrown all their eggs into one basket,' I said. 'That's why we'll win this.'

'Explain it to me,' he said.

'I'm charged with four armed robberies. The only evidence they have on three of them are the Records of Interview. Farcical fabrications that, if you handle it right, we can get thrown out of court. That leaves the bank. Even without the Record of Interview, they still have these hairs and fingerprint that they planted to counter that we have at least five witnesses who saw me in Sydney on the day of the robbery. I also signed a bail book at 8:00 pm, making it impossible for me to have committed the robbery.'

'They are claiming you arrived half an hour late.'

'Well, why would the cop write 8:00 pm in the book? Don't they have to prove their case beyond a reasonable doubt?'

'In theory, yes: in fact, it's often the reverse. The onus is often on the accused to prove his innocence.'

I was confident that I could do exactly that...

Justice Roma Mitchell CBE had more presence in a courtroom than any judge I had been involved with before or since the trial. She was the first female QC in Australia who later went on to become Governor of South Australia.

After her death, she was the subject of a South Australian float to celebrate 100 years of Federation. Immediately as the trial began I could see the lawyers were in awe of her.

After the jury was chosen, Ericksen asked for a voir dire from which the jury was excluded. If a defence lawyer challenges evidence which the Crown proposes to put forward, a voir dire is held in a closed court while the judge decides whether or not to allow it to go before the jury.

When Eriksen told the judge the three Records of Interview should be thrown out, her eyes narrowed as she stared at him. 'You had better know what you are doing, Mister Eriksen.'

After the police gave their versions of how the Records of Interview originated, I gave my evidence. I told it as it happened, emphatically denying making any confessions or even participating in the 'interviews'.

Eriksen then called Bruce Miles and a law clerk from Bruce's office. The clerk testified that he had rung the CIB on the day of the alleged confessions to Fredericks and Roberts and was told that I wasn't there.

Bruce testified that he had rung the deputy governor at Long Bay who told him two South Australian detectives and a Sydney detective had taken me to the CIB despite my having given them a statutory declaration, witnessed by him, stating I wouldn't talk to police without a lawyer present. When Bruce rang the CIB, he was told I wasn't there.

Phillips and Louis also had problems with the first Record of Interview. Despite my allegedly confessing to a bank robbery, I had been charged with possessing goods suspected of being stolen outside the state: $1600. They also couldn't explain why, if I was confessing, I wasn't asked what flight I took to get to Adelaide, what name I used to book the flight, where did we steal the car from, what make was it? Why wasn't I asked for details about the bank robbery that only I would know?

At times during the police evidence Justice Mitchell displayed open hostility towards them. After three days of listening to the evidence and the submissions she declared all three Records of Interview inadmissible.

Eriksen came to the cells to see me. 'The Crown just offered me a deal,' he said. 'If you plead guilty to the bank, they'll drop the three TABs.'

'Tell them to shove their deal. I didn't do it. Those cops should have all been charged with perjury when she threw the bullshit confessions out.'

'That won't happen. It was a heavy blow against the Crown, but it wasn't a knockout punch – they still have the hairs on the mask and the fingerprint on the car.'

'I told you – they planted them. It was impossible for me to have robbed the bank.'

'I think you should take the deal.'

'Even though I didn't do it?'

'Mitchell expects you to take it. She doesn't want a trial that could go another two months involving forty or fifty witnesses.'

'She knows I've been set up. Tell them no deal.'

I was confident Justice Mitchell was on my side against the conniving cops who wanted to send me down at any cost.

But I had read her wrong.

ROGER ROGERSON SAYS 'HI'

1979

During the trial. which went for seven weeks, Justice Mitchell's attitude towards me and my witnesses was similar to the skepticism she had displayed towards the police during the voir dire. When Gloria, David, Colleen and Margaret Sheppard all testified that they had seen me in Sydney on the afternoon of 16 June 1978, she often took a prosecutorial role asking questions in an aggressive, hostile manner. When Eriksen presented a sworn affidavit from Dad, supporting the testimony of my other witnesses, she reluctantly allowed it into evidence, commenting it held 'little weight' without being tested in cross-examination.

At one stage, I said to Eriksen: 'She's making it clear to the jury that she thinks I'm guilty. Can't you do something?'

'What can I do?' he said. 'You should have taken the Crown's offer.'

The Crown took another blow when the cop who found the mask I was alleged to have worn during the bank robbery stated that there was only one hair discovered stuck to the interior stitching of the mask. Eriksen told him it was alleged three hairs had been found. The cop then corrected his evidence stating there were indeed three hairs found.

A young girl who had been inside one of the TABs gave evidence that during the robbery some money had dropped on to the floor and the bandit had told her to pick it up and give it to him. She had noticed a large freckle on the back of his left hand. Eriksen asked her to look at the back of my left hand and see if she could discern a freckle.

It was a pivotal moment in the trial. All eyes were on this slip of a girl as she walked across the room to where I stood.

Smiling at her, I held out my left hand, wondering why an armed, masked bandit wouldn't wear gloves.

She looked closely at my outstretched hand then looked at me, returning my smile.

'Did you see a freckle?' Eriksen asked. 'No.'

I looked across at Justice Mitchell, trying to will her to swing my way again. But behind the thick rimmed glasses her eyes were hooded, her face inscrutable.

The Crown, getting desperate, called in a heavy hitter in the form of celebrity cop, Roger Rogerson.

Although I had never seen him before, he greeted me as he walked past the witness box with: 'Hi, Johnny.'

He gave evidence that during the lunch break at the extradition hearing he and Detective Phillips approached me while I was in a cell with numerous other prisoners and showed me a flight ticket in the name of D. Richards and asked me if I knew anything about it. According to Rogerson (later supported by Phillips) I said: 'Yes, that's the one I used to fly back to Sydney after the bank robbery.'

The total absurdity of this evidence is demonstrated by the fact that I had numerous witnesses in court that day swearing under oath that I was in Sydney at the time the robbery was committed. If I had confessed to police I had committed the robbery and used the flight ticket to return to Sydney I was virtually branding my witnesses perjurers. And why didn't Rogerson and Phillips give the evidence to the magistrate during the extradition hearing?

When Eriksen tried to present the statutory declaration I had made stating I wouldn't talk to police without my solicitor being present, Justice Mitchell wouldn't allow it in evidence, stating it was 'self-serving.'

Thus the jury would have to decide whether they believed my version about the flight ticket or Phillips's and Rogerson's version, unaware that Phillips's previous evidence at the voir dire regarding the three unsigned Records of Interview had been thrown out. And none of us foresaw that Rogerson, one of New South Wales most decorated policemen, would go on to become Australia's most notorious bent cop. Two years after giving evidence against me, he shot dead heroin dealer Warren Lanfranchi after Arthur 'Neddy' Smith set up a meeting on 27 June 1981 in Dangar Place, Chippendale. In the mid-seventies Rogerson had already been involved in two fatal shootings of bank robbers, Phillip Weston at Avoca Beach and Gordon Thomas at Rose Bay.

In 1999, he was convicted and gaoled for perverting the course of justice. In 2016, he was sentenced to life imprisonment for the murder of twenty-year-old student and drug dealer Jamie Gao.

It's a pity such a gifted liar will die in gaol. He could have been a good politician.

The police officer who had witnessed and signed off on my reporting for bail admitted that on the 16th June 1978 he started his shift at 3:00 pm. Thus I had been illegally extradited on the basis of false evidence given by police at the extradition hearing, stating that he had started work at 8:00 pm and I had arrived half an hour later to sign the bail register.

Rice produced a copy of a story I'd published in *Man Magazine* in 1974. The story was titled *The Perfect Alibi.*

'Here is a man who thinks alibis!' Rice proclaimed, looking at the jury as though he had just solved the case.

I was confident the Crown hadn't proved its case. The Crown must have felt the same way. They flew Greg Eyles' mother, Bessie, and his brother, Kym, from Sydney to give rebuttal evidence. Their testimony should have been inadmissible. Unless the defence gives new, previously undisclosed evidence, the Crown can't re-open its case.

Bessie and her son did their best to send me down. I wondered if the police had pressured them by using Greg's wife, Patricia, as the bargaining chip. Although she had been charged, she never spent a day in gaol.

They contradicted and twisted Gloria's evidence, claiming that when she gave them the money she was nervous and told them to hide it.

'She kept looking around,' Bessie said, 'and told us to warn Greg to keep his mouth shut about John.'

They also testified that Gloria left John with them to babysit on 16 June, contradicting our evidence that John had been with me.

This was the last evidence the jury heard and it was damaging to my case.

When Eriksen took only two hours to summarise the defence case to the jury I was nonplussed. There had been more than fifty witnesses who gave evidence over seven weeks. And despite my instructions, he didn't try to explain the alleged fingerprint on the car window or the hairs on the mask by accusing the police of planting them after extracting them from my head at the Sydney CIB.

After the jury had been sent out to deliberate on a verdict I angrily confronted Eriksen. 'You missed a lot of points in your summing up,' I said.

'The judge gave me two hours to sum up – she wants a verdict today.'

'She can't do that and you know it! Derrence Stevenson would have taken two days to sum up. He wouldn't have missed anything and he wouldn't let a judge intimidate him.'

'I'm not Derrence Stevenson. I've done my best for you.' He turned and walked out.

When the foreman of the jury announced they had found me guilty on all four counts I felt as though I had been punched in the stomach. There had been no evidence whatsoever on the three TABs.

I think even Justice Mitchell was shocked. She sentenced me to a total of eight-and-a-half years. For four armed robberies and a not guilty plea, it was a light sentence.

A few days after I had been sentenced Eriksen came to see me.

'I've spoken to a few of the best legal minds in Adelaide,' he said. 'They couldn't believe the leniency of the sentence.'

'Tell them I couldn't believe I was found guilty,' I said. 'I'm going to appeal.'

He frowned. 'It wouldn't be wise. You'll step on too many toes.'

I stared at him. 'Is that your advice – that by appealing I'll step on too many toes?'

'Yes.'

'Well, adios, Paleface. I'll find another lawyer.' That was the last time I saw him.

Within a week I had been transferred to H.M. Prison Yatala – South Australia's maximum security gaol.

As soon as I stepped off the escort truck Greg Eyles requested to be put on protection.

The governor, Mr Hughes, an overweight man of about fifty with white hair and a ruddy complexion, had me escorted to his office. 'You've only just arrived here, Killick, and I've got a bloke terrified of you. He thinks you're going to stab him to death.'

I was shocked. 'I haven't threatened anyone and I have no intention of harming anyone.'

'This fellow Eyles thinks you have. I have no choice other than to send him to Port Augusta where he'll be safe.' He paused and gave me a hard stare. 'We don't want you interstaters coming over here and robbing our banks and then threatening people when you get caught and come to prison.'

'I haven't robbed a bank since 1966,' I said, knowing I was only inflaming the situation, but frustrated with all the false accusations.

I could see he resented my attitude. 'You'll be under close scrutiny here at Yatala, Killick. If you stuff up you'll be sent to S Division.'

I assumed S Division was the Adelaide version of H Division. 'Will I have to break rocks?' I asked.

'No, only inmates get broken in S Division.' He stared at me and shook his head. 'You're a bit of a paradox, Killick. In the judge's sentencing remarks, she said you had above average intelligence. I'm giving you a chance; you'll start work in the stores. It's a privileged, trusted job – don't stuff it up.'

As far as gaols go, Yatala wasn't too bad. It held about 500 prisoners with sentences varying from twelve months to life.

My job in the stores was simple, ensuring everything was orderly and keeping a checklist on stock. I worked with two other prisoners and two civilians We had to supply stores to all prisons in the state.

Each prisoner had a one-out cell. I spent a lot of time working on my case. I also enrolled in a three-year correspondence course Writing for the Media.

When Gloria came to see me, we agreed she would have to return to Sydney to look after John.

'Don't worry,' I said. 'I'll win the appeal and soon be home.'

Instead of applying for Legal Aid, I wrote a long letter outlining my case to Michael Abbott, an up-and-coming lawyer who was highly regarded by everyone to whom I spoke.

He replied to my letter, advising me to apply for Legal Aid and he would take the case.

A few weeks later he visited me. He was a slim brown-haired man in his mid-thirties.

'Legal Aid, on my advice, has agreed to fund your appeal,' he said. 'I think we can win it.'

But the South Australian Court of Criminal Appeal disagreed. Headed by Chief Justice King, the bench of three unanimously dismissed my appeal.

Abbott's confident manner was replaced by a mood of despondency. 'This was a strong bench. The way Justice Wells has explained it leaves us with nothing.'

I was angry, frustrated. 'You people just don't get it – I'm not guilty!'

'It doesn't matter. On the evidence available the jury had an entitlement to find you guilty. We tried to get some of that evidence thrown out but the judges, in their wisdom, have deemed the evidence legal.'

'A lot of that evidence was either false or illegal. The High Court will see it that way,' I said.

'I have already spoken to Legal Aid. They won't fund you for the High Court. Three senior Supreme Court judges have said you have no grounds. You will need at least $10,000 to get there.'

'I'll do it myself.'

'John, prisoners don't do their own High Court appeals. I'm sorry.

Focus on getting parole.'

When you have been convicted for something you didn't do, you don't give up. I wrote to Legal Aid and five or six well-known lawyers. The replies I received all contained the same advice: Unless I could engage a Queen's Counsel, forget about a High Court appeal. Prisoners don't win High Court appeals.

I remembered what Eriksen had told me: 'You'll step on too many toes...'

All the negativity only made me more determined. I didn't care how many or whose toes I stepped on: I would, somehow, get a High Court hearing.

TWO'S ESCAPED!

1980–81

Early in 1980 I was asked if I would be interested in editing the Yatala magazine *Vision*. Although it was intended to be a monthly edition containing up to 24 pages of poems, letters, stories, jokes, articles and cartoons by prisoners, it had deteriorated to the point of being printed only four or five times a year.

The primary reason for the drop in contributions was censorship. A lot of the inmates resented the fact that all content had to be 'approved' by the prison officer in charge of the project.

I spoke to some of the inmates whom I knew were capable of contributing good material. 'Despite some censorship, we are better off with a magazine than without one,' I said. 'We can't write a scathing article criticising the prison or those who run it, but we can do some clever cartoons and achieve the same result. No one, even the Prime Minister, is exempt from being sent up in a cartoon. If we use humour we can get away with a lot.'

And we did. One of the guys was a brilliant artist and together we came up with some funny cartoons, a few of which ridiculed the prison system. The 'censor' gave them a pass. Our first edition was 48 pages, gradually increasing each month. We began a mailing list, sending copies to the newspapers and some of the judges and lawyers. When I wrote a story The Trial of Billy Goat, I sent a copy to Justice Mitchell. The story was a send up of my trial with Billy Goat cast as me, the police as pigs, the lawyers as weasels and the jury as sheep. The judge was a unicorn.

Justice Mitchell replied, commending the quality of the magazine and requesting to remain on the mailing list. She didn't mention The Trial of Billy Goat...

I included a section titled *The Bush Lawyer* where prisoners could send in questions on law. If I couldn't answer them I'd send the question to either Legal Aid or one of the lawyers on our mailing list.

The officer responsible for the magazine was so impressed by the popularity and quality of the material that he arranged for me to leave the store and work full-time on *Vision Magazine*. I was given an assistant editor: David Szach, the young man who had killed his lover, Derrence Stevenson. David was a good-looking blond boy who told me every chance he got that he didn't kill Derrence. After serving fourteen years in prison, he was released in 1993. He still maintains today that he was innocent.

One day a columnist named Jim Robbins with The Advertiser, came to the gaol to interview me about the magazine. Under the heading New '*Vision*' for One Man, he gave it a positive write up. I now seized the opportunity to apply pressure on Legal Aid to fund my appeal to the High Court. I wrote an article in *The Bush Lawyer* segment about rebuttal evidence, ending with a series of questions to the head of Legal Aid. It was a thinly-veiled reference to the circumstances at my trial when, after having closed its case, the Crown re-opened it by calling Bessie and Kym Eyles as rebuttal witnesses. I quoted the 1952 High Court authority on rebuttal evidence, *Shaw v* R (1952) 85 CLR 365.

A few weeks later I received a letter from Legal Aid stating they had reconsidered my application and had decided to fund an appeal to the High Court. Solicitor Marie Shaw (now a judge) was my appointed solicitor.

It was a huge relief. Now I had a real shot at acquiring justice. I immediately wrote to Gloria and Dad with the good news.

Due to the extra material we were publishing I asked for my lunchtime training partner, Marcel, to be added to our team. He was well-educated and wrote good material. The officer-in-charge approved it and eventually Marcel replaced the immature David as assistant editor.

One day a German prisoner named Fritz Werner, whom I knew, 'disappeared' from the prison. No-one knew how he had escaped. The following day, the governor, confronted by the media, said: 'At this stage we don't know if he's in or out.'

For me it was a classic line and I immediately wrote a short story titled: None's Escaped. Basically, it was about a non-existent prisoner named None whom the prison authorities thought had escaped.

The officer-in-charge of the magazine thought it was funny and gave it the all clear.

Outraged, the governor stopped the magazine. I was sent to work in the spray shop.

I contacted the Ombudsman who had recently sent me a letter praising *Vision Magazine*. Genuinely concerned, he came to see me, then negotiated with the governor to allow the publication to continue. There would be no more articles lampooning the prison system but we might be able to slip in an occasional cheeky cartoon.

I had no option other than to accept the restrictions.

One Friday afternoon in June 1980, a few months after Fritz escaped, his co-offender, Joe Tognolini, gave me two new batteries for my TV.

'I'm giving up watching television,' he said, grinning.

I had met Joe in H Division in 1971. He had been sent there after escaping from a prison van taking him to court.

I wasn't convinced Joe had suddenly lost his desire to watch television. Later that night two men broke into the prison, placed a ladder against the wall of B Division where Joe and I were housed, and began cutting the bars of his cell situated on the third floor with an oxyacetylene torch.

A prisoner who was regularly medicated and had a reputation for telling tall tales, pressed the alarm buzzer alerting the night-duty guard.

'What's your medical emergency?' the guard asked.

'Sir, there are men with a ladder cutting the bars of a prisoner's cell.'

'Hallucinating again are we?'

'No, sir. I swear it's true. It's all lit up like a Christmas tree.'

'Listen, if you wake me up again about your hallucinations I'll come up there and you will have a real nightmare. Understand?'

'But, sir...'

'I've warned you. Go back to bed!'

Joe Tognolini said his goodbyes to a few of his friends and like Fritz before him, disappeared from Yatala. Eventually a Royal Commission was held into the entire matter.

I couldn't resist writing a satirical story about it, naming it One's Escaped!

The officer-in-charge of the magazine destroyed it and gave me a warning.

But even in gaol they couldn't prevent me from scoring an Australia-wide scoop at the expense of my old rival, William John O'Mealley, who had recently been released from Pentridge after serving 25 years for killing a policeman.

O'Mealley had published an autobiography *The Man They Couldn't Break*. One of the prisoners at Yatala, a psychopath named Jorgensen, came to me with a copy of the book. He was upset. 'This bastard O'Mealley has blackened your name,' he said. 'Read this.'

O'Mealley had written about the 1968 attempted escape in E Division Pentridge. He stated I had blamed Cormick for assaulting De Boer and the guards had bashed him so badly he finished in an asylum.

I laughed. 'I called O'Mealley 'The Paper Tiger of Pentridge' in an article I wrote. This is his way of retaliating.'

I looked at Jorgensen, a blond bully who lifted weights for three hours a day and weighed about 115 kilograms.

'De Boer knew who hit him,' I said. 'Why do you think I did four years in H Division and the other two did two years or less?'

'I don't care, I'm ripping the page out so no-one can see it,' he said. My protector, Jorgensen the psychopath.

When I read the book I was shocked. I had read it before! At least the first 30 pages or so. I tried to remember where I had read it...then it came to me: Willard Motley's *Knock On Any Door*. I had read it about fifteen years ago. The early part of the book focused on the young protagonist growing up in boys' homes.

I asked the education officer if he could get me a copy.

A few days later he brought me one. 'It's out of print,' he said, 'but I found one in the local library.'

Incredibly, O'Mealley had plagiarised almost forty pages of the book. He hadn't attempted to alter it a bit – only the names of the places and characters were different. Even the dialogue was the same. He had cast himself in the role of the protagonist in Knock On Any Door.

We were close to publishing another edition of *Vision*. I went to the artist, Greg. 'I want you to draw Bill O'Mealley looking like Humpty Dumpty sitting on the ground outside a prison wall cracked and broken.'

He did a good job of it and under the cartoon I put the caption: 'The Man They Broke.' I followed it with a story revealing the way O'Mealley had plagiarised Motley's book.

The mainstream press picked up on it and soon *The Man They Couldn't Break* was taken from the shelves and pulped. Immediately, O'Mealley, refusing to comment on the accusations, went into hiding – and stayed there.

A tough 'old school' inmate told me I had 'done the wrong thing' by exposing O'Mealley as a fraud. 'He was only trying to make a buck after decades in gaol,' he said.

'Fuck him,' I said. 'He's maliciously lied about me in a book that's on the bestseller lists. What would you do?'

'I'd even up outside,' he said. 'You know the rules – you don't give anyone up, regardless.'

I was tense, ready to fight. 'What rules? I gave up a lot of screws at the Royal Commission into H Division. What do you think about that?'

We stood there staring at each other, both aware that compromise was not on the agenda. He turned and walked away. We never spoke again.

Most of the inmates supported the exposé, claiming O'Mealley got his just desserts.

JUSTICE SEEN TO BE DONE

1980–82

Encouraged by 'distinction' grades in most of my subjects in the Writing for the Media course, I sent off a story to the *Newcastle Herald* titled *End of Affaire*. They published it and sent the payment to Gloria.

I was also working on a book about the champion pacer, Paleface Adios, who had again come out of retirement and had now won more than 100 races. Gloria went to Temora to try to persuade his owner/driver, Colin Pike, to supply personal details, but he told her another writer, Graham Goffin, a quadriplegic, had been granted exclusive rights. Accepting that a convicted bank robber would lose out in a sales contest with a quadriplegic, I switched to a lengthy article and sent it to the *Adelaide Sunday Mail*. They published it in two parts. In 1982 Graham came to Harold Park Paceway to promote his book Paleface Adios and I bought an autographed copy from him. I still have this wonderful book today about one of the truly great pacing champions.

When in December John Lennon was shot dead in New York by a lunatic, 1980 became one of those years you always remember. In June, Judge David Opas (Family Court) was shot dead at the gate of his Sydney home. In July, dozens of nations, including the US boycotted the Moscow Olympics due to the Soviet invasion of Afghanistan. That same month the Shah of Iran, who had been deposed the previous year by the Ayatollah Khomeini, died of cancer in an Egyptian hospital. In August, Azaria Chamberlain disappeared from her tent and her mother Lindy claimed she had been taken by a dingo. Lindy Chamberlain was convicted of murder, served three years, then pardoned and later exonerated in one of the most controversial criminal cases in Australian history. In November, the ex B-grade movie star, Ronald Reagan, won the Presidential election.

For me, though, the highlight was an unexpected visit from Gloria and John. John asked me, 'When are you coming home from the factory, Dad?'

'Soon,' I said.

And I believed it.

In March 1981, three months after the shooting of John Lennon, another deranged misfit shot and wounded President Reagan outside the Hilton Hotel in Washington. Three others were also wounded. The shooter, John Hinckley Jr., claimed he did it to impress Jodie Foster after he watched her and De Niro in the movie *Taxi Driver*. But Jodie wasn't very impressed at all.

Six weeks later in St Peter's Square in Rome, Pope John Paul II was shot and wounded by a radical, disgruntled Turk. In October, the Egyptian President Anwar Sadat was shot dead by a rebel soldier. In a period of ten months, a Pope, two Presidents and a musical legend had been shot, two of them killed.

Things were more mundane at Yatala. James Miller, serving a life sentence for his role in the rape and murder of seven young women whose bodies were dumped in the Truro area, went on a hunger-strike protesting his innocence. He complained that all he did was get out of the car and go for a walk while his accomplice, Christopher Worrell, raped and murdered the girls. (Worrell died in a car accident before he could be brought to justice). Miller insisted that he was terrified of Worrell and if he had tried to intervene Worrell would have killed him. The court accepted that may have been the case in the first murder, but he had no excuses for accompanying Worrell when he picked up and killed the other six girls.

Most of us at Yatala hoped the authorities would allow him to starve himself to death just as Margaret Thatcher that same year allowed the IRA prisoners to die during their hunger strikes at 'the Maze' (Longkesh Prison) in Ireland, demanding to be treated as 'political' prisoners. But unlike the dedicated Irishmen, Miller didn't have the desire or the will to carry out his threat. He died in custody nearly three decades later.

I received a distinction pass for the three-year Writing for the Media course. TAFE informed the education officer that I had attained the highest mark in the state and it would be appropriate if it could be arranged for me to attend the presentation function. To my surprise, the governor approved the application. But the Commissioner, Mr Stewart, over-rode the approval, stating that I was a 'security risk.'

I later received an offer from Deakin University in Victoria to enrol in a humanities course when I was free.

But free or not, it wasn't a viable option for me.

Vision Magazine was going from strength to strength. We were now producing a ninety-six page edition and a lot of important people were on our mailing list. An officer told me the authorities were concerned about its influence and intended to do something about it.

'They tried to stop it once,' I said, 'and the Ombudsman stepped in.

The magazine is good for everyone.'

About a week later I was called into the assistant governor's office where he and two other high-ranking officers were seated.

He was an American, about forty-years-old, who had a moustache that he often stroked while he was talking to you. 'Sit down, Killick,' he said. 'We have some good news for you.'

Thinking it might be a positive result from the High Court I sat down, my heart thumping.

'You are a model prisoner,' he said, stroking his moustache, 'and we've decided to reward you by classifying you as a minimum security prisoner so you can go to Cadell.'

Cadell was an open prison farm about 100 kilometres away.

'Well, thanks,' I said, caught totally unaware. 'But I don't want to go to Cadell, I'm happy here.'

'Nonsense,' he said, again stroking his moustache, 'you'll be much better off at Cadell. And it will help you when you come up for parole.'

'I'm not worried about parole – I expect to win my High Court appeal. Meanwhile I enjoy working on the magazine. I'm not interested in going to a prison farm.'

'Look, Killick, you've done a good job on the magazine, but it's time for you to move on. Most prisoners would jump at the chance to go to Cadell.'

'Not me. I'd never get a visit.'

'This is for your own good, Killick. You are now a minimum security prisoner and you'll be going to Cadell.'

I stared at him. 'If you send me to Cadell, I'll escape.'

One of the other officers banged his fist on the table. 'Enough of that talk, Killick! You're going to Cadell and you won't escape.'

'I will.'

'I said you won't!'

The assistant governor stood up. 'The interview is over. Don't push your luck, Killick. You'll go to Cadell and you won't escape.'

I turned and walked out. Whether or not I would have escaped if I'd have been sent to Cadell is a moot point. Within a week of the interview I was working on the magazine when a high-ranking senior approached me. 'I have some news for you, Killick,' he said, waving a piece of paper in his hand. 'The High Court has quashed all your convictions. You have been given a retrial.'

It was almost like being granted a reprieve from a death sentence. Except the relief was short lived as the reality of the word 'retrial' sank in. I'd have to go through the entire trial process again. But surely this time, after three-and-a-half years in custody, they would have to grant me bail?

The next day Michael Abbott, who had been working with Marie Shaw on the case, visited me. He was in a buoyant mood. 'This is an historical win,' he said. 'They've virtually said three of the State's leading justices got it wrong. Four if you count the trial.'

I nodded, but my excitement had waned. I was still inside a maximum security prison facing another arduous trial. 'I want to apply for bail.'

'Wrong move,' he said. 'You have to be patient. I'm working something out for you but it will take a week or two.'

I met his gaze. 'What do you mean, working something out?'

'I'm talking to the Crown. They aren't keen to go through it all again, but we need to give them something.'

'I'm not pleading guilty if that's what you have in mind.'

He spoke calmly, but his voice rose a little. 'You have to understand, they don't like you. They believe you are guilty and that you have had your convictions overturned on a technicality. We are at a crucial stage of your case – we have to give them something.'

'I won't be pleading guilty. Get me bail.'

'Just hang in here for a little while and trust me. Give me two weeks.' Ten days later I was told to get ready, I was going to the Supreme Court.

On arrival, Abbott came to the cell to see me. 'We haven't got much time,' he said. 'We've got Justice Sangster and he's got a trial beginning at ten.'

I couldn't believe my luck. 'Sangster! He's the toughest judge in the state.'

He gave a dismissive wave of his arm. 'It doesn't matter. Everything is settled. You'll plead guilty to the bank and the Plympton TAB and you will walk from court a free man.'

'I told you, I'm not pleading guilty.'

'It's up to you. But I've gone to great lengths to secure this agreement. If you decline it, you'll be on your own.' He paused, staring intently at me. 'If they have to put on a second trial involving fifty witnesses, some from interstate, they will crucify you. I won't be a part of it. This is your chance to walk away.'

I thought of Dad, he wasn't well. Young John, nearly seven-years-old – he had rarely seen me in the past three years. And Gloria, battling to bring him up on her own. I could be with them tonight.

But my mind was screaming: 'I didn't do it!' A prison officer called out. 'You're on, Killick.'

'Well,' Abbott said. 'What's it to be?'

'Are you certain about this?'

'Guaranteed.'

'Let's do it.'

In the courtroom, when I was asked how I pleaded to the two robberies I stood mute for about five seconds before uttering 'guilty'.

I had been forcibly taught that life was about compromises which always came with a cost. At that moment something inside me died.

Justice Sangster stared at me as he listened to Abbott's submissions. When Abbott handed up my certificates for the Writing For The Media course and a few copies of *Vision Magazine*, the judge turned to my old nemesis, Rice, and asked: 'Any submissions, Mister Rice?'

Rice smiled. 'No, Your Honour. It would appear Mister Killick has made every effort to rehabilitate himself.'

The judge nodded. 'Mister Killick, these are serious crimes. The state has had to go to great lengths to bring you to justice. However, you have the advantage of coming before me after three-and-a-half years in custody and during that time one can only applaud your attitude and application towards rehabilitation. Quite exceptional. I hope you have learned your lesson that crime doesn't pay?'

It was a question and he stared at me, eyebrows raised, awaiting my assent.

I wanted to tell him that I had learnt justice was a complicated game and I was angry. Very angry. But I said nothing.

'Yes,' he said, nodding to himself. 'I sentence you to three years and six months on each count, the sentences to run concurrently and to start from the day of your arrest. You are therefore free to go. Justice has not only been done, but seen to be done.'

It was as simple as that.

The two prison guards stood near me, wide-eyed with stunned looks on their faces.

I grinned. 'Put your handcuffs away, fellas. I'm going home.' Abbott shook my hand. 'How do you feel?'

'Amazed at the total of fuck ups this case has produced. And now another one.'

He gave me a quizzical look. 'How so?'

'He sentenced me to three and a half years, backdated to the day of my arrest. I spent the first four months in Long Bay before being extradited. This judge didn't have the authority to backdate it including the New South Wales time.'

'I didn't hear that. Do you want to go back into court and explain to the judge how he got it wrong?'

I grinned. 'I'd like to. But I'll give him a break.'

'Very wise. Anything else I can do for you?'

'Lend me ten bucks – I haven't got a cent on me.'

'You are supposed to be paying me,' he mocked, handing me ten dollars.

Mr Schneider, my parole officer, who had watched the proceedings, came over. 'Congratulations, John. You don't have to worry about parole now. But I need you to come to the office and sign off on all the paperwork.'

He was a nice old guy who had been filing good reports on me. 'Sure. Let's go now and get it done.'

Walking through the city among civilians instead of prisoners and guards,

I once again relished the feeling of freedom. Even the air seemed different.

As we entered the main entrance of the Corrective Services building, a man who looked to be in his late forties approached me. It was the commissioner.

'Hello, Mister Stewart,' Schneider said. 'This is John Killick: the court just released him and I've brought him here to close his parole file.'

Stewart stared at me. I could sense his resentment. 'Yes, I just heard about it – unofficially. Nothing is official yet.'

He pulled out his wallet and proffered three $2 notes. 'What I want you to do, Killick, is to take this money and catch a taxi to Yatala. I'll let them know you're coming. You may have to stay there overnight but I'll try to arrange for the paperwork to be done immediately so you can be released tonight. We need to make it all official.'

'Do I need an escort to catch the taxi?' I asked, deadpan. He looked surprised. 'Well, no, why would you?'

'You over-ruled the governor and wouldn't allow me to go to my writing award presentation – even with an escort. You claimed I was a security risk.'

He flushed. 'But at that point you hadn't won your appeal.'

'No. But now the court has told me to go home and that's where I'm going. What I want you to do is to ring Yatala and tell them that I told you it's official.'

I turned to Schneider. 'Let's get this paperwork done.'

He was embarrassed. As we walked away he said: 'You shouldn't have spoken to Mister Stewart like that, John.'

'I told him what he needed to know.'

To my delight, old Schneider grinned. 'You did, John. You fucking did...'

THE BEAST BEGINS TO STIR

1981–82

My life has always been one of highs and lows. One of the great highs was walking through Sydney Airport to be greeted by Gloria and my beautiful boy, now a month from his seventh birthday. Picking him up and hugging him I realised how much he had grown since my arrest. Gloria looked radiant. Any doubt I had about my decision to plead guilty in exchange for unconditional freedom was immediately dispelled.

Gloria had rented a small two-bedroom unit in Waverton. John insisted on my undivided attention and Gloria prepared us dinner while John told me about his friends, his school and his interest in cricket and rugby league. He and Gloria were staunch Parramatta Eels supporters and the Eels had recently won the grand final for the first time.

After John had gone to bed Gloria and I had a long talk. Without a doubt, prison is the great destroyer of relationships. My three-and-a-half years in maximum security gaols, 1,600 kilometres from Sydney, had killed something in our marriage. We both knew it, but pretended nothing had changed.

I had a great reunion with Dad. It had always been at the back of my mind that, by the time I was released, he wouldn't be around.

'Just put it all behind you, Johnny,' he said.

But I couldn't. Behind the calm facade, I was raging inside. I wanted the world to know how easy it was for the system to go wrong. I conveniently blocked out the fact I had instigated my own downfall by planning the robbery before withdrawing. I wanted people to know that, innocent or not, once you are in prison, it's almost impossible to get out before serving your sentence.

I rang Roger Holden, the editor of the *Adelaide Sunday Mail* who had published my Paleface Adios articles. He had been an avid supporter of *Vision Magazine*. I told him I had won my High Court appeal and was in the process of writing an article about the case. He advised me to come and see him after the Christmas break so we could discuss a possible feature article.

Although Gloria was working for a lawyer, she had taken her holidays to coincide with the school break.

For the next few weeks I spent a lot of time with John. We went to Luna Park, played cricket and football, went to a few movies and even did the shopping for Gloria. We made up stories and John illustrated them and stood outside Waverton Railway Station selling them for 20 cents to anyone who was interested. A sort of 7-year-old paperboy who wrote his own news stories.

Gloria commented that John and I were gradually restoring the once strong bond between us that had been withered by my long absence. It was almost like old times.

I wrote a 10,000 word article entitled '*The Perfect Alibi* Case'. My memory of the events was almost photographic: the first draft needed very little editing.

About mid-January, after advising Roger Holden that I was on the way, I hired a car and drove to Adelaide, only stopping for petrol. I was running on adrenalin and didn't feel tired.

On arrival I didn't have to wait. His secretary ushered me into his office and served us coffee and cakes.

He was a good style of a man, middle-aged, with thick brown hair and a trim moustache. His manner was pleasant.

While I gave him a rundown of the article he flicked through it, occasionally raising his eyebrows and shaking his head.

Eventually he handed the manuscript back to me. 'I'll be honest with you, John – we couldn't print this.'

'It's all true,' I said.

'I don't doubt it, but if I print this I'll be out of a job.'

'Roger, you knew what this was about. Why bring me all this way for a few cakes and coffee?'

'Because I know you can write. How about another article like the Paleface Adios story?'

I stood up and shook his hand. 'I'll keep it in mind. Thanks for your time.'

At that stage I had no intention of writing an article about sport or anything else other than my case. I felt certain that Roger had intended to publish my article but someone had intervened. Probably, the only way I could make the story public would be to write a book. In the meantime what would I do for money? I had anticipated receiving a handsome payment for the article.

Maybe I should go and rob a bank in Adelaide. That would even the scorecard. It would never compensate me for the past three-and-a-half years, but it would be a start.

Even as it occurred to me, I dismissed the idea. If something went wrong and I returned to prison, the impact on John, Gloria and Dad would be irreversible.

But I realised that I was far from a rehabilitated man. If I knew I could rob a bank and get away with it, I wouldn't hesitate to do it. This had been my mindset in 1966. Now, in 1982, I had returned to that place. In 1966 I had lost Cathy and I had no brakes. This time I had John and Gloria. Had I been rehabilitated in the seventies when I wrote stories, owned businesses and worked hard, living an honest life? Probably. But is 'rehabilitation' a permanent thing? Obviously, not.

It's a mindset! I had tried hard to live a normal life, but that other side of me that was prepared to risk all if the prize was worthwhile, that part of me had never gone away...it had lain dormant but alive – ready to take control if things went wrong. That's why I had planned the Plympton bank robbery. Withdrawing from it days before the event had been too little too late.

Now the beast within me was stirring again – for how long could I contain it?

These were my thoughts as I booked into a motel for the night – too tired to drive to Sydney.

The next morning I dropped in to see June and her family in Sturt. She was a devout churchgoer who regularly visited prisoners who otherwise didn't receive any. She and her daughter, Jackie, had come to see me on a number of occasions. Jackie, a pretty teenager with light brown hair, was slim and athletic – unlike her Mum, Dad and brother Peter who were all on the stout side.

She told me she was leaving her boyfriend, Sam, who was ten years older than her and going to live with her half-brother, Robert, in Toronto New South Wales. She had a new boyfriend, Phillip, who lived in that area.

'How does Sam feel about it?'

'He's upset.'

'Does he know about Phillip?'

'Are you serious? He'd do anything he could to stop me if he knew.'

'What about your parents?'

'They don't know either.'

Although I wondered why she had confided in me, I said nothing. I had more important things to worry about.

Ten minutes later I was on my way to Sydney. Jackie was the last person on my mind.

Although I had failed before as a professional punter, I decided to try again – this time using a different system, one that I had trialled successfully whilst in Yatala. But experience had taught me that what works in theory sometimes failed in practice.

I called it the Charthorse System. The idea was to choose a 'stable' of twenty good – not champion – horses and, regardless of form, back them every start. If, after four starts, one didn't win, I would drop it from the 'stable.' Over the years I had noticed that often a horse would fail as a short-priced favourite and then, at one of its next few starts, win at lucrative odds.

When I outlined the plan to Gloria she loaned me $1000 to get started. Within a month I had some good priced winners and then I hit a 20-to-1 winner. This enabled me to reimburse Gloria and continue to operate with my own bank. After a few more wins I bought an old white Kingswood. Although

I wasn't making a fortune, I was winning. Past losses – some of them disastrous – became distant memories. I had become a successful professional punter. If only I'd have used this system in the past.

In April, Jackie arrived on our doorstep at 6:30 am. She had a black eye. I brought her inside. 'Who hit you?'

She wouldn't tell me. She was upset. 'Could I stay here for a couple of days until I decide what to do?'

Gloria, who had joined us, comforted her. 'Of course you can.'

'Where's Phillip?' I asked.

'He's still in Toronto. It's over.' That was all she would say about it.

A few days would have been fine. But Jackie slotted in well. Days became weeks. She often cooked, cleaned and shopped for us. She played her guitar and sang for us. She played with John.

Her parents tried to persuade her to return home but she was finished with Sam and refused to go. She was happy with us. She had become one of the family.

I should have thought of her as the daughter I never had. But I didn't. I had become attracted to her. Eventually I made a pass at her. Although I was twenty years her senior, it led to a hot affair. In eight years of marriage it was the first time I had been unfaithful. But once you are caught up in a passionate affair, remorse and guilt become inconsequential.

Gloria soon found out. When she angrily told Jackie to leave, Jackie broke down and said she was sorry.

'There's no point in being sorry,' Gloria said. 'I take you into my house, I trusted you and you do this!'

I cut in. 'It's my fault.'

Gloria turned on me. 'Of course it's your fault. And what's your excuse?'

I didn't have one. 'Something's missing,' I said. 'Blame me, blame all the years in gaol, but sometimes I think I'm only twenty.'

That was probably as close to the truth as I'd ever get.

I knew that Gloria was shattered. She had received a raw deal from me all the way down the line.

We looked at each other. My comment about 'something's missing' didn't leave her much choice.

'I want you to leave.'

I nodded. 'All right. What about John?'

'You can come and see him.' She looked across at Jackie. 'Don't bring her.'

Fifteen minutes later, with Jackie seated beside me, I drove off in the Kingswood. I had about $500 in cash and nothing in the bank. I had no idea of where we were going or how we would survive.

THE CORNFLAKES SCAM

1982

Believing Jackie would soon become homesick and want to return home, I drove towards Adelaide. On the first night we stayed in a motel at Wagga Wagga.

I explained the situation to her. 'We have nowhere to live. We have no income. In a few days we'll have no money.'

She shrugged, seemingly unperturbed. 'We can get jobs.'

'I can take you home – then you can get a job.'

'I'm not going home. I want to stay with you.'

'If you stay with me we'll have to steal to live.' She was resolute. 'Whatever it takes.'

And that's how it began...

My experience as a shoplifter with Scotty had taught me that it could produce maximum profits with, if caught, minimum penalties. It was relatively easy to steal items from supermarkets and department stores, but selling the goods was more difficult: the one exception being cigarettes. In those days most of the supermarkets stocked cigarettes in open steel cabinets from which the customers could serve themselves. I figured that if I bought one of those canvas covered, two-wheeled trolleys that Scotty had nearly always used for stealing from shops, I could put an empty Cornflakes box inside the trolley, put cartons of cigarettes inside the box and, using double sided tape, seal it. It was the era before supermarkets in Australia used scanners. The checkout girls simply looked at the price on the label of the item and rang it through the register. I would be able to pay for the Cornflakes and walk out with the cigarettes inside.

I outlined the idea to Jackie. She was enthusiastic about giving it a try. We headed for Melbourne, discussing and fine tuning the plan on the way.

In Albury I bought a canvas trolley, some double sided tape, a packet of Kellogg's Cornflakes and a packet of Skippy Cornflakes, which were different in size. The cartons of cigarettes also came in two different sizes. I purchased a carton of Marlboro and a carton of Benson and Hedges (B&H). The Marlboro was longer and thinner than the carton of B&H. The B&H and other brands in similar sized cartons fitted perfectly into the Skippy Cornflakes box. Measuring it, I figured I could cram five cartons into one box. Almost out of cash, we put the plan into action in the supermarket from which I had purchased the cornflakes.

Applying the double-sided tape to the underside of the top flap of the empty Skippy Cornflakes box, I placed the box inside the trolley, pulled the canvas flap over the top, then walked into the supermarket. Jackie followed me at a discreet distance.

Going to a cigarette cabinet I grabbed three cartons of B&H and two of Dunhill and dropped them into the trolley. I walked halfway down the aisle, then quickly pushed the cartons into the box and sealed it. I glanced at Jackie: she nodded. No one had taken any notice of me.

I walked to the breakfast foods section and placed the box alongside the other Skippy Cornflakes and picked up a smaller carton. Jackie came over and picked up the box with the cigarettes inside. As she walked towards the checkout I followed, watching to see if we had aroused anyone's suspicions.

Everything seemed to be okay.

Jackie paid for the cornflakes and went through the checkout without a problem.

Outside, she was excited. 'It's unbelievable! 'she said. 'We can be rich.'

'Maybe. But every time we do it, it's a risk. If we get caught, you'll have a criminal record.'

'As long as we look out for each other, we won't get caught,' she said.

On the way to Melbourne, Jackie went into a small shop that sold cigarettes and told the owner she had won five cartons in a raffle and she didn't smoke. Would he like to buy them for half the retail price?

He didn't hesitate to hand her the cash. Before arriving in Melbourne we worked the scam twice more. Again, selling the cigarettes wasn't a problem.

In Melbourne we booked into a motel and spent a day driving around the suburbs buying the cornflakes from various supermarkets. After opening the boxes we dropped all the cornflakes off at a Salvation Army centre.

Within a few days we were hitting ten supermarkets a day.

Jackie became expert at selling the cigarettes. Her 'won a raffle and don't smoke' routine gave the honest shopkeepers a clear conscience when they bought them. She was selling ten cartons per shop.

A few of the shopkeepers asked her to 'come back if you win any more raffles'.

We soon had a small network of buyers. One of them, a Greek guy, whom she said was always sweating, commented when she returned a third time. 'You win a lot of raffles.'

By now, Jackie was very sure of herself. 'Oh, well, I guess I'll have to take them somewhere else.'

'No! Every raffle you win, no matter how many cigarettes, you bring them to me.'

Later that week she walked into his shop with a grin and told him she had won a 'big one'.

He gave her a knowing look. 'How many?'

'One hundred.'

He paid cash.

I regularly phoned John and Gloria. Sometimes Gloria was pleasant; at other times curt. John was missing me and I assured him I'd return to Sydney soon.

Although Jackie rang her parents a few times, it became an ordeal for her. They threatened that if she didn't immediately come home, they would go to the police and have me put in gaol again.

But Jackie still had raffles to win and cigarettes to sell. She hung up and didn't ring again for a month.

We stayed in Melbourne for about six weeks. During that time my charthorses had a bad run. Frustrated, I began betting on other horses trying to recoup losses. By the time we departed Melbourne, despite having stolen thousands of cartons of cigarettes, we had less than $1000.

DARCY DUGAN

1982

On arrival in Sydney I took Jackie to meet Dad. I could see he liked her. But he was also very fond of Gloria. For once in his life he didn't try to tell me what I should do: probably because he didn't know. My life was in a mess, we both knew it. Best to pretend everything was 'normal'.

Jackie and I rented a little unit above the shops in Campbell Parade, Bondi. It was a quick drive to Waverton to see John and Gloria.

Sometimes Jackie resented my spending time with them. Once, she stood in front of me, hands on her hips, barring my exit from the unit.

'Can I come, too?'

'You know you can't.'

'Well, if I can't come, you shouldn't go.'

'Don't be ridiculous. John needs to see his father.'

'And I need you here.'

'Need me here for what? You're acting like a six-year-old. I'll see John as often as I can. If you don't like it, go back to Adelaide.'

I was angry and I meant it. I pushed past her and she hit me in the back. Ignoring her I ran down the stairs, glad to be away from her. We were together twenty-four hours every day and that can destroy any relationship. Particularly when we were daily risking our freedom.

When I returned home she had passed out after drinking half a flask of Bacardi.

In Sydney we continued with the cornflakes scam. I gave the old reliable Kingswood to Gloria and we rented vehicles by the month.

Using her 'I won a raffle, but...' routine, Jackie soon established a new group of willing buyers. The cigarettes were as good as cash. I nicknamed her 'Imp'. She loved the name and often referred to herself as 'The Imp'.

It was winter – not a good time to gamble on the inferior class of horses that generally raced during this period. Some heavy losses in the past had taught me that. Unless a charthorse was running, which was rare in winter, I curtailed gambling, waiting for the spring when the top class gallopers resume racing.

We began to build up a bit of a bank. When it came to stealing the cigarettes our luck was remarkable. No-one seemed to have a clue about what we were doing. 'We can probably do another month here, then move on to Queensland,' I told Jackie.

I was wrong about that.

Although we generally avoided hitting the same store twice, sometimes the procedure went so quickly and smoothly that we did it again. When staff became aware that they were down five or ten cartons of cigarettes they realised that someone was walking out of the store with them. But how? A circular was sent to all the stores with a directive for staff and store detectives to be particularly vigilant regarding the cigarette cupboards. They were also advised to be on the lookout for a mysterious canvas covered two-wheeled trolley which had been seen on numerous occasions near the cigarette cupboards.

When we walked into Kmart at Merrylands on 25 August they were immediately on to us. They were good – neither of us noticed anything suspicious.

They grabbed hold of Jackie first. She was sunk: she was holding a cornflakes box full of cigarettes. When they tried to grab me, I pushed them away and showed them the trolley. It was empty.

'You've got the wrong guy,' I said and walked outside before they could gather their wits. If I could get away, Jackie would be straight out on bail. At worst she would get a fine. But if they found our car we were both in big trouble – the boot was half-full of cigarettes.

I realised things were serious when a female police officer withdrew her gun and pointed it at me. They must have called the police the moment we entered the store.

'You're making a big mistake,' I said to the cop. 'I've got nothing on me.'

Some of the Kmart staff were holding on to me. She handcuffed me. 'Where's your car?' she asked.

'I always travel by train,' I said.

A quick search found my car keys.

I refused to tell her where the car was. We were in Merrylands. Maybe an enterprising lad would steal it.

We were taken to Merrylands Police Station where detective Peters, a tall, dark-haired but balding guy in his forties was in charge.

He told us the charges weren't very serious but he needed to know the make and model of our vehicle. I protested that I was being illegally detained after an unlawful arrest at gunpoint. 'Either let me go now,' I said, 'or let me ring my lawyer, Bruce Miles.'

Peters knew if I could contact a lawyer he would be forced to release me. He stalled. When Kmart closed and everyone went home, the rental car stood out like a beacon in the vacant carpark.

We were both charged with goods in custody and stealing. Although Jackie was granted bail, I was refused.

Peters had another ace up his sleeve. 'John, we just found out about this,' he said, smirking.

He showed me a warrant issued for my arrest in the District Court in August 1979. It was for the break and enter charge at Flemings in 1975. I had forgotten about it.

'Judge Goran held this over so I could be extradited to South Australia to fight charges of bank robbery,' I said.

'Well, there's been a warrant out for you for three years now,' Peters said. 'When this is added to the present charges you'll be going away for quite a while.'

I was taken to Long Bay Remand Centre. On the Saturday morning, Gloria and Jackie visited me. If nothing else, the arrest initiated an uneasy truce between them. But I could see by their manner that it was a fragile peace.

'Ask Bruce to put in an urgent bail application to the Supreme Court,' I said. 'These charges aren't serious enough to deny me bail.'

'And what will you do when you are out?' Gloria asked. 'Carry on as usual?'

'No. Me and the canvas-covered trolley are through.'

'I hope so. You are in enough trouble already.'

When I returned to the yards I enquired about the library. I was told that it was closed on weekends but if I asked the librarian he might open it for me.

'Who's the librarian?'

'Darcy Dugan.'

Darcy Dugan! The legend. Australia's most notorious bank robber/ escapee. I had always wanted to meet him.

I waited for about an hour for him to come out of his Wing. 'Here he comes now,' one of the guys said.

As he walked past the yard I called out to him. He stopped and turned to look at me. He was sixty-one but looked older. He was much smaller than I had imagined.

'Could I see you for a moment, Darcy?'

He walked over to me, scowling. 'Do I know you?'

'No. We've never met. But I've heard a lot about you. When I was a kid everyone was talking about the shoot-out you and Mears had at the bank in Pyrmont.'

'That was 30 years ago. I was sentenced to death for it. See you.' He started to walk away.

'That's not what I wanted to see to you about,' I said. 'They tell me you're the librarian.'

He turned and stared at me. 'So?'

'Well, I've just come in. I'm in a cell with nothing. I'd really appreciate it if you'd open the library and get me a couple of books. I'll look after them.'

'You'd really appreciate it, would you? What are you in for?'

'Shoplifting. I should get bail next week.'

He stepped back and announced loudly to the yard: 'A fucking shoplifter wants me to go and open the library for him because he's got nothing to do until he gets bail next week!'

A few guys laughed. I stared at him, shocked by his attitude. I was on the verge of telling him that I had probably robbed more banks than him and I didn't have to shoot anyone to get away. But I controlled the impulse. He was old and bitter. He had been through incredibly tough times, particularly at Grafton where even the toughest of men had broken down. He was a great survivor and once he had nearly escaped from Grafton. In his view I was just a petty crim asking the legend for an undeserved favour. Watching him walk away with a swagger, I smiled and silently wished him well. He died a free man but frail and sick in 1991, aged seventy.

Ironically, within two years of my only meeting with Darcy Dugan, 'the fucking shoplifter' would again be on '*Australia's Most Wanted*' list – for bank robbery and escape.

AN UNDESERVED CHANCE

1982–83

On Monday, Bruce Miles managed to get me into the Supreme Court. The judge granted bail, ordering me to appear before Judge Goran in the District Court on Thursday for the Flemings matter.

On Thursday he briefly explained the situation to the judge.

'Yes, I remember Mister Killick,' the judge said. 'We sent him off to Adelaide to deal with some bank robbery matters.' He turned to me. 'You told me six to nine months. It has taken four years.'

I nodded. 'I had to go to the High Court, Your Honour.'

'Yes, I noted that. A technicality, no doubt?'

'Not at all, Your Honour.'

'Hmmm. What about these stealing charges you are on bail for?'

'I'm pleading Not Guilty, Your Honour.'

'I thought you might. You haven't been found guilty on them so I can't take them into account.' He turned his attention to Bruce. 'What do you think, Mister Miles? He said he would come back, it has taken four years, but here he is. Should I give him a chance?'

Bruce smiled. 'I think you should, Your Honour.'

For a few moments the judge studied me. 'I remember you told me you made a living from installing those peepholes in doors,' he said. 'It reminds me of that song, 'Jeepers, creepers, where did you get those peepers?' Do you remember that song?'

Everyone, including the prosecutor was smiling.

'Yes, I do, Your Honour.'

He raised his eyebrows. 'Why don't you try doing it again.'

'That's a good idea, Your Honour.'

'Yes, I think it is. Will keep you busy – and honest. I wish you luck with the stealing charges. On this offence I sentence you to the rising of the court.'

I was thankful for Judge Goran's clemency. But I had little doubt that when I fronted for the cigarettes caper, the magistrate would send me to gaol.

During the next few weeks I spent a lot of time with John. Once, I mentioned that I might have to go away for a while.

'When will you be back, Dad?'

'Well, I mightn't go yet. Let's wait and see.' I was a lousy father. I knew it.

Almost broke, I hit a hot streak on the horses. Using an 'all or nothing' approach, I built our paltry bank up to more than $3000.

At Rosehill races I collected on five consecutive winners. Then, sitting in the dining room area studying the form for the next race, I heard a lot of yelling and screaming. Looking towards the direction of the commotion, I was shocked to see Jackie standing behind a young woman who was seated at a table, holding her by the hair with both hands and yanking her head from side to side. The woman was screaming. A young guy seated next to the woman grabbed hold of Jackie but she wouldn't let go.

I rushed over and, none too gently, managed to break her grip and pull her aside.

'This bitch was laughing at us!' she said. 'What? What the hell you are talking about?'

'At our age difference!' Jackie yelled. 'She was calling you my white-haired sugar daddy!'

The victim retorted, 'I did not. You're crazy'.

The young guy said: 'You had better leave or we'll call the police.'

Everyone was staring at us. I was amazed that no security people had arrived.

'Don't worry, we're going,' I said.

We were fortunate to get out without further incident. I decided then to dye my hair black. My shock of white hair stood out and added at least ten years to my age. The girl Jackie had attacked probably thought I was about fifty – and Jackie looked her age, eighteen.

By dyeing my hair I had made the decision that I wouldn't appear in court. It was easy for me to justify my actions. Why should I go to gaol for stealing cigarettes when I had recently spent three-and-a-half years inside for crimes I hadn't committed? It was time to balance the books. Now we'll play 'catch me if you can!' What will they do – set up a taskforce to catch a shoplifter for absconding bail? No, they will simply wait until I'm arrested again. History almost guaranteed that it would happen. But in the meantime I'd travel around Australia with Jackie, living by my wits. It was a challenge. I'd spent nearly all of my twenties in gaol and a part of me had died. Now, I'd turn back the clock, black hair, young girl, travelling, gambling and taking risks!

I was forty years old – about to be twenty again.

On 21 September, Bruce accompanied Jackie to the magistrate's court. He made a strenuous plea for mercy. The magistrate was scathing in his assessment of Jackie's behaviour. He told her that he had considered sending her to prison but had decided to place her on probation.

As expected, he immediately issued a bench warrant for my arrest. 'He would have given you two years,' she said.

'He still might. We have to leave the state for a while.'

I bought an old Ford with a good engine. A few hours later we set off for Melbourne.

We reverted to shoplifting. This time it was a hard slog. One of us would go into a store or shop, steal an item, then the other would return it, requesting a refund. Sometimes the person responsible would refuse to refund the money, offering an exchange instead. But most of the time we received the refund.

We operated in country towns as well as the city. On a good day we would make two hundred dollars. But expenses were heavy.

My good luck with the horses continued. One of my charthorses, Gurner's Lane, won the Caulfield and Melbourne Cups double. When he beat the champion Kingston Town in the Melbourne Cup I had $200 on him at 6 to 1.

A few weeks later I was nearly caught after stealing a camera from Kmart. A fit-looking store detective, who looked to be in his early thirties, ran up to me as I was walking towards the car where Jackie was waiting. He grabbed me by the arm.

'You've got one of our cameras under your jumper,' he said. 'You're coming back to the store with me.'

I jerked my arm free. He tried to grab hold of me and I pushed him back and went into a fighting stance. 'Touch me again and I'll put you in hospital.'

He stared at me, sizing me up. He didn't look intimidated. Then he looked around. There were a couple of teenage boys nearby, rounding up trolleys. 'Hey! You two – give me a hand with this bloke.'

Turning, I ran as fast I could to the end of the carpark, dashed across the busy highway and ran down the side passageway of a house and jumped over the back fence, landing in a paddock. A few hundred metres away I could see a school. No-one had tried to follow me.

Jogging towards the school I saw our Ford cruising past. Jackie had figured out where I would be. Waving, I ran towards her.

Getting into the car, I grinned. 'I think it's time we robbed a bank – it's less risky.' I was only half joking.

But we persisted with the shoplifting, working our way through suburbs and towns towards Adelaide. We were bickering over minor things and Jackie decided she wanted to go home.

We arrived in Adelaide two days before my forty-first birthday. Jackie insisted we stay together for a few more days because she wanted to get me a special present.

We booked into a motel at the bottom of the Adelaide Hills. Now that we were in Adelaide I sensed that she was in two minds about returning home.

For my part, I knew that although I'd miss her, I would also feel a sense of relief that the unlikely affair was over. Jackie demanded constant attention and I couldn't provide it. Although I'd never admit it to her, I didn't love her. I doubted if I was capable of love in the true sense of the word. The trauma I had experienced over losing Cathy while I was in H Division had mortally wounded my belief in 'true' love. Then the three-and-a-half years away from Gloria had killed any remaining illusions I had about 'romantic' love. You can love someone for a lifetime. But 'romantic love' was an ephemeral thing.

Somehow, for my birthday, Jackie managed to get me a copy of Norman Mailer's In the Belly of the Beast. It was about a supposedly reformed criminal whom Mailer had helped to get parole. The ex-con, Abbott, soon reverted to character and killed someone. I had tried a few times to purchase it but without success.

On 16 February we were still at the motel. Out of control bushfires in both Victoria and Adelaide were so catastrophic that this day became known as Ash Wednesday. Extreme fires were raging in the Hills above us. We saw news reports of people in their vehicles trying to outpace the flames, being burnt to death.

In South Australia 28 people died; Victoria had 47 deaths. At least 3,700 buildings were destroyed. Some of the fires had been deliberately lit. During my time in prison I had met a number of arsonists and firebugs.

They were regarded by most inmates as weirdos. It's doubtful if a stint in prison had any deterrent value. They needed intense psychiatric therapy – and usually they didn't get it.

Jackie decided she didn't want to go home. 'I'll stay with you until the end,' she said. I figured she expected that it was only a matter of time before I returned to gaol.

Again low on funds, we returned to Melbourne with the intention of working our way through to Sydney, then on to Brisbane.

For about a week we focused on shoplifting and refunds. During this period I didn't gamble – not on the horses, anyway. Every time I stole from a store I was gambling with my freedom. I was constantly aware of it but carried on regardless.

We left Melbourne without incident, arriving in Albury on 2 March. The next day our luck ran out. We had worked four stores, getting the refund each time. On the fifth occasion I stole an expensive iron. When Jackie returned it the male sales assistant refused to give her a refund because she didn't have a docket. She demanded the refund. When the man refused to back down Jackie abused him before walking out.

A store detective followed her and wrote down the number of our vehicle.

Ten minutes later we were pulled over by police. Although I protested, we were taken to Albury Police Station.

They soon discovered there was a warrant out for my arrest. After a while, two detectives took me to an interview room. For a few hours they questioned me about a number of unsolved armed robberies around the state. I told them the truth: I knew nothing about any of them.

'These days I'm just a petty shoplifter,' I said.

Eventually both Jackie and I were charged with stealing. I agreed to plead guilty if they gave her bail on her own recognizance. They complied with my offer.

The magistrate remanded us for a week, continuing Jackie's bail. I was refused bail.

We agreed that Jackie would take the car and drive to Sydney. Hopefully, Gloria would let her stay there until she returned for court. Failing that, she would go to Dad. I had no doubts he would be happy for her to stay with him.

Before leaving she bought me four paperbacks, a couple of hamburgers and some sweets. The cops were decent and gave them to me.

I spent the next week in a cell at the police station. At least they didn't put anyone in the cell with me. But they obviously considered me to be a security risk because they wouldn't allow me out of the cell for exercise.

On the scheduled court date, Jackie arrived in time to visit me. She had stayed with Gloria and John. Gloria had been upset that I was almost certain to return to prison. Neither John nor Dad were told – just in case I miraculously avoided a prison sentence.

The only positive factor for me was the Albury magistrate. The cops told me he was lenient on property crime – tough on violence. He would sentence me on all the offences, including the Sydney charges for which there was an outstanding warrant.

The magistrate dealt with Jackie first. He told her that if she didn't change her ways she would finish in gaol. He ordered her to report to a probation office in Burwood where she would be assigned some weekend community service.

Then he turned his attention to me. After the prosecutor read out the charges, urging a custodial sentence, the magistrate asked me if I had anything to say.

The prosecutor had placed a lot of emphasis on my criminal history, particularly the armed robberies.

'Your Worship,' I said. 'It's true that I have a record of violence. But four of those robberies I didn't commit. It's not on the record that the prosecutor read to the court, but if you check you'll find the High Court in 1981, quashed the four 1979 convictions. I then pleaded guilty to two of them in order to secure my release. There were reasons why I did that. But I still spent three-and-a-half years in gaol for crimes I didn't commit.' The prosecutor jumped up. 'I must object, Your Worship. There is no evidence in this Court that he won a High Court appeal. And, in any case, he pleaded guilty to two of them, then tells us he wasn't guilty.'

I cut in. 'Your Worship, I'm willing for you to adjourn this matter until you can ascertain whether or not I did win in the High Court. If I didn't, I ask that you sentence me to two years for being an idiot.'

There was some laughter at the back of the court.

Even the magistrate smiled. 'There will be no need for that, Mr Killick.

I'm aware of your history.'

I nodded. 'I didn't do those two robberies I pleaded guilty to – but there have been others in the past that I got away with. So I can't complain.'

The prosecutor who was a local cop, shook his head in disbelief.

I ignored him. 'But those three and a half years took their toll on not just me, but my family. It cost me my marriage and as you can see I'm now involved with a girl half my age. The entire experience destabilised me. But there's one important point here that the prosecution has missed.'

I paused and looked around. For some reason the courtroom was full.

Jackie was watching me intently.

I again focused on the magistrate. He arched his eyebrows. 'I'm listening, Mr Killick.'

I've spent half my adult life in prison – mostly for bank robberies. Now I've been arrested twice in the past six months for stealing from shops. I've gone from the top of the criminal hierarchy to the bottom. From a bank robber to a shoplifter. My proclivity for violence has gone. It's not total rehabilitation but it's a huge drop in criminality. Now, spending the last week locked in a cell again, I've come to my senses. Your Worship, I'm not only finished with violent crime, I'm finished with crime altogether. Returning me to gaol where I'll be mixing with hardened criminals again won't help me and it won't be in the public interest.'

The magistrate surprised everyone, including me, when he gave me a three year bond.

I was free to go. Incredibly, I had fared better than Jackie who would have to do community service.

After a decent meal and coffee, we drove to Sydney, stopping only for petrol.

GOOD TIME REG

1983

Jackie and I rented a flatette in Burwood from where she only had to walk down the street to see her probation officer. She was assigned community work every Saturday at Brush Farm near Marsden. She did various projects helping the handicapped.

For an income we bought chocolates, nuts and candy and assorted them into little baskets which we wrapped in cellophane and tied ribbons around. Jackie sold them for $10 each at clubs and pubs. We barely managed to eke a living from it. John told me he had developed a keen interest in chess and wanted to join a club. I took him to the Anzac Memorial Club at Cammeray where, on Saturdays, they held junior competitions. He was a good player but needed the experience of competition.

While there I was told their annual open competition would soon be starting. It was conducted during weeknights.

'You should enter it, Dad,' John said.

I filled in the entry form and paid the fee.

For the next few days I played out and analysed a lot of Bobby Fischer's games. Fischer is still regarded by many as the greatest ever chess genius. I mainly studied the openings – if you can gain an advantage in the opening fifteen moves, you are generally favoured to win.

I went through the competition unbeaten, winning the final in a seven hour marathon against a guy who was rated much higher than me.

It was the last time I played competition chess.

• • •

One morning in late June I went for a jog around Burwood. When I returned I received a phone call from Dad's neighbour, Maye.

Dad was dead.

In a state of shock I drove with Jackie to Waterloo. When I entered the flat I saw Dad slumped in his chair near the kitchen sink. Standing near him was an undertaker who fitted the term to perfection: tall, thin, dressed in black, pale complexioned, hooded eyes.

Maye had called him, let him inside, then returned to her own unit to grieve.

He told me there was nothing I could do, that they were about to take the body to the funeral parlour.

I looked at the table where Dad always kept his prized possession: a gold Rolex watch without a band. It wasn't there.

I stared at the undertaker: had he stolen it? Or had Maye taken it? It would have been so easy for this guy to have pocketed it. I was almost certain he had. Rage surged through me. Look at this guy – stealing from the dead! I had the urge to grab him, throw him against the wall and demand he give me the watch.

But what if I was wrong? My father was dead – I didn't care about the watch. I let it pass. I had to break the terrible news to David and Gloria. Both would be devastated.

Dad, independent to the end, had left a bank account to cover his funeral. He had told me he wanted to be cremated.

Gloria accompanied me to arrange all the details. I silently thanked the Albury magistrate for his magnanimity which had resulted in my being able to do it. One of my fears had been that I would be in gaol when Dad died.

The lady at the funeral parlour showed us three different coffins: a cheap, no frills model; a medium priced one and an expensive one. I chose the latter – they were going to burn it, but Dad was entitled to go out in style.

'You did the right thing,' Gloria said.

There were a few discussions among different family members about whether Jackie should be allowed to attend the service and cremation. I made it clear that Dad had been fond of her and she wanted to be there. Eventually, any opposition was withdrawn.

At the cremation David was emotional. 'I should have been there more often for him,' he said.

'How about me?' I replied. 'I was away for years at a time. We weren't ideal sons, but he wasn't an ideal father either. That's the way life really is.'

After that we talked about the 'good old days' with Dad. He had been a one-off character. On his death certificate, his doctor had written: Sir Reginald Killick.

Not bad for a Waterloo pensioner.

That night, after the cremation, I took Jackie to Harold Park trots. In the first race, there was a pacer named Good Time Reg. He was 16 to 1 and should have been 50 to 1 – at his past three starts he had finished 000. I put $50 on him to win $800.

He won by four lengths.

After collecting, we left without placing another bet.

I have no idea how that horse managed such a huge form reversal or why I had risked $50 on him!

'That was Dad's parting gift to us,' I told Jackie.

IMP COMES UNSTUCK

1983

In July, Joe, one of the shopkeepers who had often bought cigarettes from me told me there was good money to be made in collecting stamps. He had begun collecting them a few years ago and had a proposition to put to me. Being a fast runner, I could walk into a stamp shop, ask to see an expensive album and run out the door with it.

'The owners are nearly all old or middle-aged men,' he said. 'They could never catch you.'

I was reminded of when, in 1963, I had run out of the jewellery store in Burwood with a pad of diamond rings and realised it had been twenty years ago. I wasn't as fast now.

I told him I'd think about it. He stipulated that he would only buy Australian albums for which he would pay, depending on the content, between $2000 to $4000.

I discussed it with Jackie who was an exceptionally fast runner. We agreed it would be easier for her to disguise herself with a wig than for me to try to change my appearance. Plus the proprietor would be less likely to suspect that a young woman would run off with the album.

We drove around the suburbs checking out the stamp shops, eventually choosing two with ideal getaway routes.

A few days later Jackie, wearing a dark brown wig, entered one of the shops and asked to see the latest Australian stamp album. When the proprietor, a middle-aged, overweight man, handed it to her she dropped it into her bag and ran out of the shop. She ran for about 50 metres, then cut down a lane to the next street where I was waiting for her, the motor running. We drove off without incident.

That afternoon she hit the other shop we had chosen. It went smoothly – no-one pursued her.

After a lot of haggling Joe gave me $5000 for the two albums.

About a week later Jackie struck again. This time the proprietor was a middle-aged lady who screamed as Jackie ran outside with the album. Luckily, no-one chased her.

At the time, I was breaking about even on the horses. Financially, we were okay for a while so we decided to take a break from the stamp stealing and resume selling chocolates and nuts.

I knew it was a good decision when Joe told me that a monthly stamp journal did a write up about a 'fleet-footed young woman' who was running out of philatelist shops with expensive Australian stamp albums.

If we did it again, it would have to be interstate. We chose Adelaide.

Jackie's Saturday community work necessitated the trip would have to be a hit and run mission. Not prepared to risk the old Kingswood breaking down, I rented a new Falcon.

We did the trip in about eighteen hours. I booked a motel for three days and we slept for about ten hours.

That afternoon we checked the philatelist shops. There weren't many. The one we chose lacked the type of getaway route I preferred but all she had to do was run to the car and we'd be away. As a precaution, I stole a set of South Australian number plates and used Blu-tack to stick them to the New South Wales plates.

The night before the scheduled stamp album theft we had dinner and a few drinks with Frank, a guy I had known in Yatala. He offered to sell me an automatic .38 pistol for $1000. I told him I only had $600, take it or leave it. He took it and I took the pistol.

The next morning Jackie had a bit of a hangover. After a few strong coffees, she insisted she was ready for the task.

I dropped her off at the entrance to the shop then parked about 80 metres away near a corner street. The plan was that when I saw her run out of the shop I would drive into the side street where she would jump into the car.

But this time she didn't make it to the vehicle. When she ran out of the shop, the proprietor was only a few metres behind her, screaming blue murder. Two guys walking towards the shop, realising what had happened, intercepted her and grabbed hold of her. She began struggling, looking towards me and yelling out for help.

The proprietor joined in and the three of them began dragging her towards the shop.

I could have saved her. All I had to do was run across the street brandishing the pistol. I doubted they would resist freeing her but what then? As it stood, she would be charged with the theft of one item and bailed. If I rescued her by holding up and threatening three citizens who were simply doing their public duty there would be a manhunt for us. A Bonnie and Clyde situation. The media would love it. Sanity had to prevail. Jackie would have to go through the process of arrest, questioning, finger printing, court and bail before she was free.

I returned to the motel and waited. She arrived at about 6:00 pm. She looked tired and bedraggled.

'I've had enough,' she said, sitting on the bed. 'Did your parents bail you?'

'No. Thank God I didn't have to ring them. I was given self-recognisance.'

'We're in a bind,' I said. 'If you don't turn up for community work in Sydney they'll issue a warrant. If you do turn up, they'll issue a warrant for you here.'

'Bloody hell! I'm sick of it.' She gave me a questioning look. 'You could have rescued me from those bastards. You watched while they manhandled me.'

'How far do you think we would have got? Bonnie and Clyde in a new red Falcon at large in the city of churches. Bail was better.'

'Well, I won't be stealing any more stamps.'

'Nope. Stamps are off the menu.'

'What are we going to do?'

'I might have to rob a bank. I've been thinking about it for a while.' She shrugged. 'I'll help.'

'We'll see. Right now, you have to make a decision: do you want to stay here and risk going to gaol as well as having a warrant issued for your arrest in Sydney for not doing community work, or do you want to return to Sydney and have a warrant issued for you here?'

She looked at me and I saw the child. She didn't know what to do. Nor did I. What a bastard I was.

'I want to go back to Sydney with you,' she said. An hour later we were on our way.

In those pre-digital days, there wasn't a great deal of co-operation between the police in different states. I knew that when Jackie didn't appear in court in South Australia the magistrate would issue a warrant for her arrest. But I doubted the New South Wales police would be notified. The offence wouldn't be considered serious enough.

We rented a flat at Glebe. Resisting the urge to rob a bank, I opted to again try an 'honest' living. Jackie and I again focused on the chocolates and nuts venture. On Saturdays, she continued to do her community service at Brush Farm.

For a while we lived an uneventful life. I was spending a lot of time with John; Jackie was again regularly ringing her mother. Eventually she disclosed our address to enable the family to send Christmas gifts.

Soon afterwards the police came and arrested her. She was taken to court and remanded for a few days until her extradition to South Australia could be arranged.

They held her at Mulawa, the Silverwater women's prison. Before visiting her, I rang to find out what I could bring her. It was as strict as a men's prison: I brought her a few dresses, underwear and put some money in her account.

Although she tried to be brave, she soon became teary when she saw me.

'You won't get long,' I reassured her. 'A few months – maybe even a bond.

Your family will be able to visit you and I'll come over when I can.'

'Make sure you water the pot plants,' were her parting words to me. The next day she was flown to Adelaide.

LUCY GETS MARRIED AND MIGRATES TO AUSTRALIA

1983–1993

Meanwhile, in Russia, 1983 was a memorable year for Lucy. After graduating in Librarianship from the Samara Institute of Culture, she started work in the Moscow State Library as a librarian. She was also doing post-graduate study in History at the Academy of Sciences.

While working in the library, she met Alexei Dudko, who often went there to study scientific articles. He had graduated in Computer Science and Mathematics. Eventually he asked her to a movie and they began dating. He was her first serious boyfriend and they were married in April 1983. Their only child, Anna, (not her real name) was born in September 1988.

By all accounts the marriage from the start was unstable.

According to Alex, in an interview with the weekly Russian magazine *Ogonyk* in June 1999, he was part of Moscow's elite society while the 'provincial' Lucy felt out of her depth and had difficulty making friends. She usually stayed at home while he partied on. Although she was doing a post-graduate course she hadn't finished it after ten years, according to Alex. He boasted of controlling her spending, even to the point of taking her credit cards.

Alex also told Ogonyk that Lucy's father earned plenty of money and his wife just spent it, and Lucy was a very beautiful girl who never really had to work for anything, she was given everything. She never really had to face life. She was like a princess.

Angered by this article, Lucy's father, Vitali, responded when given the opportunity by Ogonyk. He said that after the wedding Alex controlled all finances and when they argued, which was often, he sometimes threw her out. On one occasion when her mother visited them he threw her out too. After one particularly heated argument in 1990 she decided to leave him. But he managed to persuade her to give it another try.

Vitali described his son-in-law in these words: 'In his family, he was almost a stepson. His parents called him an idiot and an imbecile, didn't respect him and never gave him any money. This is what made him what he is: a mixture of snobbishness, charm, horrible tight-fistedness and a wish to prove that he is also a human being.'

After the dissolution of the Soviet Union in 1991, the science sector was one of the chief institutes to suffer severe cuts. Alex couldn't find employment in the new Russian Federation. Australia beckoned. A bright, sophisticated young Russian scientist such as Alexei Dudko would have no difficulties in getting a plumb job in that provincial land of kangaroos and koala bears. And the provincial Lucy would surely feel at home.

But while in Russia Lucy had the support of her parents and brother. When Alex, Lucy and Anna migrated to Australia she had no support system.

Lucy also wrote to Ogonyk in 1999 countering what Alex had told them. She wrote:

'Strictly speaking my marriage couldn't be named 'normal' from any point of view. Once Alex came home drunk and said to me: 'I was cheating on you, I am cheating on you and will cheat on you for the rest of my life.'

I said to him: 'I've never cheated on you, not since today. And I'll make sure that the ends of your horns will stick in the walls of our flat.'

'He did not believe what he heard and laughed. 'You are not capable to turn on me. You are too loyal. Try to understand monogamy is utterly alien to men's nature. And by the way, jealousy is a sign of your provinciality.

If you were born in Moscow you would not have experienced this cheap feeling.'

'Really? It was a challenge! And suddenly rage was gone. I thought that this is a time to find out if he was able to experience jealousy or was he indeed too sophisticated for this simple feeling.'

Soon afterwards, Lucy began to indulge in affairs.

This was the state of the disintegrating marriage when they arrived in Australia in July 1993.

THE LADY GOT MY NUMBER

1983–84

With Jackie gone I had no desire to continue the 'chocolates and nuts' venture. For a long time, I had quelled the desire to solve financial problems by robbing a bank. Now, the restraints were gone. I decided to go into unchartered waters to do it – Queensland.

Retrieving the pistol from where I had hidden it under the house next door, I caught a train to Newcastle. From there I took a taxi to Raymond Terrace – about 25 kilometres north. There, I rented a late model Holden Commodore for a week with unlimited kilometres. I figured that if my name ever came up as a suspect, and police did a check on rental cars, they would only focus on metropolitan areas. I hadn't forgotten the 1978 debacle when Eyles had put us both in prison due to his rental car being seen and partly identified by a curious kid.

I drove to Queensland, booking into a motel about 10 kilometres south of the city. The next day, using a street directory, I drove to various suburbs checking out the banks and suitable getaway routes. The one I chose had a small arcade to run through, leading to an open grassy area where I could jump a fence and run to the next street where I would have the car parked. If anyone tried to follow me they would have to be athletic.

On the morning of the robbery I parked the car in the street that I had chosen. Wearing transparent gloves and carrying a shopping bag which contained the pistol, a mask and an aerosol can of paint, I walked to the main road where the bank was situated. At the entrance, I put the mask on and, pistol in hand, walked inside. There were four or five customers, all facing the counter. The three tellers were busy and took no notice of me as I took the aerosol can from the bag, stood on a chair and sprayed the camera which was positioned above the door to my left.

Walking towards the counter I yelled: 'This is a hold-up! I'm here for the bank's money. Everybody stay calm.'

The customers turned to look at me. No-one said anything.

I pointed the pistol at a young blond male teller and placed the bag on the counter. 'Fill it up – be quick!'

An old lady walked towards the exit.

I stepped back and pointed the pistol at her. 'Sorry, madam, you can't go outside yet. Stay where you are.'

She stared at me. 'Certainly not! I'm going home.' She walked out the door.

I had visions of her outside the bank screaming: 'Robbery! Robbery!' (Apparently, she simply went home. There was no mention of her in the media reports).

There wouldn't be time to collect from the other tellers. When the young guy handed me the bag I turned and, slipping the mask off as I reached the door, dashed outside and ran through the arcade and across the open area. I was over the fence in seconds and jogged down the street to where I had parked the vehicle. I looked around – there was no-one in sight.

I drove nonstop until I arrived in Ballina where I booked into a motel. Being back in New South Wales eased the pressure on me. The local cops wouldn't be looking for a Queensland bank robber.

The robbery had netted a little more than $11,000. I figured the old lady walking out had saved the bank at least another $10,000.

The next morning before setting off for Sydney I bought the Queensland newspapers. The reports about the robbery sent a chill through me: a woman sitting in a car three or four back from mine had noticed me hurrying to my vehicle and for some reason, she had written down the registration number. When she heard on the news that the bank had been held up she contacted police. I stared at the number of my rental car printed in the newspaper. I knew this was one of those life-changing moments. My life would never be the same again. Soon I would again be on the run. The fact I had rented the car at Raymond Terrace would buy me some time. But the police, in possession of the correct registration number, would soon ascertain who had rented the vehicle.

First, I had to dump it. Driving to a parking area I wiped the car of prints and left it there. Walking to the shopping centre, I bought the local newspaper and checked it for vehicles for sale. There was a green Mini Cooper advertised for $800. I rang the number and spoke to the owner, a young woman, who arranged to meet me at the shopping centre.

The car looked to be in good condition and ran well. When I didn't haggle, paying her cash, the woman was delighted.

I then rang the car rental firm and told them the vehicle had been stolen in Brisbane. When the girl began asking for more details I hung up.

Although the drive to Sydney was uneventful, the Mini was so small that I felt uncomfortable in it.

At Glebe, I packed Jackie's belongings with a few of mine and took them to a storage unit. I thought about leaving the pistol there but considered it to be too risky. No matter what I did with it, if the police found it and connected it to me I would be convicted on the robbery – a replay of 1966 in Melbourne. Without it, I had a good chance. If I was arrested I would insist the car had been stolen. There was no other evidence to link me to the robbery. I resolved that this would be my last bank robbery. There were too many uncertainties that couldn't be foreseen, let alone controlled. To ensure that I didn't change my mind I threw the weapon in the Parramatta River.

I found new accommodation in Ryde, sharing a house with Kerry, a young woman whose housemate had gone overseas. She was a pleasant lady in her late twenties whose boyfriend sometimes stayed over. I told her I had split from my marriage and had taken a month off work to adjust to single life again.

My next task was to make Gloria aware that the police might call on her, looking for me. She wasn't happy but there was nothing either of us could do about it. I spent precious time with John, knowing that soon it would be dangerous to see him.

Looking back, 1983 in Australia had been one of those memorable years: Bob Hawke had brought Labor back into power after eight years in opposition; Australia had done the impossible and won the America's Cup; Ash Wednesday had taken 75 lives in Victoria and South Australia and destroyed 3,700 buildings.

On a personal note, it had been a disastrous year for me: Dad had died; Jackie was in gaol and I was on the run for bank robbery. Once again, my life was in a mess – as were the lives of those close to me.

The New Year was almost upon us but I found it difficult to be optimistic. I felt as though I was back in 1966: different girls, different horses losing, different banks, but the same old story all over again.

In early January, I rang Frank and asked him to visit Jackie at the women's prison in Northfield – not far from Yatala.

He reported back that Jackie had received six months and wasn't coping well. Unaware of my problem in Queensland, she couldn't understand why I hadn't travelled to South Australia to visit her.

I had no alternative other than to go and see her. I reasoned that it was unlikely the Queensland police would notify a women's prison in South Australia to be on the lookout for John Killick. Why would they?

I paid $2000 for a blue Ford Fairlane that was mechanically A-1. After telling Kerry that I'd be away for three or four days I set off for Adelaide.

Security at the prison was lax. I was allowed to visit Jackie without booking ahead. Only one door, locked from the inside, separated the small visiting room from outside the prison. There were two female prison officers.

Although Frank had prepared me for a downcast Jackie, when she entered the room I was shocked at her appearance. She was wearing a grey-white coarse cotton frock that was two or three sizes too large and her head was shaved. She was pale and tired looking.

Trying to mask my shock, I smiled and gave her a hug. 'Hi, Imp.'

She burst into tears. 'I caught lice and they shaved off my hair.'

We sat down. I held her hand. 'Listen, Imp, are they giving you a hard time?'

'No. But I miss you. Can you stay in Adelaide?'

Conscious of the guards who were politely looking away, I whispered: 'I can't. They're looking for me for a bank robbery in Queensland.'

It was her turn to be shocked. 'Bloody hell! What a mess. You have to live quietly until I get out. Don't take any more risks.'

'Don't worry, I won't.' I paused. 'I'll write to you most days and send you money. You can write to me care of my brother, David. He'll pass it on to me.'

She began crying again. 'If they catch you I might never see you again.'

'They won't catch me. I'll be waiting for you in Sydney.'

After leaving her some money I drove away – well aware that it should have been me, not her, in prison.

A few days later in Sydney I had a discussion with Gloria concerning John. He was missing regular contact with me and wanted to live with me for a while. He couldn't stay with me at Kerry's where I only had the one room. We decided that I would take him for a holiday, including a visit to the renowned theme park, Dreamworld, on the Gold Coast – a place he had always wanted to see.

I figured that the police wouldn't be on the lookout for a man with a nine-year-old boy.

Staying in motels along the way we enjoyed a terrific two weeks. We made up stories that would have been plausible movie scripts. We went swimming, played mini-golf, visited a koala park and an animal sanctuary, watched a few movies, and spent two days at Dreamworld. At Byron Bay, we watched the migrating whales.

On the return drive to Sydney I told him a story about a father and his son who went to Tasmania to try to find a Tasmanian Tiger and found one!

'Can we go to Tasmania to find a Tasmanian Tiger, Dad?'

'I don't think there are any left.'

'But there might be. We'll be famous.'

'Okay. One day when you are older we'll give it a try.' I paused, knowing that while I was on the run I'd rarely see him. 'But first I have to go away for a while.'

'How long for, Dad?'

It is situations like this that tear at your heart. Suddenly I was depressed and I paused before answering. 'Most of the year.'

He thought about it. 'When you come home do you promise we can go to Tasmania to find a Tasmanian Tiger?'

'I promise.'

But by the time I was able to come home he was sixteen – and wasn't interested in going to Tasmania to try and find a Tasmanian Tiger.

BOGGO ROAD PENITENTIARY

1984

On 31 January, Hakki Atahan, a Turk wanted by police for numerous armed robberies, tried to rob a bank in the city. When he became aware that the police had surrounded the building, he took five hostages, including the bank manager, and using them as shields around him, shuffled to a waiting car. With Atahan giving directions, one of the hostages drove as far as the Spit Bridge over the Middle Harbour where they were forced to halt due to the bridge opening (normally for give-way-to sea traffic, but in this instance to place Atahan in a 'no escape' situation).

As the police rushed the car Atahan shot Detective Constable Steve Canellis between the eyes at an angle, the bullet passing through the nose and lodging in his shoulder. Canellis survived – Atahan didn't, other police shooting him dead.

Police and media choppers and vehicles had tracked every movement from the time Atahan and the hostages had exited the bank.

Jackie had watched it live on television and for a while had feared I was the robber.

Although I only heard about it after it was over, I immediately saw it as an opportunity to create doubt about who had robbed the bank in Queensland. Atahan was a known heavy gambler. (I had met him in a TAB; I had a losing day; he offered me $500 for a loan of my rental car for two days; he must have driven to Queensland and robbed a bank.)

I knew the cops wouldn't buy it and I couldn't prove it – but they couldn't prove it didn't happen either. At least it would give me a chance.

Frank had learnt from Jackie that the police had called in for tea and scones with Jackie's parents. The subject of discussion was John Killick. It had taken a while but police Australia-wide were now aware of the connection between Jackie and I. Although I doubted they had the resources for a twenty-four hour watch on Gloria's place I was certain they would, from time to time, put her under surveillance.

Over the past few weeks I'd had a good run on the horses – my bank was healthy. I decided to get out of town for a while – the cops would soon get tired of coming up with zero results. They would drop off, wait for me to make a mistake.

First, I had to get another driver's licence. In 1984 the licences were just a strip of paper containing your name, address and date of birth. If you lost your licence you simply went to the RTA office, supplied your details and, for a few dollars, they would issue you with another licence marked 'Duplicate'.

I went to an unemployment office, waited until I saw a guy close to my age and approached him. 'Hi, mate. Are you looking for a job?'

'Why, yes, as a matter of fact I am.'

'Do you have a current driver's licence?'

'Yes, I do. What type of job?'

'Walking people's dogs. It pays $8 an hour and I have thirty-five dogs on my books.'

'Gee, that would do me.'

'Could I see your driver's licence?'

He took out his wallet and handed me his licence.

I scribbled down the details. 'I'll have to do a police check – some people are banned from working with animals. If you check out okay I'll call you tomorrow. Do you have a number I can contact you on?'

He gave me his number.

Driving to the nearest RTA office I soon had a duplicate licence in the name of the would-be dog-walker. I was confident that if the police pulled me over for any reason they would have no reason to suspect I was a wanted man.

That night I rang the owner of the original licence and told him that a lady with experience in walking dogs had been given the job.

One night about a week after I had resumed living at Kerry's house in Gladesville, I received a surprise: I found Jackie sitting in the lounge room. Instead of greeting me, she gave me a hard stare. 'Who's the floozy you're living with?'

'I'm not living with her – I'm sharing.'

She continued to stare at me, searching my eyes. 'Okay, I believe you.' She jumped up and hugged me. 'I got out two weeks early – good behaviour.'

For a while we lived a quiet life. But I never forgot that I was a wanted man.

The police were setting little traps for me; spasmodically placing either members of my family or friends under twenty-four hour surveillance. Imp's family remained in close contact with the police.

When we had less than a thousand dollars remaining, I said to her. 'Winter's almost here. How about a trip to sunny Queensland for a few weeks? We can sell the Mini.'

'Okay. I could do with some sun.'

I drove the Ford while Jackie followed in the Mini. On arrival in Brisbane the best offer we had for the Mini was $600 which I refused to accept.

After a week in Brisbane funds were low. We decided to again try shoplifting.

This time, instead of Cornflakes, we used two empty Ry-Vita cartons each time to stash two cartons of cigarettes inside – negating the need to use the trolley.

It had taken them twelve months to figure out the cornflakes caper; now with no trolley to draw attention to us the Ry-Vita rort should be a safe venture for months.

Because we only took two cartons of cigarettes per store it took us most of the day to earn $200.

Jackie wasn't her usual confident self. She was a bit apprehensive about getting caught and spending another stretch in gaol. Sure enough, by being hesitant she brought attention to herself and was arrested.

Trying to remain calm, I told myself it was only a minor charge – stealing two cartons of cigarettes. They would have to bail her. But once they discovered who she was they would know I was nearby. I would have to hire a solicitor to ensure they didn't illegally hold her. First, I had to drive to the motel and move the Mini – Imp had the ownership papers in her handbag. If the police traced me to the motel they would get the number of my Ford.

The motel was on the other side of town – it took me fifty minutes to drive there. After parking the Mini about a kilometre away I jogged back to the motel, packed our suitcases and booked out. The manager and his wife were both nervous: when he offered to refund my money because I was prematurely checking out, fear and alarm surged through me – he was trying to stall me! I had walked into a trap!

I rushed out the door – too late. Police, guns drawn, appeared from every direction, screaming at me to get face down on the ground. Numb with shock I did as they ordered.

Jackie had given me an hour's start and then informed the police about the motel. They had told her that she would be fined $100 for the cigarette theft, but before the magistrate could release her, the court needed her current address.

On arrival at the police headquarters Detective Arch MacDonald, a slim balding man who looked to be about forty, informed me that I was suspected of robbing six banks. I told him that he must be getting me confused with the Turk they shot on the Spit Bridge.

'I loaned him my car once,' I said, trying hard not to grin at the absurdity of it.

Another cop who had the red complexion of a drunk stared at me, a knowing look on his face: 'You're the only one who sprays the cameras,' he said.

After about six hours of questioning, they were becoming agitated. Despite the late hour, they brought in the blond bank teller to identify me. Although I recognised him, he didn't recognise me without my disguise. Eventually they brought Imp, handcuffed, into the room and then quickly dragged her out again – but not before she gave me a wink.

'We can hold her without bail until the trial,' MacDonald said. 'That could be twelve months away.' He paused and stared at me, his eyes narrowed. 'Don't you think she's been through enough?'

I nodded. 'What's the deal?'

He told me that unless I wrote a statement admitting to six bank robberies, he would charge both of us. If I wrote the statement, Imp would be released without being charged.

Although the only evidence they had against me was the statement of the woman who wrote down the number of the hire car, police verbal was at that time in Queensland a powerful weapon.

'I'll admit to the one where the woman took the number of the car,' I said grudgingly, hating it, but knowing there was no real alternative.

'We know you did the six,' MacDonald said, handing me a pen and paper, 'but, okay, seeing you're doing the right thing by the girl I'll only charge you with four and put the other two on some other bastard's brief.' True to his word he released Imp. I was sent to Boggo Road on remand, one of the most notorious gaols in Australia. (Condemned for years, Boggo Road was finally shut down for good in 1992.) I could sense the tension in the gaol as soon as I had arrived. A few months prior there had been two violent riots there.

My old friend Robert 'Bertie' Kidd was there. He told me that now the prisoners and the guards hated each other. It was the type of situation that could violently erupt at any time. Most of the prisoners' privileges had been taken from them. In the mornings, we were herded from our dingy little cells while it was still dark; we didn't return to the cells until 9:00 pm. We were confined all day in 'exercise yards' – small yards each containing forty to fifty prisoners. When it rained we had to crowd together for shelter under the awnings. Each yard contained a television that was usually controlled by the toughest prisoners in the yard. A strong odour of disinfectant pervaded the entire gaol. After a few days, I could think of only one thing. I had to get out.

Jackie wasn't permitted to see me until the Monday. During the visit, we were separated by a see-through Perspex partition. We had to converse via phone.

We stared at each other.

'I want you to go home,' I said. 'I'm staying.'

'It's finished, Imp. I'll get ten years.'

'No you won't – I'm going to get you out.'

I smiled. This girl never gave up. 'How? We haven't even got a gun.'

Her composure vanished. 'I don't know. But it's my fault you're in here and I'm going to find a way to get you out.'

'Don't blame yourself. They would have got me sooner or later.'

Living on the dole and the money from the sale of the two cars, she took a room not far from the gaol. She wrote every day and visited me twice a week. After a while she managed to sweet talk one of the old chief prison officers into granting her an occasional extra visit. Sometimes she would arrive in tears – depressed to the point where she talked of suicide.

'I want to get you out,' she sobbed, 'but I don't know how.'

I had looked hard at the possible avenues of escape. Some of the prisoners had grandiose schemes such as rushing the front gate or taking hostages. Although, due to their sheer audacity such radical actions could succeed, I was circumspect enough to realise that the chances of failure or even being shot were far greater. I figured the best chances to make a bid for freedom would occur once you were outside the main walls. A trip to hospital would achieve that.

I asked Jackie to buy a replica pistol – the nearest she could get resembling the real thing.

On the next visit, she was excited. 'I bought one,' she said. 'But the barrel is blocked in. You can see it doesn't work.'

'You have to return home to your parents for a while,' I said. 'Until I send you a message to return. While there, get a drill and drill a hole in the barrel and paint the inside black.'

She didn't want to leave but eventually I persuaded her.

After she returned to Adelaide I worked on a scheme to get to hospital. I was born with Iritis – if I didn't eat the correct foods and vitamins my eyes became inflamed to the point where I couldn't open them. I began starving myself – surviving only on bread, water and weak tea. Every chance I had I read something – books, magazines, anything I could obtain to enable me to put extra strain on my eyes. I stayed up late until I was sleep deprived.

It took a month and four visits to the gaol doctor before he finally relented and ordered that I be escorted to hospital to see an eye specialist. Handcuffed, I was taken to the Princess Alexandra Hospital. I noticed only one of the three escorting guards was armed. After we arrived the driver of the van drove off to pick up another escort. It was a flawed system: half an hour ago I had been securely confined behind huge walls manned by guards with high powered rifles; now, I was walking through the foyer of a hospital with only two guards and a pair of handcuffs restricting my freedom.

As anticipated, the specialist prescribed me some special drops and told me to return in a few weeks for a check-up. For security reasons, the authorities always ensured that prisoners were not informed of their hospital appointment dates. Turning my back, I deliberately stood away from the desk while the guards made the appointment; but as the nurse handed one of the guards the appointment slip I spun around and asked to go to the toilet.

'You'll be home soon,' the guard said. 'You can wait until then.' Despite the inflamed eyes, I caught a glimpse of the slip: 9th August! Now all I had to do was inform Imp.

That afternoon I put my name down to see a welfare officer. Three days later I was called to the welfare office. A small, harassed looking man with horn-rimmed glasses greeted me. 'Sorry it has taken so long to see you, but nearly everyone in gaol wants to see a welfare officer.'

I explained that it was important for me to get a phone call to Jackie. I had an unexpected court date on the 8th August and needed her to hire me a solicitor.

Although he wouldn't allow me to use the phone (regulations), he phoned her while I was there. She assured him she would arrange it.

Thanking him, I left the office. If he didn't check my court date, I would, on the 9th August, either be free or dead.

In the middle of all this wheeling, dealing and conniving, Gloria, travelling by bus, brought John to visit me. A chief prison officer had assured me I'd be given a special 'contact' visit for two hours due to the distance travelled and the fact that they would only be able to make the trip on rare occasions. An ex-doctor who had been sentenced to twelve years for drugging and raping his female patients was allowed regular contact visits with his children. But someone over-rode the chief 's instructions: we were given twenty minutes with Perspex separating us and we were forced to speak by phone. I was refused any contact with John and when they were told to leave, he began to cry. If I had ever needed motivation to try to escape, this traumatic incident provided it as I vividly recalled the way young John had reached up to the Perspex with his hand and tried to touch me.

E DAY

9 AUGUST 1984

On the 8 August, I was called to the visiting room. A worried Imp gave me a brave smile. 'What have you got in mind?'

She had flown from Adelaide to Sydney, picked up the old Kingswood and drove to Brisbane. I had arranged for Gloria to give her some extra money while she was in Sydney.

Mindful of what might be overheard by other prisoners or their visitors, I gradually informed her of my scheme.

'You will have to hire another vehicle,' I said. 'Get it for a week. If everything goes right, no-one will see it.'

Although Jackie was nervous, she assured me she would do it. Before leaving she whispered, 'We'll be together soon.'

The 9th August 1984, a day I'll never forget. The three guards that came for me were all big – that's the first thing I noticed. The authorities seemed to think that size intimidated; maybe it did, but in this instance size would count for little. One of them, the biggest of the three, handed me a clothing bag and told me to strip off and put my civvies on – I was going to hospital. Feigning surprise, I did as I was told. It was important that they didn't suspect I knew of the hospital appointment, otherwise they would increase the security on me and that was going to be tough as it was. I finished dressing except for my shoes. I looked longingly at my runners – then dismissed the thought; if I put on my runners it could make them wonder why. Reluctantly, I put on my Karondonis slip-ons.

The guard took from his back pocket a pair of handcuffs. 'I'll just put these on you.' He fastened the handcuffs on me securely.

I looked around me. The austere buildings behind me with their tiny cells, cages and yards would, I hoped, soon be a thing of the past for me.

The prison van pulled up outside the office. 'Okay, Killick,' guard number one said, 'let's go.'

I got in the back of the van; the three guards got into the front with guard number three driving. At the front gate one of the guards inside the main gate area pressed a button and the gate opened, but the one leading to outside the gaol remained closed. A different switch operated it. The van stopped between the gates and guard number one got out and walked over to a desk. I saw him handed something which he placed inside his left jacket pocket. He then signed a book and got back inside the van. The main gate opened and we were on our way. At least I knew who had the gun.

When we arrived at the hospital, guard number three drove off after the other two and myself reached the hospital entrance door.

Inside, the hospital was crowded. A lot of people stared at us with curiosity, even in some cases with open hostility. I looked around for Jackie but I couldn't see her anywhere. Had she decided not to go ahead with it? Guard number one told me to follow him, while number two followed behind. We had to go through a few corridors to where the eye specialist was. The guard seemed to know where to go which didn't surprise me as they usually rostered the same men for hospital duty. As we approached the Eye Specialist section I saw Jackie. Although she was wearing a long brown wig and dark glasses, I immediately recognised her. Without a glance, she walked past us. My heart started to pound...it was on! Not here, in this crowded area – too many things could go wrong. It would have to be as we were leaving. Jackie would wait for the signal from me before she acted. Number one gave the nurse at the desk some papers. She immediately beckoned us to follow her. She took us through a corridor into a small waiting room.

Ignoring the two guards she looked at me and smiled. 'The doctor will see you soon, Mr Killick.'

I returned the smile. 'Thank you.'

'Sit down Killick,' number one growled.

The three of us sat down. We were the only ones in the small waiting room. It was time for me to not only psyche myself for what was coming, but also try to unnerve the guards into believing I really was a dangerous violent criminal.

I stared at number one; he seemed to be the meanest of the two and I knew he was armed. 'Why do I have such heavy security?' I asked aggressively.

'Because you're an armed robber,' he said. 'I haven't been convicted yet.'

Number one gave a cynical smile. 'You blokes are all the same. You get caught and then you cry innocent. Well in this state you are guilty until proven innocent.'

Number two laughed. 'You should have stayed away from Queensland.

It's a bad state to be caught in.'

I shrugged. 'I suppose they don't trust me because I bashed that guard's head in with an iron bar at Pentridge. He got thirty-six stitches in his head and was pensioned off.' I paused, then added: 'I had to hit him – he tried to stop me from escaping.'

They stared at me.

'That was years ago,' I said. 'But I'd never use an iron bar again – it's too messy. Sure, if I had a gun I might shoot someone, but I haven't got a gun.'

'Just keep your mouth shut,' number one said.

I glanced at him. The arrogant manner was gone. Until now he thought I might be dangerous. Now he had no doubts I was a dangerous psychopath. It could be a deciding factor when the time came for action.

After a few quick tests, the specialist informed me that my eyes had healed. There was no need to come back.

Still handcuffed, I was escorted back through the corridors to the foyer of the main waiting room. I looked for Jackie – she was sitting to the left of where we had entered the foyer. I glanced quickly at her: she was white. Poor little Imp – if I was uptight, I could imagine how she felt. As we walked towards the exit I was tempted to look around to see if she was following, but I knew it could alarm the guards, so I resisted the urge.

'Wonder what's for dinner tonight,' I said.

No-one answered. They couldn't give a damn.

I was feeling calm now. I'd waited for this moment from the time I was arrested nearly three months ago; I knew the danger and the risk involved; I was prepared to take those risks. In a few minutes, I would either be free or dead – of that I was certain. Consequences were insignificant to me now: I had decided on a certain course of action and would carry it through. Whatever happened, Jackie should have enough time to get away.

When we approached the phone box which was situated to the right near the exit, the guards stopped as I knew they would.

'I have to phone through for a van to come and pick us up,' number two said. He entered the booth. Number one stood by my side. We were standing about 5 metres from the exit.

I looked towards Jackie – she had stopped about 10 metres behind.

Number one was facing me with his back to her.

I coughed loudly. She stood there, big-eyed and staring – unable to move.

I coughed again. Number one gave me a questioning look. My face must have given me away. I saw the alarm in his eyes. He began to undo his jacket as Jackie rushed forward with the butt of the replica protruding from a folded newspaper. She thrust it towards me and ran to the exit.

The guard had reached inside his jacket.

Grabbing the replica by the butt, I pointed the barrel at his head. 'Put your hands in the air or you're dead!'

Our eyes locked. Slowly he raised his hands. It flashed through my mind that if Jackie hadn't drilled a hole in the barrel to give the pistol an authentic look, I would have then and there, been shot dead.

I glanced across at number two. He was looking at us and shouting into the phone.

'Come after me and I'll kill you!' I said, before spinning around and, untroubled by the handcuffs, running out the exit.

I saw Jackie waving to me across a small park area. I ran towards her and down a street to where she had a car parked. No-one had followed me.

As we drove down the street we could hear sirens coming from everywhere.

Two streets away Jackie had a rental car waiting. Not bad for a twenty-year-old!

She drove nonstop until we crossed the New South Wales border. Then she booked into a motel.

Using a nail file, we spent hours severing the chain link of the handcuffs. During the process, the left cuff had tightened, cutting into my wrist. By morning it was blue and swollen.

We drove to a hardware store where she bought some small hacksaws. She also bought newspapers. Both of our photos were on the front page. Police had already named Jackie as the woman who had helped me escape.

She was upset. It wasn't a good photo.

'Don't worry,' I said. 'If we can prove you weren't the culprit you can sue them for millions.'

But we both knew that wouldn't happen.

We drove to a motel in Port Macquarie where, using the hacksaw blades, it took over three hours to cut through both handcuffs.

In their efforts to apprehend us the police enlisted the aid of the media. A lot of fanciful stories were printed about us. One article claimed I had been broken out of gaol by Sydney gangsters to enable me to rob a bank to repay gambling debts. Some of the newspapers couldn't resist the temptation to call us 'Bonnie and Clyde.'

The comparison was odious. Bonnie and Clyde were killers. But I was now a true outlaw. No point looking for a nine to five job. Shoplifting and stamp stealing were out. Bank robberies were in. Over the next ten months I robbed quite a few. We kept moving from state to state, mainly basing ourselves in Victoria.

I mailed a letter to a friend in Queensland asking her to post it to the Courier Mail. Including a fingerprint for authentication, I described the atrocious conditions at Boggo Road. Having the letter posted in Queensland would confuse the police as to where I might be.

The newspapers published the letter, including comments from Detective Arch MacDonald that during a bank robbery I had pushed a loaded rifle against the stomach of a nine months' pregnant woman.

MacDonald made it up to incense the public against me. I was never charged with it and surely I would have been – if it hadn't been a figment of his imagination. I did use a rifle in my first bank robbery at Canley Heights in January 1966. As far as I know there weren't any pregnant ladies there either.

ONE BANK TOO MANY

1984–85

We rented a house in Caulfield near the racecourse. Although I began gambling again, I stayed away from the racecourse.

Jackie took a job serving coffee and cakes to the beautiful people in Toorak. Every morning I bought the Melbourne and interstate newspapers to keep abreast of what was being printed about us. I was concerned they might publish our photos in the Melbourne press. If this happened we would have to again move on.

I wondered how, to some of the press, we could be more newsworthy than the horrific famine in Ethiopia where nearly one million people had died that year. I think that the magnitude of the tragedy is beyond our capacity to accept it. We shut it out of our mind. If we see someone killed in an accident we always remember it. But a million people dying of starvation and disease? Can't comprehend it.

For us, Christmas and New Year passed uneventfully. Although I arranged for Gloria to give John gifts from me, not being able to see him depressed me. It was the fourth Christmas I had missed with him.

Low on funds, we drove to Sydney in late January where, using the replica, I raided a bank in Mona Vale, escaping with $22,000. I increased the risk by spending a few hours with John and Gloria in the city.

Returning to Melbourne, we continued to live in the house at Caulfield. A few days after my forty-third birthday, a former associate from the Pentridge days, Michael 'Mick' John Sayers, was gunned down outside his house in Bronte, New South Wales. I had always liked Mick. Even in gaol he was a larrikin and a hopeless gambler. Another ex H Division inmate to meet a violent death.

I thought of Bertie Kidd who was still at Boggo Road. Mick was like a brother to him. He would be devastated.

Despite our improved financial funds, life wasn't easy 'on the run'. We couldn't plan ahead, we were forced to live one day at a time. We were together twenty-four hours a day, unable to vent our frustrations on anyone except each other. We had no friends we could turn to, only acquaintances. We couldn't let anyone get close for fear of them seeing through our flimsy facade.

After about eight months of life on the run Jackie turned to me one day and asked: 'Do you love me? I mean really love me?'

I could see she wanted reassurance about us, about our future – about the babies she wanted to have, the home she dreamed about.

I met her gaze. 'No, I don't. Not like you want, anyway.' She nodded and walked away. It was over.

The following day she booked a flight to Adelaide. I gave her $4000 – half of our bank. 'Make sure you get a lawyer. Don't make a statement to police. They have no real evidence against you.'

As she walked to the tarmac she was crying. I was also emotional. She had been by my side for three years. But now she had a chance to live a normal life again.

Shortly after arriving in Adelaide she went to police headquarters accompanied by a lawyer and her parents. The lawyer informed the police that his client would only answer any questions they may want to ask in his presence.

The police declined to either interview or arrest her. I figured they may see her as bait, hoping eventually she would lead them to me.

If that was the case they would be waiting a long time.

I returned to Sydney where I rented a unit in beachside Coogee. A few times I managed to see John and Gloria and once I called on David. He advised me to go to Western Australia, just as Dad had urged me to do in 1966. Naturally, I again didn't heed the advice.

My money held out for two months. During that time, I bought a .32 automatic pistol from an Italian guy who boasted he was a mafia man. He charged me $1000 for it. There's always a risk when you buy an illegal second-hand firearm. It could have been used in a serious crime. But I didn't feel safe with just a replica. There was an undeclared gang war going on in Sydney and I had known some of the victims. Another ex H Division inmate had gone missing on 9 May – never to be seen again. None other than Mr Rentakill – Christopher Dale Flannery.

On 20 May 1985, I pushed my luck to the extreme. I again robbed the bank in Mona Vale from which, in January, I had stolen $22,000.

This time they only gave me about $17,000. I escaped on foot, running down a back lane, across a park into a small shopping centre, out to a side lane and up a flight of steps leading to a no-through road where I had my car parked.

An old lady looking through her window saw me run to the vehicle. She had never seen the car in her street before so she wrote down the number.

Déjà vu – Brisbane, December 1983.

It was the break the police had been waiting for. That night, in Newport, I was surrounded by a posse of detectives from the Armed Hold Up Squad. One of them pressed the barrel of his firearm against the side of my head and shouted: 'Blink, and I'll blow your brains out.' His hand was trembling.

Later that night I was charged with three bank robberies.

'We are going light on you,' one of the cops said. 'You are in enough trouble in Queensland. I reckon you'll do twenty years.'

The next day I was taken to the MRC at Long Bay. A distraught Gloria came to visit me. I tried to cheer her up by telling her that it might have been just as well I'd been caught or eventually I might've been killed. Our main concern was John. We decided at this stage she wouldn't tell him. I asked her to ring Jackie and break the news. When Gloria told her of my arrest she collapsed. A few days later she caught a flight to Sydney and came to see me. She didn't realise the danger she was in.

'Imp,' I said, gently, 'I'm surprised they haven't arrested you. As soon as you leave here go to Bruce Miles and make a statutory declaration stating you had nothing to do with my escape. I'll support it.'

She promised she would do it.

As she tearfully waved me goodbye I doubted that I would ever see her again.

She was arrested before she could consult Bruce. Within a few days she was extradited to Queensland where she was charged with assisting my escape. She pleaded guilty and was eventually sentenced to two years' imprisonment. After eight months, she was released on parole.

The high-profile prisoners at the MRC on this occasion were the former British military man, Scott William 'Jock' Ross, and his team of Comancheros bikies. On 2 September 1984 at the Milperra Tavern, Ross had led his team into a gun battle against thirty Bandidos. Four Comancheros, two Bandidos and a fourteen-year-old girl, who had been a bystander, were killed. Twenty others finished in hospital. It became known as 'The Milperra Massacre'. I found all the bikies to be friendly enough – including Jock. But I think he thought he was still in the military: he liked to give orders to his men – even in gaol. Most of them went along with it. Oddly enough the guards made no attempt to interfere.

Eventually Jock and a number of others received non-parole periods of seven years. Others had the charges reduced and received lesser sentences.

It was one occasion where the judiciary could be seen to be lenient on serious crime. Very lenient...

I went to the District Court for sentence on my 'jinx' day: 16 June. On 16 June 1968, I was involved in the disastrous escape attempt in Pentridge; on 16 June 1978, the Plympton bank was robbed and – even though I had a 'perfect alibi' – I was convicted for it. Now, on 16 June 1986 I was due to be sentenced for three bank robberies.

The judge gave me twelve years. He fixed a non-parole period of eight years. But at that time remissions were still effective in New South Wales and I knew that with good behaviour I could be out in less than six years. Then I'd have to deal with the mess in Queensland. Bruce Miles told me that the amount of time I would spend in New South Wales prisons would be taken into consideration and I'd only spend a couple of years in Queensland.

I took a good look at the situation; I had been in custody for thirteen months. If I did everything right I could be free in less than seven years. It would be tough, but what were the alternatives? I was only forty-four...if I looked after myself – and I would – I'd be fifty-one on release. Still time to achieve good things. John would be eighteen and a young adult. That's the price I'd have to pay. At least he could visit me. If I escaped again I'd never see him. No. I had prepared myself for the tough times ahead – my escaping days were over.

In August, I was transferred to the new maximum security prison at Parklea. Compared to the other seven gaols I'd been in – all of them maximum security – Parklea had five-star conditions. Each cell had only one bed in it and was equipped with a shower, a writing desk and a window that opened onto a small ledge allowing a person to stand outside the window – enclosed by large steel bars. Each wing had its own two cooks and the food was good. I concluded that if I had to spend years in maximum security, Parklea was the place to do it.

All the Bandidos were there. I befriended a few of them. They caused no trouble in the gaol.

I had been at Parklea for about six months when John Robinson arrived. John, a slim prematurely grey-haired man of about forty, was openly gay. I'd met him, and his boyfriend Graham, at Yatala where they had both been serving a sentence for bank robbery.

At Parklea, he told me he had applied for an interstate transfer to Yatala. 'Graham is back in Yatala and has a new boyfriend there,' he said, visibly upset. 'I know he still loves me, he's only with that little slut because I'm not there.'

There wasn't much I could say. 'Yeah, you two were good together,' I said lamely.

'We love each other. If they don't let me go I'm going to turn out the lights.'

Although I was a little shocked at his claim, I didn't take him seriously. Bank robbers don't kill themselves when love doesn't run smoothly. Junkies maybe...

'Don't worry,' I said. 'South Australia is pretty progressive in these things. Jackie had no problems getting transferred from Queensland.'

But the South Australian authorities refused his application, reasoning that a gay boyfriend was not family.

The morning after John received the news, a prison officer found him hanging from the railing of his shower curtain – his feet only 6 centimetres from the floor.

Things ran uneventfully for me until September 1987 when, a few inmates, drugged out of their minds, decided that conditions at Parklea were too harsh. Before a lot of us knew what was happening we were all involved in a full-scale riot. Shots were fired and most of us were tear-gassed. Seventeen guards and eight prisoners were injured. As far as riots were concerned I'd rate this one six out of ten.

In 1988, I was transferred to Long Bay for six months to the Special Care Unit. It was based on a similar programme to one in Scotland where hardened criminals were given special privileges, including wearing civilian clothing, all day visits and unlimited phone calls. While there they had to participate in daily groups with the other inmates, psychologists and prison officers. The programme had a good strike rate when it came to rehabilitating recidivist criminals.

I found it to be a total turnaround from the normal prison environment. All the inmates were on a first-name basis with the prison officers and the psychologists. We could remain out of our cells until 9:00 pm. It was good to be able to phone Gloria and John late at night and the all-day visits helped to re-establish a rapport with John. We played chess, batball and had a lot of fun on the visits. Gloria said it was the only time she actually enjoyed visiting me in prison.

One day Jackie unexpectedly came to visit me. We spent most of the day talking about old times. She told me she'd met a nice guy but the relationship was now over.

Before she left we had some photos taken. It was a pleasant reunion but our time together as a team was over and we both knew it.

The Special Care Unit taught me a lot about myself. Although gambling had been the catalyst behind my errant ways, I was often selfish and I hated to lose. This was the main reason I lost at gambling: I chased my losses, throwing caution to the wind. But looking back, I realised that I lived my life that way – risking everything when I was losing.

In late 1989 at Parklea I was approached by the former Marrickville Alderman, George Savvas, who was serving twenty years for a major drug importation.

'John,' he said. 'I need your job. I'll give you $300 for it.'

At the time, I had what was regarded as the best job in the gaol: I was the clinic sweeper. I worked unsupervised with the nurses, cleaning and looking after the stores in the clinic. Savvas was offering me fifteen weeks' wages for my job.

'Sorry, George. I wouldn't give this job up for a thousand.'

Two weeks later at about 9:00 pm the 'Special Squad' came to my cell, put me in handcuffs and placed me on an escort truck with a few other prisoners. I wasn't permitted to take any property with me – only the clothes I was wearing.

We arrived at Goulburn at about midnight. No explanation was ever given for my shock 'shanghai'. Savvas was given my clinic job. Fifteen years later a reliable source told me that Savvas had paid a high-ranking prison officer to remove me south.

Maybe Savvas was looking for an escape route and mistakenly believed the clinic was his best option.

About five years later he also was transferred to Goulburn where he managed to escape from the visiting section by putting on civilian clothing while other prisoners caused a distraction. He simply walked out through the gates.

A few months later he was arrested in a Sydney restaurant while dining with two females.

In 1997 at Maitland Gaol he was accused of planning an escape with Ivan Milat, the notorious backpacker serial killer.

It was all too much for George and he hanged himself at Maitland on the 23rd May 1997. He was forty-eight.

My unexpected 'transfer' to Goulburn was something of a culture shock. Nearly twenty-eight years had passed since that day in March 1962 when the still idealistic twenty-year-old John Killick was released from what was then known as Goulburn Training Centre – a gaol for first-time prisoners. Now it was the dreaded Goulburn Gaol – the dumping ground for recidivists and incorrigibles – soon to become known as 'the killing fields'.

One of the resident psychopaths there when I arrived was Billy Munday. He was one of many who had been unlawfully brutalised at Tamworth Boys' Home, and gone on to become a violent criminal. He was doing about fifty years for rapes, kidnapping, murder and other crimes of violence. Most of the prisoners – and a lot of the guards – were intimidated by him because, as he always put it, he had nothing to lose by killing someone.

I had first met him at Parklea where he asked me to play him chess. After I beat him – rather easily – he stood up, shook my hand and said: 'Too good, mate.'

He then went to his cell and wrecked it. A lot of the guys told me I was lucky to be alive. After that I avoided playing him.

Soon afterwards he bashed another prisoner and was sent to Goulburn. After a bit of time in segregation he was given the plumb job as 'head sweeper' of C Wing. He and a few other sweepers had the task of maintaining a clean wing and handing out the meals to the other prisoners. There were always extra meals, milk and desserts for the sweepers.

For Munday, being head sweeper had one other perk – he was able to choose which prisoner he shared his cell with. He would wait for the escort truck to bring in the new inmates. Then, while they were lined up and being 'processed,' he would check to see if any good-looking boys were among them. If he saw one he fancied he would arrange with the wing officer to put the boy in his cell.

'He's a nephew of mine,' he'd tell the officer. 'I'll keep an eye on him.'

It was a standard joke that Bill Munday shared his cell with a lot of 'nephews.'

When I arrived without any property he arranged the next day for me to have a TV in my cell. 'Bank robbers are good blokes,' he said. 'Anything you need, let me know.'

I knew that as long as I avoided playing him chess, I would have no problems with him.

For me, life at Goulburn was depressing. There was no education or work available to me. I wrote to the head psychologist at the Special Care Unit (SCU) at Long Bay and requested to return there for a 'refresher' course. I explained that, after all the positive work I had completed at the SCU, Goulburn was not the ideal environment for me to finish my sentence in. It was a totally retrogressive move and I didn't even know why I was there. I didn't hold out a lot of hope. I knew there was a long list of inmates waiting to be accepted into the programme where rehabilitation actually worked. But I had established a good rapport with the head psychologist and when she received my letter she arranged for my transfer.

A few days later a guard told me to pack my gear. 'You're going back to the Scum Unit at Long Bay,' he said.

A lot of guards resented the SCU and what it stood for. They thought that by adding an M to the name they were being clever.

I gave him a polite smile. 'Us prisoners appreciate you hard-working taxpayers funding such an important project as the SCU.'

His face reddened. 'The Scum Unit, that's what it is.' He obviously wasn't much of a debater.

That afternoon I was on the escort van – en route to the SCU at Long Bay.

Bill Munday, a renowned drug user, died in the mid-nineties, reportedly from an aneurism. Not one nephew went to his funeral.

THE KILLICK PRINCIPLE

1989–91

My stay at the SCU was much the same as that in 1988. Same staff, same programmes, same routine but with different inmates. Compared to Goulburn it was a holiday resort. Sometimes, wearing civilian clothing and playing chess or batball with John, or sitting at the table and having lunch with him and Gloria, I didn't feel like a prisoner. I can understand why some of the guards resented the SCU, claiming prisoners got it too easy. They were ignoring the fact that the SCU actually achieved its goal by rehabilitating some criminals and that the unit dealt with less than two per cent of prisoners in New South Wales.

When, in May, they transferred me to Cessnock, I was seven months away from my release date. Although I was expecting the Queensland authorities to try and extradite me, I was told by my parole officer and the Classification Board that no warrant had been issued.

As far as gaols go, Cessnock wasn't too bad. But gaol is gaol – it's the people you have to deal with inside the gaol that, for me, determines whether it's a 'good' gaol or not. There were no Billy Mundays at Cessnock. But one guy I had no time for was Robert 'Bobby' Chapman – a onetime associate of Neddy Smith until they had a fall out. Chapman was a tough, arrogant drug dealer and rapist who had a team of cronies doing his dirty work for him. In the seven months I was there, we didn't speak to each other once. A few weeks after I arrived, he and a few of his thugs beat up on some poor fool who owed him money for drugs. The victim was big and strong but had no chance. I figured that after that incident all those owing Chapman for drugs would pay up. Those who couldn't would go on protection.

A few years later Chapman was shot in the chest and wrapped in a carpet by a couple of his enemies. They put him in the back of a car and were driving somewhere to bury him when, still wrapped in the carpet, he kicked out the rear panel window and somehow forced himself through the opening and fell onto the roadside.

Nearby residents rushed out to see what the commotion was about and the car drove off. After being rushed to hospital, he was still alive. When police arrived, they asked him who had shot him. Legend has it that, with his dying breath, he said: 'Get fucked!'

A tough, bad guy, Bobby Chapman...

At Cessnock, I was given a job working with two female librarians. They were both nice people and I enjoyed the job. I also completed a TAFE correspondence course on 'TV and Film Scriptwriting'. I had some good stories to tell and I figured television and movies were the way to go. During my stay at Parklea I had written a script for the popular Rafferty's Rules and sent it to Channel 7. One of the executives, Louise Holmes, wrote back telling me that another scriptwriter, John Upton, had read it and declared it an 'acceptable episode'. The problem was the series was coming to an end – the remaining episodes had been contracted and written. But it gave me confidence that I could succeed in the industry.

After work, I usually played tennis. I also arranged a chess tournament but there weren't many good chess players at Cessnock. Billy Munday would have beaten most of them.

A few months before my release date, Parklea was again the subject of a riot – this time full scale. Fires were lit, buildings were wrecked and both prisoners and guards were injured.

It was a consequence of months of unrest throughout the New South Wales prison system. The newly elected Greiner Liberal Government had allowed the Minister for Corrective Services, Michael Yabsley, to implement, all at the one time, his ideas of how to improve the system. Nearly all of it was punitive in nature, involving taking away property, privileges and cutting visiting times. The 'one-out' cells at Parklea were suddenly 'two-out' – with an extra bed installed in each cell. In many ways, the system had retrogressed to the sixties. Remissions for good behaviour were abolished and the new 'truth in sentencing' laws had been introduced – resulting in harsher sentences with no respite for good behaviour. The system was like a powder keg, ready to erupt just as it had been at Bathurst in 1974.

When news of the Parklea riots spread, other gaols followed suit. One of those being Cessnock. Although there had been talk between some of the inmates about a possible protest over conditions, it had, to that stage, been nothing more than talk. I was totally unaware of any rioting activity until guards rushed into the library and, none too gently, escorted me to my cell where they took most of my property including writing materials. Fires had been lit around the gaol and some property damaged. The gaol was locked down for about a week, but compared to the damage done at Parklea, the Cessnock 'riot' had been low on the Richter scale.

The day before my release on parole on Sunday, 23 December 1990, Gloria hired a car for the weekend and drove up to see me. While at the gaol she asked the Assistant Governor if I was going to be arrested for extradition or whether she could come and pick me up.

He assured her that there would be no extradition – I would be released at 8:00 am.

That night she told John I'd be home for Christmas. He helped to place presents on the Christmas tree.

The next morning when I was taken to the front gate for release, the police were there to arrest me. 'You were told you wouldn't be arrested,' one of the cops said, 'because we didn't want you escaping.'

When Gloria arrived, I was already in a cell at the local police station. 'Detective Arch MacDonald is on his way from Queensland to collect you,' the desk sergeant said.

When Gloria drove home she had the task of explaining to John why his Dad would be absent for another Christmas.

Gloria arranged for Bruce Miles to drive to Cessnock to appear for me before a local magistrate. Arch MacDonald, who looked much the same as he had nearly seven years ago – with the exception he now had a pot-belly – produced a warrant signed by a Brisbane magistrate ordering my extradition.

Bruce, off the cuff without notes, made an impassioned plea that it was an abuse of process, that for years I had been told that no extradition would be sought. But as expected, the magistrate confirmed the order. Bruce – pointing out that most of the courts would be closed during the Christmas/New Year period requested, and was given, time to apply to the Supreme Court for a review of the order.

Although MacDonald wasn't happy about having to return to Queensland empty-handed he was grimly resolute: 'I'll be back,' he told me.

I spent Christmas in the local police cells before being transferred to Maitland Gaol. It was one of the gaols that, during the Nagle Royal Commission, came under criticism for the bashing and ill-treatment of prisoners in the 'Intractable' section of the prison. But, for the most part, those days of systematic bashings were gone.

Within a week I was driven to Sydney and placed in one of the cells at Surry Hills Police Centre. There were about eight of us in the one large cell. The lights were on all night and we had to sleep on the concrete benches. After a while, with no way of keeping track of the time, it was difficult to know if it was night or day.

Not long after arriving there I had a headache so severe I felt as though my head was going to burst. Although at first the police ignored my complaints, after a few days a nurse took my blood pressure and told them to take me to St Vincent's Hospital.

My headache had become even more severe. Maybe I had a brain tumour? If I did, Arch MacDonald would never get his man. He was the sort of guy who would think I somehow got a brain tumour deliberately – just to spite him.

The doctor diagnosed me with severe hypertension. He prescribed me some medication and told the cops I was okay to go back.

The next day I was transferred to the MRC at Long Bay. On a visit, Gloria told me my Supreme Court hearing was scheduled for late January. Bruce wouldn't be available.

'In that case I'll do it myself,' I said.

She gave me a surprised look. 'Are you sure that's the right decision?'

'Yes. I know every detail of this case. We don't have the money for a top barrister and there's not enough time to properly brief a Legal Aid lawyer. I'd be lucky to see him once before we got to court.'

Gloria had some other news. She had taken a position as a Judge's associate in the Industrial Court. The irony of the situation wasn't lost on me.

In the Supreme Court, the judge gave me a good hearing. I enjoyed the opportunity to cross-examine MacDonald about some of the unsubstantiated statements he had made to the media regarding the charges. But, as the judge emphasised, the seriousness of the alleged four bank robberies left him with no alternative other than to dismiss my application.

That afternoon I was on a plane. Even during the flight MacDonald wouldn't take the handcuffs off me.

After arriving in Brisbane, I was taken to the Police Watch House where I spent the night in a cell by myself. The next morning, I appeared before a magistrate. When I asked him for bail he said it was nice to see I had a good sense of humour.

Surprisingly, I wasn't charged with the escape. When I asked MacDonald why, he gave me a frustrated look.

'There was a stuff up. You won't be charged with it, but you'll get a big whack for the banks.'

A few hours later I was taken to Boggo Road. It had been seven years since I had been there and some parts, including the showers, were in disrepair.

'It will be closing down next year,' an old prison guard said. 'Never thought I'd see the day. In its day, it was the toughest gaol in Australia.'

I wasn't convinced of that. But I wasn't about to debate him. No doubt the government wouldn't spend money on renovations when it was soon to be shut down.

I had expected a hostile reception from the guards and management when I arrived but there wasn't a hint of it. Most of them were faces unfamiliar to me.

Due to experience of having worked in the Parklea clinic I was given a job in the records section of the medical centre. Two other prisoners worked with me. It was a position of trust – we had access to all of the prisoners' medical files and, incredibly, the dates for hospital appointments. Our boss, Kris Waters, a civilian, trusted the three of us. She told us that if one of us broke that trust she would be disillusioned and would resign immediately. I enjoyed working with someone like that.

One of my co-workers, Brian, was in gaol for bank robbery. He had kidnapped the manager of a Gold Coast bank with the intention of driving with him to the bank and emptying the vault. But the manager told him that he could only gain access with the assistance of the accountant. Brian found himself in the absurd situation of driving around the Gold Coast while holding the bank manager at gunpoint, trying to locate the accountant.

The police found Brian before he found the accountant. He was sentenced to seven years with a non-parole period of four years. It was his first offence. When he learned of my criminal past he became concerned for me.

'John, if you go down on four banks they'll give you at least fifteen years.'

'I won't be going down, I'm innocent.'

Although I knew that some judges could be biased, and that some police lied in court, I still had faith in the legal system. The High Court had given me that faith ten years ago when it had quashed four wrongful convictions for armed robbery.

My Legal Aid appointed solicitor, Vicky Zammit, proved to be one of the best and hardest working lawyers I have known.nThe first time she visited me, she stared at me and asked: 'Did you rob these banks?'

I met her gaze. She was an exceptionally pretty, dark-haired girl who looked to be in her mid-twenties. 'No,' I said.

She nodded, more to herself than to me. 'Then we are going to fight these charges to the death.'

I was immediately taken by her. She meticulously went through the details and witness statements of each charge. She flew to Adelaide and interviewed Jackie. She wanted her to come to my trial and testify on my behalf. Jackie had been with me at the time three of the banks were held up. She hadn't been charged with any of them and could testify as to my whereabouts at the crucial times.

She told Vicki she had only been married for a few months and her husband, a respectable accountant, didn't want her to get involved.

Vicki was insistent. 'One way or another,' she said, 'you are involved.

It's essential that you testify.'

'I'll try to persuade him,' Jackie said. Vicki left without a definite commitment.

'We could subpoena her,' she said when she came to see me.

'No,' I said. 'Either she comes voluntarily, or we do it without her.' I paused. 'Don't worry, I know her. She'll come.'

'I'm not sure about that,' Vicki said.

She filed an application to the Supreme Court for me to be given bail, outlining the fact that I had been in custody for six years. Although it failed, she forced the prosecution to give an assurance that I would have a trial date within six months of my having re-entered Queensland custody in January.

While Vicki worked diligently on my case, I also received help from Bernie Matthews, an old-school bank robber who had done hard time in the brutal Grafton intractable section as well as the 'electronic zoo' Katingal. He was now in custody for a bank robbery – an offence he didn't commit. (He was released later that year, police admitting they had the wrong man).

About fifteen years later he published a book, Intractables, vividly relating his experiences in some of the harshest prisons in Australia.

Although Legal Aid wouldn't fund another bail application, I applied again in July. Representing myself I emphasised that I still didn't have a trial date.

The prosecution complained that the offences had occurred more than seven years ago and police were having problems locating some of the witnesses.

I pointed out that they had been aware since my sentencing in 1986 of when I would be released from New South Wales custody. Ample time to locate witnesses.

The prosecution argued that the charges were too serious for bail to be granted.

'Well, he has been in custody for over six years,' the judge said. 'If I grant him bail and he absconds he'll lose the benefit of all that.'

'Your Honour, he has a history of –'

The judge cut in: 'I understand.' He turned to me. 'Mr Killick, if I grant you bail and you don't honour it, anyone charged with armed robbery appearing in my court will automatically be refused bail. We will call it the "Killick Principle".'

He granted me bail with a $5000 cash surety required. Despite more protests from the prosecution, he gave me permission to live in New South Wales until it was time to return for trial.

I feel he did it to send a message to the prosecution: when unconvicted people are being held in custody it should be a priority to get the matters dealt with within the allocated timeframe.

I thanked him and assured him I'd be there for trial.

Before being returned to the gaol I asked a duty solicitor at the court to contact Vicki and ask her to arrange with Gloria to post the $5000 bail.

It took two days for the money to be transferred from Sydney and accepted by the authorities.

When I walked through the gates to at least temporary freedom, I was half-expecting MacDonald to be waiting to arrest me and charge me with the

1984 escape. But there wasn't a cop in sight. I caught a taxi to the city, finally savouring my first taste of freedom for seventy-four months.

Before going to the airport, I met up with Vicki and shared a drink with her.

She was excited that against the odds, I had managed to obtain bail. 'It's a good sign,' she said.

'Vicki, with you in my corner, how can I lose?'

She gave me a serious look. 'We need to persuade Jackie to testify for you,' she said.

'Leave it with me,' I said. 'She'll be there when it counts.'

Ninety minutes later I was on a flight to Sydney – this time without handcuffs.

FIFTY AND OUT!

1991–92

For me, the hardest part about prison is the separation from loved ones and friends. Even though I had been fortunate enough to receive visits from Gloria, and occasionally, John, it was a poor substitute for the real thing – being free to go anywhere with them and do as we please. Now I again could do that – at least for a while. John, now sixteen, slightly taller than me and blessed with classic good looks, gave me a big hug. 'Welcome home, Dad.'

It was still prominent in my mind that I was only out on bail – for four armed robberies. The pressures of a coming trial in another state with the real prospect of another long prison sentence, separated from these people I loved, was impossible to trivialise. But I tried to mask my mood from John. There would be time later, as the trial date loomed, to break the news to him. At the moment, he thought I was home free.

Despite the fact that I'd languished in prison for eight of his sixteen years, we still had a great rapport. Over the next six months we had a lot of fun times together. We played tennis, Trivial Pursuit, chess, tenpin bowling and cricket at the local park. The three of us went for long drives, picnics and even to a drive-in.

My work at the SCU hadn't eradicated my interest in gambling. I still believed I could win. There was a fine line between winning and losing. It was a matter of fine tuning my past strategies: this time I would be more circumspect with my bets. I'd only bet on top horses, ridden by top jockeys and trained by top trainers. And the tracks would have to be good – not rain affected. Research over the past few years had convinced me this method was a recipe for success. And from now on, I told myself, gambling would be a hobby – not a career.

I managed to obtain some casual work tutoring English to three Asian students. They needed tuition in comprehension and enjoyed the way I'd sit with them and together we would make up a story which I would teach them to construct properly.

John, when he finished school the following year, intended to study journalism at university. His marks were high and I felt he could, if he pushed himself, attain the standard required to study law. But he wasn't interested. Journalism was his goal.

I read some of his work: there was nothing I could teach him, he was already a superior wordsmith to me.

A few weeks after I had returned home, Jackie rang me. I immediately recognised the voice. 'Am I talking to Mrs James Walters?' I said.

'Yes. I'm a married woman.'

'I'm shattered.'

'Well, you had your chance. Now, John, I don't want you to go back to gaol, but it will be difficult for me to testify at your trial.'

'Nonsense. All you have to do is get in the box and tell the truth as you and I understand it to be, rather than MacDonald's version of it.'

'James doesn't want me to do it. He said it will be too much pressure on me.'

'Tell him you thrive on pressure. Or do you want me to come and tell him?'

She hung up.

I knew that if I wanted her at my trial, I'd have to go to Adelaide and try to persuade her to change her mind.

About fifteen minutes later Vicki rang me. Her attitude was a bit stern. 'Jackie just rang me – she said you were rude to her and she won't be testifying. What did you say to her?'

'Nothing, really. Jackie hasn't changed. It's her nature to throw a tantrum when she can't get her own way. She got us both arrested in Albury after she threw a tantrum.'

'But what did you say to her?'

'Not much, honestly. Listen, don't worry, I'm going over to see her next week. She'll testify – I promise you.'

'Well, if she doesn't, we're in trouble.'

'It's not a problem. You just focus on the rest of the evidence and leave Jackie to me.'

A few days later, after hiring a new Falcon, I rang Jackie and told her I was on my way. She agreed to meet me in two days' time at the motel we had stayed in during the 1983 Ash Wednesday bushfires.

I tried to analyse how I really felt about her now. Did it bother me that she was married? This girl who had pleaded with me on numerous occasions to divorce Gloria. Had I harboured a desire to rekindle the relationship? The answer was no. It was over between us. Together, we had been through some incredible experiences and you never forget those times. But I had confined them to my memory bank where they belonged. Team John and Jackie was past history.

Nevertheless, when she knocked on the motel door I knew I had been looking forward to this moment. I opened the door and she stood there with a silly grin on her face. 'Well?' she said, her arms open wide, ready for a hug.

I gave her one. 'You look great,' I said.

And she did. She was dressed in a stylishly cut skirt and blouse and had obviously just had her hair done. This 27-year-old woman now standing before me was no longer the young girl I had always called 'Imp.' She looked every bit of what she had become – a middle class housewife enjoying life.

'Does James know you are here with me?'

'Yes. He expects me to make it clear to you that I can't come to the trial.'

'Let's discuss it over a few drinks,' I said.

We went to a hotel. For old time's sake, we both drank Bacardi and Cokes. 'Brings back memories,' I said.

She nodded. 'Two drinks and I was drunk.'

For a while we brought each other up to date on the past few years.

When we started on our third drink, I said: 'Vicki believes that without you, I can't win the trial.'

'John, they'll bring out my background. The jury won't believe anything I say.'

'Look at you. You're a respectable housewife. When it's explained that you've come 2,000 miles against the wishes of your husband, a respected professional man, because you want the truth to be known, they will believe you.'

'What if they don't?'

'Then I go down. But at least we will have tried. Do you want MacDonald to win without a fight?'

'Is he still around?'

'Of course. He's the one who insisted that I be extradited.'

'What about the escape? I've already been convicted for it.'

'MacDonald said there's been a stuff up. He's really pissed off about it. I'm only charged with the four banks.'

'Bloody hell. I did nine months for that escape and you get nothing.'

'They should have given you seven years for the audacity of it,' I said. We both laughed.

Eventually, she said 'I'll testify for you. I wouldn't do it for anyone else. I don't want to see you go back to gaol'.

I nodded. 'I never lost faith that you'd do it. When will you tell James?'

'Tonight. He won't like it, but I'll handle him.'

When she drove me to the motel we agreed to meet again the next day. She wanted to show me her wedding photos.

When she showed them to me I told her the truth: she was a beautiful bride. But on their wedding days all brides are beautiful.

We met again on the third day. 'Vicki will arrange everything for you,' I told her. 'You'll fly up the day before the trial begins and stay in a hotel. You won't have to pay. Vicki and the barrister will go over all the evidence with you. You have nothing to worry about.'

'When will it be?' she asked.

'In three months. January. I'll see you up there – we'll have dinner.'

'I'd like that.'

'Consider it done.'

I drove to Sydney without an overnight stay.

For the next three months, I spent as much time with John and Gloria as I could. I reunited with my brother, David, and met his new wife, Trudie. We went to his place for barbeques where John spent time with his cousins.

Two days before the scheduled trial date of 24 January 1992 I flew to Brisbane.

Gloria arranged for me to stay with a lady friend of hers, Pearl. She was a lovely lady and made me feel at home. 'I'm sure they will realise you are an innocent man and let you go,' she said.

The morning before the trial, Jackie arrived. I met up with her at Vicki's office. Both of us were introduced to the barrister with whom I was impressed. When we went over the details of each robbery I realised he had put a lot of work into it. Of course, Vicki had done all the groundwork. I was confident we would beat at least three of the charges. The fourth bank, involving the hire car, which occurred while Jackie was in gaol, was a concern.

Vicki had booked Jackie into a nice hotel. 'Are we still having dinner?' Jackie asked.

'Of course, we are. We'll call it the last supper.'

After dinner, we walked around the city. The strain was beginning to get to me and I wasn't good company. After a while I decided to go back to Pearl's place and prepare for the ordeal ahead.

'I'll pack my bag in case the judge pulls the bail,' I said. Jackie looked at me. 'He won't do that. Why would he?'

'If the evidence is strong he will. You never know what surprises MacDonald might come up with.'

We said goodnight and I caught a train to Pearl's place.

There was no trial. The Crown case on three of the banks was weakened by the fact a lot of the witnesses couldn't be located. My barrister pushed home the advantage and persuaded the Crown to drop three of the charges if I pleaded guilty to the other one.

'How long will I get?' I asked. 'Two years,' the barrister said.

Two years. They still had remissions in Queensland. If I stayed out of trouble I would be out in eighteen months. I didn't like it, but I decided to take it.

Jackie flew home without having to testify. Before she left I thanked her. She gave me a hug. 'Don't escape,' she said.

I grinned. 'I need an Imp for that.'

The next time I saw her she was seven months' pregnant.

When the judge sentenced me, he surprised everyone – especially MacDonald. He gave me two-and-a-half years but recommended I be released immediately on parole. He gave weight to the almost six years I had spent in custody in maximum security in New South Wales before being extradited and then another six months on remand in Boggo Road. My behaviour had been good, I had lived in Sydney for the past six months without incident and I had honoured my bail.

Although the recommendation was for immediate parole, I had to return to prison until the Parole Board arranged all the paperwork, including my parole transfer to New South Wales.

On 18 February 1992, five days after my fiftieth birthday I was released on the condition that I return immediately to New South Wales.

Vicki met me in town and we went to a hotel for a drink. 'One day you'll be a Senior Counsel,' I said confidently.

'I'm afraid not,' she said. 'I'm giving up law soon to get married.'

I was stunned. 'He's a lucky guy. We can't afford to lose lawyers with your tenacity.'

'I'll be satisfied with my career if you stay out of trouble. When I took your matter on I thought you would finish with ten years.' She raised her glass. 'You've been lucky, John. You won a High Court appeal on four armed robberies. And now you've walked away again after being charged with four bank robberies. Make the best of it.'

I met her gaze and touched my glass to hers. 'For you, I'll stay out of trouble.'

After she had gone I bought another drink before going to the airport. In the past, I'd had some bad decisions by the judiciary; this time I had indeed been fortunate. Overall, I figured I'd broken about even with the judicial system. I had no idea that the two-and-a-half years' sentence would take twenty-four years to finish.

As I finished my drink and walked out of the hotel my mood was buoyant. I was free! No more trials. I could go home and focus on the future. I was fifty but I was fit, healthy and my mind was sharp. Whatever I did from here would have to be legal. Yes, the future was bright.

A FAVOUR FOR A FRIEND

1992–97

The next twelve months were uneventful. I returned to Sydney where I lived with Gloria and John at Milson's Point. John was now seventeen.

In his HSC exams, he finished in the top four per cent in the State.

The rapport between the three of us was good. But the years with Jackie and then the long years of separation while in prison had effectively destroyed what was left of the marriage. Gloria and I were now good friends. In fact, she was and always will be my best friend.

After advertising on the noticeboard of the local supermarket, I again managed to find some part-time work tutoring composition English to five students. Combined with unemployment benefits it was enough to live on. At this stage, my gambling was almost non-existent.

In early 1993 John enrolled in journalism at the University of Canberra. Gloria and I often drove down to see him. Although my lifestyle was unexciting I was enjoying the freedom.

But in March 1993 disaster again struck. An ex-prison officer (I'll call him Max) knocked on my door. I had met him in 1991 during my six months' stay at Boggo Road. He was one of the good ones who simply did his job without being judgmental. But in 1992 Boggo Road was closed down and Max found himself unemployed.

He was a member of a pistol club and had two pistols which he kept in a safe at home. With mounting debts, he decided to sell them – on the black market where he could get a much better price.

I agreed to try to arrange a buyer for them. Wrong move.

Leaving one weapon at home, I drove to a hotel to meet a prospective buyer. After taking him to my car and showing him the pistol he said he would buy it but not at the requested price. I told him I would get back to him after the owner considered the counter offer. I'd arranged to meet Max about 2 kilometres away in a quiet, leafy little street in Wollstonecraft. Unknown to both of us there had been a few house break-ins in the area and it was being staked out by undercover police. While waiting for me Max had approached one of the undercovers. She was a nice-looking blonde who was wearing tight shorts. When she told him who she was and asked him for his name, for some reason he gave her a false one. She was checking it out on the radio when I drove up alongside them. If he'd have signalled to me I would have driven off. But he looked at me and shrugged. Figuring he was trying to chat up the girl I got out of the car. Suddenly other undercover police came out of hiding.

The girl took me aside and asked me Max's name. I told her. The fact that this simple detail didn't coincide aroused enough suspicion for them to search my car where they found the pistol.

When Max saw it, he yelled out: 'He stole my pistol!'

Max had applied for a position with the Victorian police. If he was convicted of trying to sell his weapons illegally he wouldn't be accepted.

'Cuff him!' the girl said.

Both of us were taken to North Sydney police station. At my place, they found the other pistol.

A couple of detectives told me that unless I pleaded guilty to the theft of the pistols Max's career was over.

'If you plead guilty,' one of them said, 'we will do our best to get you a bond.'

Even if I pleaded not guilty, I would be guilty of illegal possession of two firearms. With my background and the certainty of the police going in hard against me, I would almost certainly pull a gaol sentence. With the police on side, I had a chance of a bond and at the same time could save Max's career.

I took the deal. I had to spend a short time on remand at Long Bay Correctional Centre, where I met up with a few old lags again. Eventually I was given bail and in October 1993, represented by my good friend, Bruce Miles, I was given a five-year bond.

While I'd been in gaol for possession of the pistols my students had found other tutors.

A lady, Lyn Warner, at the Commonwealth Employment Service (CES) took a genuine interest in me. She was a slim, attractive blonde lady who, despite being aware of my background, did everything she could to get me employment. But my age and criminal history proved to be major stumbling blocks.

Unperturbed, Lyn enrolled me in a computer course where, incredibly, I was seated beside the undercover blonde cop who had arrested me for the pistols. We got along fine and she even helped me with my toolbar when it malfunctioned.

After the computer course Lyn, using precious resources, enrolled me in a comprehensive three months' course: Introduction to TV – Motion Pictures Production (Screen Production Academy), learning how to write, direct and produce television and film scripts. Thanks to Lyn I learned a lot. I wrote a few quality scripts for television and although Louise Holmes at Channel 7 was supportive, I soon learnt that all doors in the industry were closed to me.

Lyn and I became good friends. Sometimes I would drive to her unit at

Collaroy where we would have a drink and a chat. Our relationship was strictly platonic. She had a teenage daughter, Mia, who was a talented singer. I went to a concert to hear her sing and I was impressed with not only her voice, but her confident, professional presentation.

A few weeks later there was a huge scandal when it was revealed that Mia's music teacher had been drugging, photographing and sexually assaulting a number of his young female students. Fortunately, Mia wasn't one of the victims. The sexual predator was sentenced to about nine years in prison, strict protection of course.

One night in November 1993 I came home late and saw a lady I knew, Faye, sitting on the steps near my unit crying. Her right eye was bruised. It was well-known in the area that her husband, Tom, often became violent towards her when he was drunk – which was often.

It was a sad sight to see this good woman in the state that she was in.

She reminded me of my mother four decades ago when she would be too frightened to enter the house due to the drunken raging of my father.

I asked Faye why she didn't leave Tom. She gave the same answer my mother had always given: she had nowhere to go.

Although she was beautiful and had a kind, gentle nature, Tom treated her more like a slave than a wife. She was a good worker, often holding down two jobs. He received the disability pension and often used her wages to travel solo overseas.

We sat in my car for about an hour until she was certain Tom would have fallen asleep. Before she returned home I arranged to meet her the next day with her bags packed ready to leave.

Without Tom being aware that his wife was leaving him, I drove her to Eastwood where a friend of mine rented a unit. When I explained the situation to her, she offered Faye the spare room until something else could be arranged.

But Faye phoned her son and told him where she was. Later that day Tom arrived and forced her to return home.

About a month later he again assaulted her. I decided to permanently get her out of his clutches. I rented a small unit for her in Marks Point on the Central Coast – 135 kilometres away from Sydney and Tom.

After that I saw her often and eventually I moved in with her. She told me that she finally felt safe.

He had no idea of where his wife was. He drank more heavily and told people that when he found her he would kill her.

Sometimes I would drive her to Sydney where she would visit her son. She made him swear he wouldn't reveal to anyone that she was with me. He wasn't privy to where we lived.

Life ran smoothly for us but I couldn't get work in the area. When the director of Collmark College rang me with the offer of twenty hours per week tutoring students in their homes I decided to return to Sydney. It was a position I had applied for when I was tutoring the Asian students.

Although Faye had a job in a Newcastle cafe she resigned and came with me. We rented a unit in Eastwood where she soon found work at a nearby fruit and vegetable shop.

A few weeks later Lyn arranged an interview for me with International Correspondence School (ICS) in Artarmon. It supplied correspondence courses on numerous subjects as diverse as child care, French language and locksmithing. A team of glib telemarketers persuaded people to sign up to these courses. A deposit would be taken from their credit cards. Often some of them would later change their minds and want to pull out of the contract. My job as the liaison officer would be to convince them not to cancel.

After the interview, I was hired. I became fairly good at it achieving an eighty per cent success rate.

Another positive that came from my friendship with Lyn was her introducing to me her good friend, Emeritus Professor Ian Plimer. They had known each other since their university days.

At our first meeting in 1994 he took Lyn, Mia and myself to an expensive restaurant at Palm Beach. We immediately established a rapport. Despite our contrasting backgrounds, this charismatic academic chatted with me on many subjects as though we were two labourers meeting for a beer at the local pub. I later discovered that this in fact was what he liked to do – go to a local pub and chat with the boys. As I got to know him better I often managed to get to Broken Hill and join him at his favourite watering hole for a beer or six.

At the time of meeting him he was the Head of the School of Geology in the University of Melbourne and one of Australia's most experienced and respected geologists. (He later had a mineral, Plimerite, named after him.) Over dinner Lyn mentioned Ian had just finished a new book, *Telling Lies For God.*

'A non-controversial book,' Ian said, grinning.

It would, in keeping with many other books he has written, become a bestseller.

Although he didn't mention it at our initial meeting, he was embroiled in a controversial court case that would ultimately financially ruin him. Although he recovered from this setback, the long drawn out five-year struggle took its toll on both Ian and his wife.

It began in April 1992 when he attended a lecture in Melbourne by Dr Allen Roberts, a creationist representing a recently formed organisation Ark Search. Roberts was on a fundraising tour showing photos and stating scientific tests proved he had found the remains of Noah's Ark in Eastern Turkey about 20 kilometres from the summit of Greater Mount Ararat. When Ian publicly challenged Roberts on his statements about geology, the chairman had him evicted.

A month later at the Wesley Centre in Central Sydney Ian joined a group of about thirty friends, science students and members of Australian Skeptics where Doctor Roberts was lecturing.

On arrival Ian was handed a writ for defamation concerning remarks he had made about Roberts's scientific qualifications as well as claiming as false the alleged discovery of Noah's Ark.

Ian counter claimed against Roberts stating Roberts and Ark Search had traded in manifestly false claims.

In April 1997, the trial was held in the Sydney Federal Court with Justice Ronald Sackville presiding.

A week earlier Ark Search went into liquidation.

On 2 June 1997, the judge found that Dr Roberts's claims to have personally carried out scientific tests were false but he couldn't be persecuted under the Trades and Practices Act because his activities did not occur 'in trade or commerce' pursuant to the Fair Trading Acts.

After the verdict Professor Plimer said: 'This gives the green light to every snake oil salesman.'

An appeal to the Federal Court of Appeal brought no joy. The judges ruled 3–0 against him.

Apart from his own costs he was ordered to pay the court costs of Roberts.

Despite these setbacks, Professor Plimer, who had already been given the 1995 Australian Humanist of the Year award was, in 1997, made an Honorary Fellow by the Geological Society of London for his 'courageous stand' against creationism – international recognition of the fact that he is 'a man of enormous courage who has put his money where his mouth is'.

Probably half a million dollars...

Dr Roberts boasted that his technical legal victory (technically he wasn't in trade or commerce) was a victory for 'free speech' – ignoring the elephant in the room: The judge had found him to be 'misleading and deceptive'.

JOHN MEETS LUCY

1993–1996

One day, after driving to Canberra to see John, I visited the Canberra Casino and won a few hundred dollars playing baccarat. For a while in the early sixties, I had frequented the illegal casinos at Kings Cross and had often won playing baccarat. The win at Canberra rekindled my interest in the game and I worked at developing a mathematical system to beat the odds.

Working as a tutor and a liaison officer from Monday to Friday, I drove to Canberra on Friday nights, booked a motel for two days and spent the weekends at the casino. In the first twelve months I won $21,000, not a fortune but for the first time in my life I was consistently winning at gambling. I still had a few wagers on the horses and lost overall, but I had cut down drastically on this form of betting and the losses were minor. I was enjoying life.

Eventually the lengthy hours I spent working at ICS and then tutoring at nights, combined with the weekend trips to Canberra began to wear me down.

I was making more money – tax free – from the baccarat than I was clearing from tutoring. But my main concern was the work I was doing for ICS. Sometimes when a person phoned wanting to cancel their contract for one of the courses I wouldn't argue. Before enrolling someone in a course the telemarketers always took a deposit after obtaining credit card details. But by later cancelling the course the person would be free of the contract. My job was to convince them to continue – not cancel.

But when you had a woman call up and say: 'My husband went off his brain when he saw what I had done. We are behind in our payments on the mortgage. If I don't cancel I'm frightened of what he might do.'

What are you going to do? You let her cancel instead of bluffing her that debt collectors will be knocking on the door with a garnishee order against her husband's wages.

A few times the manager called me to her office and asked me why I had cancelled without a fight.

'She couldn't afford it,' I would say.

'That's not our problem. She wanted to do the course. She paid the deposit. You have a splendid strike rate – don't spoil it.'

It was ironic. I had never had any qualms or feelings of guilt when I robbed a bank. But I had remorse about having sold raffle tickets for a non-existent prize to battlers. And this job at ICS was giving me similar feelings of guilt.

One morning I walked into the manager's office and told her I didn't want to work there. She allowed me to leave without notice.

In December 1995 Faye and I were at a party in Five Dock where we met Lucy and Alex Dudko. He was tall and thin with dark brown hair and thick-rimmed glasses. Lucy, wearing similar glasses, was slim with long blonde hair. To me she was the most attractive woman in the room.

The four of us sat with drinks and chatted for a while. He revealed that two years ago they had emigrated from Russia. When Faye showed interest, he began a monologue about himself, Russia and the flaws he had found in the Australian way of life, in particular its poor academic standards.

I diverted to Lucy. She was still in the process of learning English and her accent was strong.

'Seems to me, not much of a party,' she said. I laughed. 'Parties bore me.'

She gave me a serious look. 'But you come. Maybe for you a book is best.'

I smiled. 'Russian I suppose.'

'Of course. Have you read any?'

'Quite a few.'

Whilst Alex tried to impress Faye with his worldly views, Lucy and I discussed Russian literature.

She was surprised that I had read Dostoyevsky, Tolstoy, Chekov and Pushkin. I didn't reveal that I had read most of these books while in gaol. Years later, when I thought of her, I was reminded of Tolstoy's tragic Anna Karenina.

While Alex was still charming Faye, I asked Lucy for her phone number. For a few moments she stared at me, then with the faintest of smiles she gave it to me. Maybe she thought that I would soon forget it. But I didn't.

About a month later, in January 1996, I met Lucy in a cafe at the Macquarie Centre. Although we had spoken on the phone a few times, this was our first meeting since the party. Sometimes two people meet and instantaneously know what type of person the other is. It wasn't that way with us. We both misjudged each other. I saw her as a bored housewife looking for excitement; she saw me as a mild-mannered, educated gentleman who would play by the rules. When she asked me what I did for a living I told her I was an English tutor and a part-time writer. This wasn't a lie: I had recently had a story published in HQ Magazine and had applied for a literary grant to write a book.

We began to meet every second week. I took her to motels, ensuring she was back in time to pick up her seven-year-old daughter, Anna, from school. After a while, the rendezvous became weekly. Occasionally I took her to a movie in the city, or to a restaurant. She rarely had money, explaining that Alex made her account for every cent she spent. She told me that if she overspent he would punish her.

A few months after we became involved she told me she had another lover. 'I gave my husband horns in Russia and Slovakia and I made certain he would also wear them in Australia.'

I laughed. 'So now you are giving me horns.'

She gave me a serious look. 'He was before you. If it bothers you, I will stop.'

'It doesn't bother me.'

How could I be critical? I was separated from my wife, living with Faye, and having an affair with Lucy. We were two of a kind. I felt that with her we could push the boundaries and see where it led us.

A few weeks later when I went home Faye was upset. She told me Tom had found out where she was working. She would have to leave.

'You go to Canberra all the time,' she said. 'Why don't we go down there to live?'

At first, I wondered if she had discovered I was seeing Lucy and this was a ploy to get me away from Sydney. But she wasn't a devious person. I knew that if we stayed in Eastwood, Tom would cause us major problems. Faye was in fear of him. I decided it was time to confront him.

Driving to Milson's Point, I went to his unit but he wasn't there. It was a good opportunity to see John and Gloria and I spent a few hours with them. As I came out of the building Tom was waiting for me. He had a mate with him. A little plump guy who had a foreign accent.

'You bastard!' Tom said, moving towards me aggressively.

I shoved him in the chest and he stumbled backwards but managed to stay upright.

John, who had followed me outside, grabbed hold of me. 'Let it go, Dad, he's not worth it!'

Tom was clutching his chest. His mate yelled: 'Tom! Are you all right?'

'My heart,' Tom said.

I stared at him. Was he having a heart attack? I hadn't hit him that hard. 'I saw what happened,' his mate said to me.

'He attacked Dad,' John said. He was angry.

Ignoring his mate, I walked up close to Tom. He was still clutching his chest.

'Leave Faye alone. She's divorcing you. If you ever assault her again it will be the last thing you ever do.'

'She's my wife!' he yelled. Heart attack was gone. 'No. She's your ex-wife. Go find another one.'

'I'm a witness,' his mate said.

'Good,' I said. 'Just tell the truth.'

John and I walked away. As I got into my car Tom yelled: 'You bastard! You are going back to gaol for assault!'

He tried to have me charged. But even his mate admitted that he rushed at me aggressively and swearing. I truthfully said I pushed him back. Not to be denied, he took out an Apprehended Violence Order (AVO) against me and the magistrate forbid me to go within 500 metres of him – effectively preventing me from visiting John and Gloria. This was later changed to allow me to come to the units to see my family but to avoid Tom. If I saw him I had to walk away.

Faye retaliated by applying for an AVO against him and it was granted. Once while I was at Gloria's place someone slashed the four tyres of my car and inflicted deep scratches on two of the doors. I never found out who the culprit was.

Faye insisted on us leaving Eastwood and we rented a unit in Queanbeyan – 290 kilometres from Sydney and only a twenty minute drive to Canberra. The rent was only $100 per week.

Faye soon found work in a local cafe and again felt safe.

Every day I went to the casino and, using a bank of $1000, I would walk out as soon as I won $100. Working on the premise that if I lost my bank once, I would finish $1900 ahead per month – tax free. Financially we were better off than when I was working for ICS and tutoring at nights.

A SERIOUS AFFAIR

1996

By mid-1996 I was driving the 600 kilometre return trip twice a week to meet Lucy. At least once a week after leaving her close to Anna's school before she finished class I would drive to Milson's Point and visit John and Gloria. Sometimes I would do a third trip on the weekend to bring Faye to visit her son.

When I could manage it, I would drive to Collaroy to see Lyn.

I began to get pains in the chest and the doctor told me to slow down – I had high blood pressure. He wanted to prescribe some medication but I refused. The medication often produced side effects and I preferred to risk it. I began to feel guilty that Lucy had no idea about my background. I decided the best way to make her cognisant with all the facts was to give her a copy of a 1994 HQ Magazine which had published an article I had written about robbing banks and my escape from Queensland. Unaware of what the article was about she assured me she would read it while Alex was at work. When we parted that day, I had grave doubts that I would hear from her again.

I didn't call her, figuring that if she was still interested she would call me.

She rang on the third day. 'Did you read the article?'

'Yes. You are the mystery man.'

I laughed, relieved that she seemed okay about it. 'I wouldn't call it that, but can I see you tomorrow?'

'This can be arranged. I will be at the cafe ten o'clock. I want you to tell me more about you and this girl.'

'Well the story covers most of it. She's married now.'

'I would like to meet her.'

'She's in South Australia.'

'Still. Tomorrow you can tell me everything. This is exciting story.'

The next morning, I drove to Macquarie Centre and met her at a cafe. I immediately noticed she had cuts and bruising around her left eye.

'What happened to your eye?'

'Big scandal over a pot plant.'

'I have to confront him, Luce.'

'No. He mustn't know about you. Not yet.'

'Well do me a favour and go and make a report to a doctor. I'll drive you.'

'No, Boy. I'm okay. Let's go to a motel.'

We spent a couple of hours at a motel at West Ryde which had become a regular rendezvous spot for us. There was a golf links at the back of the motel where Lucy liked to go for a walk.

'No dobbers will see us here,' she said. 'If Alex knew about you there would be the world's biggest scandal. Now tell me about this girl who risked her life to get you from the hospital, Boy.'

'Her name is Jackie. We spent about three years together. We didn't work, we stole and sometimes I robbed banks.'

'So...you really are a bad guy. A Ned Kelly.'

I laughed. 'Ned Kelly wasn't such a bad guy. But yes, I am a bad guy, or at least I was.'

'Do you still see Jackie?'

'Since she got married I've seen her three times.'

'You know exactly how many times you've seen her, this to me means you still think about her.'

'It means I've got a good memory.' I grabbed her and pulled her towards me. 'When you are finished with me will you still think about me?'

She grinned. 'It's probable that I won't. When it's finished, it's finished.'

'So your previous lovers, you don't think about them?'

'No, I think about you, Boy. You are different to all the men I have met.'

'Different in what way?'

'All those years wasted in prison. Other men were living their lives, you were in a cell.'

'But you couldn't tell that when you met me. You thought I was a gentleman.'

'You are a gentleman, more than Alex could ever be. But how was it, living in normal world after forever in prison. How could you adapt?'

'I've never had problems with it. But when you spend a long period in prison a lot changes in society. In the sixties and early seventies, I didn't have access to newspapers or TV and I didn't even know a man had walked on the moon until months later. Nowadays most prisoners have access to televisions and radios. They know what is going on in the outside world.'

'You missed out on a lot, Boy. But you are having good time now, eh?'

She was grinning her sexy grin.

'True. But you Russians can be big trouble.' An understatement.

Until June 1997 the affair with Lucy ran smoothly without anyone being the wiser. The previous year she had terminated the affair with her other lover and our relationship grew stronger. Then she decided it was time for her to leave Alex.

Her main concern was Anna. During the past six months she had brought Anna to meet me on four or five occasions. We often went to a park or a cafe.

She told me that Anna liked me but thought I was a bit 'old.'

'We should go on a holiday together for two weeks,' Lucy said. 'If Anna accepts you I will leave Alex and we will live with you.'

'I have to tell you that I like to gamble at the casinos, sometimes late at night,' I said.

'No matter. You told me this before and that you win.' She smiled. 'Otherwise where do you get your money, eh? Is poor boy robbing banks again, eh? Tell me.'

I laughed. 'No, I am not robbing banks again. If I do, you will be the first to know.'

We arranged for a trip for late June. When I told Faye that I was involved with Lucy, she demanded that I finish it. 'I don't want to finish it, Faye.'

'You take this trip with her and you decide. It's her or me. You can't have both.'

About a week before the proposed holiday I met Lucy in our favourite cafe. She again had bruising around her eye.

'Why did he hit you this time?'

'I told Alex I was going to leave him. This information caused great scandal. According to Alex, when time comes he will leave me. Until then I will remain slave. Last time I got bashed over pot plant. This time for more serious reason.'

'That's it. I'll go and give him some of his own medicine.'

'No. He will run screaming to police. He is a coward. Last night we had fight, but his arms are longer than mine so I picked up a chair and chased him into Anna's room and he locked the door.'

(Three years later Lucy wrote: 'Probably in any family, husband and wife get upset of each other time to time, but not every day! What always surprised me was the cause for scandals. Say, how many husbands can make an ugly scandal with bashing because of tiny indoor plant? I think 99 per cent of them even wouldn't notice it. The meal, plants, furniture weren't real cause of scandals. I think it was execution of Alex idea: 'You suppress me, or I suppress you.' So you can make your choice why I left Alex. There is plenty to choose out of...')

Lucy left all the furniture, even the computer for Alex. She also left a note explaining that the marriage was a torture and she was leaving him. She had done his washing and after that he would manage...

We drove to Broadbeach on the Gold Coast where I rented a small unit for two weeks. Alex was ringing her three or four times a day. Sometimes the phone calls went for thirty minutes. Lucy would pace up and down outside the motel while talking to him in Russian. Most of the time she looked stressed. In 1999, she wrote:

'...Alex rang every day asked me to come back promising everything possible and impossible, threatening me with suicide. Once he rang and said that he is HIV positive. I was horrified.

'One day the owner of motel said to John:

'Do you know tall, dark haired, very skinny man with glasses?' We looked at each other. It can't be true. He is in Sydney!

'You see yesterday in the night this man fell off the tree. The neighbour's dog was chasing him. Our neighbours awoke up and called the police. This man told police that he was watching his wife. I asked him to leave the motel.'

Lucy had told Alex where we were and while pretending to be in Sydney he had driven to the Gold Coast and rented a room directly opposite us. He had been watching us all the time. He had also hired a private detective to follow me, probably hoping to find me engaged in some criminal activity. The detective had checked me out and revealed to Alex my criminal record. Apart from spending a few hours each day at Jupiter's Casino, I was always with Lucy and Anna. I had no idea at the time that I was being spied on. The private dick came up with zero. In his report, he stated that we seemed like an ordinary happy family. Lucy told me this upset Alex.

After learning about the tree incident we packed and left. We had only travelled 50 metres when the car broke down. I arranged for it to be towed to a mechanic who told me sand had been put into the petrol tank. It cost a few hundred and a half a day to get it fixed.

We drove to Sydney where we booked into a motel. When Alex rang Lucy and said that he had moved out of the unit into a place near the New South Wales University she believed him and returned home, on the understanding she would soon take Anna to Russia to see her grandparents while she decided what she would do regarding me and Alex.

Returning to Queanbeyan and Faye, I brought her up to date on the situation. 'She's returning to Russia,' I said.

Lucy rang me the next day complaining that Alex had moved back in and had cut his wrists in front of Anna. Now she was feeling guilty.

'The best thing you can do,' I said, 'is to fly to Russia as soon as you can.' The day before she left for Russia I met her in town. Alex had bought return tickets for her and Anna but had only given her a paltry amount of money to spend.

'He said everything is cheap in Russia,' Lucy told me. 'I will have to rely on my parents for everything while I am there. The only reason he sends me to Russia is so I get away from you.'

I gave her $500 and grinned. 'It's not much, but things are cheap in Russia.'

Normally she would have laughed but she was stressed: 'I don't think I want to go, Boy. Anna and I should come and live with you in this Quean Bay place.'

'It's too late, you have the tickets and your parents want to see Anna. You'll only be gone for three weeks. Anyway, I will have to arrange for another place. Faye wouldn't be too happy about us all living together.'

They flew out early the next morning.

At this stage, I had applied for a job with Juvenile Justice – working with kids in trouble in the Queanbeyan area. After a positive interview with the Director General, Ken Buttram, at his city office I was confident of being given the position. I would supervise juveniles doing community service on court orders around Queanbeyan. I could also help illiterate kids to read and write as I had a certificate in teaching Literacy and Numeracy. The local juvenile justice officers were supportive, believing I was better equipped to deal with tough kids on the brink of incarceration than the fresh-faced, inexperienced university graduates who were often intimidated by them. After being given a police clearance I received the following letter from the NSW Juvenile Justice Department: (29 September 1997)

'Dear Mr Killick – I am pleased to advise after careful consideration of your recent representations and the favourable outcome of referee checks, the department will be able to offer you employment as a sessional supervisor on a three-month trial period when work becomes available...'

But work never became available. Every day I called into the office only to be told: 'Nothing for you today.'

I was later informed that the local magistrate had learnt of the intention to give me work and had declared: 'I won't have this man working with my children.'

'Her children' were the same kids she was locking up in juvenile detention centres.

When the job offer was withdrawn I was depressed. For a few years I had developed a great rapport with my students when tutoring composition English – most of them from middle class or rich households. When it came to dealing with kids from dysfunctional families around Queanbeyan who were close to being incarcerated, I felt I was the right man for the job. When Lucy returned, Alex nearly pulled off a masterstroke. My licence had been suspended for three months due to speeding fines. Alex had learned this information via numerous phone calls to Lucy during her stay there. Why she told him I have no idea. It was later revealed that he was recording all phone calls with her, me and quite a few other people. Some of the conversations with Lucy were quite bizarre.

She later wrote: 'Alex rang very often and every time he gave me "some news".'

'Do you know that John gave you drugs without your knowledge?'

???

'Yes, I sent your underwear to USA and I've got result.'

'Then he listed long list of drugs with very complicated names. The easiest to recall was marijuana. 'But Alex, marijuana is for smoking and I don't smoke at all. Plus, if John gave me drugs I have to feel that because I am in Russia without John's supply.'

'Silence. Then: 'Let's drop the subject. Do you know that as soon as your plane lands in Sydney you'll be arrested?'

'What for?'

'Police'll let you know then. And John is going to kill you and Anna.'

'Non-stop nonsense. At airport instead of police there were John and Alex.'

I was lucky to be there. Alex had contacted Queanbeyan police and told them I was driving without a licence. When I set off for the airport the police were waiting for me at the turnoff on to the highway. I had two weeks left before the disqualification ran out. I was taken to Queanbeyan Police Station where I had to wait two hours until Faye arrived to bail me out. There was no way I could get to the airport in time. But the best laid plans of rats and men... Lucy's plane was delayed in Vietnam. Her brother rang me from Russia with the news and Faye drove me to the airport in time for the arrival. When Alex saw me he came over and told me to go.

'She is my wife,' he said.

'If she tells me to go, I'll go,' I said. 'But she won't – she's finished with you.'

When Lucy confirmed that their marriage was over and she was going with me, he persuaded her to let him take Anna for an ice cream so he could spend some time with her. We didn't see Anna again for three days. Alex, who was now working and living in Canberra, drove her the 300 kilometres to his place. Although Lucy called the police, there was nothing they could do. Thus began a series of drawn out Family Court battles that stressed all of us to the limit. Custody of Anna was shared: usually she lived with Lucy on weekdays and with Alex on weekends. I rented a two-bedroom unit in Queanbeyan for Lucy and Anna. At this stage I had moved out of the unit I shared with Faye and moved into a caravan park. The court wouldn't allow me to live with Anna after Alex complained that I was a dangerous criminal.

After a while I challenged this decision and the ruling was rescinded. Not long after I had moved in with Lucy, Alex was twice discovered by a neighbour outside our door with sound equipment. On the second occasion the neighbour called the police who gave him a caution. Alex later stated in an affidavit that when he listened outside our door he heard the unmistakable sounds of sexual intercourse while his daughter was living there.

The full extent of Alex's snooping became apparent in a document filed by police in the Queanbeyan Magistrate's court when Lucy made an Apprehended Domestic/Personal Violence application. It stated:

'...About 10.30 pm on the 23.9.97 the defendant was located outside the PINOP's home by police and told to leave. About 2.50 am on the 24.9.97

the defendant was located by police outside the PINOP's home. He was in possession of a video camera and told police he was conducting surveillance of his ex-wife for the case before the Family Law Court. About 1.25 am on the 26.9.97 the defendant was again located by police outside the PINOP's home. He left after he was directed to do so by S/C HUGHES of the Queanbeyan Police...'

One night Anna rang Lucy, she was crying. Alex had overturned the car while driving. Both were okay but shook up.

'This is my worry,' Lucy said to me. 'Alex is hopeless driver. Always in accidents. This time they were lucky, next time Anna could get hurt.'

It must be a Russian thing. Lucy was also a hopeless driver. She told me about the time in Russia when her father commanded a military base and had a military jeep with a driver supplied. The driver, Anatoliy, decided to teach teenage Lucy to drive. They drove on open fields and hills with no trees or other traffic around. The chances of being involved in an accident were almost non-existent. But Lucy found a way. She drove it straight into a small lake. Both of them had to be rescued. Furious, her father decided to teach her to drive. On the first lesson she drove into a large hole. A military truck was used to drag it out.

Her father declared: 'Lucy should never drive a car.'

But on 22 November 1997 I wasn't aware of these disasters. I remember the date because later that night the singer Michael Hutchens was found dead in his hotel room. It was also the thirty-fourth anniversary of John F. Kennedy's assassination.

It was a Saturday. We had a winning day at Canberra Casino and in high spirits we decided to drive to Sydney. Lucy wanted to drive. I had been at the casino until the early hours of the morning and didn't argue.

'Keep in the left lane and don't go over 110 and you'll be fine,' I said.

I must have dozed off. About 10 kilometres from Goulburn I came to my senses with a jolt. We were swerving from side to side! The car smashed into a railing that prevented us from going over a small bridge down onto an embankment, where no doubt we would have been killed.

Apart from Lucy breaking her glasses and receiving a slight cut above the eye, both of us escaped unscathed. The car, my last remaining asset, was a write off.

'What happened?'

'Rabbit,' she said.

'Okay, keep your cool. That was one lucky rabbit.'

A guy had pulled up behind us. He was talking into his phone. I walked to his vehicle.

'I just called the police,' he said. 'Are you all right?'

'Both of us are fine, thanks.' I gave him a hard stare. 'I was driving.' He met my gaze. 'Okay.'

Two police cars came. An old sergeant was in charge. He was a no-nonsense type of a guy. 'How did it happen?'

I felt like an idiot when I said: 'A rabbit ran out onto the road and I instinctively hit the brakes. The car began to swerve and I hit the railing.'

'A fucken rabbit! Why didn't you run over it?' I shrugged. 'Reflexes.'

He got angry. 'Listen, it's Saturday night, later I will have a town full of drunks and we are understaffed. I'm seriously thinking of charging you with negligent driving. And on top of that you will be getting a bill for the damage to the railing.'

But he didn't charge me and I never received a bill. After arranging a tow truck we were driven into Goulburn by two young cops who told us not to worry about the sergeant, he was always like that. We booked into a hotel for the night. The next morning I rented a car and we drove to Sydney where we spent some time with John and Gloria. Lucy and Gloria always got along well which eased the pressure on us during difficult times.

OFFICER – THAT MAN'S GOT A GUN!

1997–98

Alex twice tried to impose an AVO against me but the magistrate refused to comply. There were incidents and once Alex accused me of hitting him and breaking his glasses after he smashed a new pair of glasses we had bought for Anna. Lucy and I told police Alex had hit his head on the steering wheel when he jumped into his car while I, admittedly, was chasing him. All storms in a teacup stuff.

Apart from Family Court appearances, we also had to deal with various matters in the Magistrate's Court, due to the occasional AVO taken out by Alex against me, another taken out against him by Lucy and another one filed against him by Faye after he began harassing her. Add to that my traffic matters and a property hearing and we were in and out of court nearly every week.

Early in 1998 I obtained for Lucy a small, silver Derringer .22 pistol. It was nicknamed the 'assassin's gun'. Small enough to cover in the hand, it had twin barrels each holding one bullet. Most of the time she carried it in her purse. When I wasn't around, it made her feel safe.

One day we were waiting outside Canberra Magistrate's Court where Lucy was scheduled to be heard on a property dispute. Alex had refused to give her any of the property they had accumulated together, including important documents and photos.

About ten minutes before we were due to enter court I saw Alex talking to two uniformed cops and pointing in my direction.

I glanced at Lucy. 'What's he up to now?' They began to walk towards us.

'Careful, Boy.'

'He probably told them I hit him again. I'm getting sick of it.'

'We've had a complaint that you are carrying a weapon on you,' one of the cops said. They stood either side of me.

'Let me guess,' I said. 'You received your misinformation from that ugly cretin standing over there smirking at us.'

'It doesn't matter where we received our information, it is a serious complaint and we have to follow it up. I want you to stand with your face to the wall and place your hands in the air while I search you.'

'I have a mobile phone in the left hand pocket of my jacket,' I said.

Apart from the phone, they found nothing. 'Sorry, sir, we have to check these things.'

'This guy is a vexatious litigant – he is always making false accusations against me.'

'Well, you should make a complaint about that.' They walked away. I turned to Lucy. 'Did you bring your gun?'

'Of course.'

We both burst out laughing. Alex was watching, he was grinning. 'Look at him. He has no idea how close he came to spoiling our party.'

We were in for another shock. I was banned from entering the court, ordered by the magistrate. He had been told about the incident and didn't want to risk my being present. So Lucy, assassin's gun in her purse, went into court and argued valiantly for a share of their property. But the magistrate knew about me and told her that she would have to rely on me to provide her with new property.

'We reap what we sow,' he told her.

When Lucy joined me she was upset. 'I am sure I will never see my history thesis again,' she said. 'He has probably destroyed it.'

Not long afterwards the Family Court ordered us to move to Canberra if we wanted to share custody of Anna. Short on funds, I borrowed $10,000 from a well-known Sydney criminal. My credit was good: I always paid back.

About this time a lone bandit, who according to witness accounts was a very fast runner, entered the Commonwealth Bank in Mittagong, disarmed a security guard, took his pistol and escaped with a large sum of money.

Lucy and I often dropped into Mittagong when returning to Queanbeyan from Sydney, usually for coffee or to place a bet on the TAB which was across the road from the bank. The lady in the cafe told us about the robbery.

'The police station was closed down and the bandit must have known this,' she said.

I kept in mind what she told us. A country town of this size should have a police station.

And, over the next four months, that's the way it played out. To Anna it was a game, organised, I have no doubts, by Alex.

• • •

We rented a three-bedroom house in Aranda, not far from where Alex now lived in Cook. The fight for Anna was in full swing. The Family Court judge gave us custody Monday to Saturday morning, when Alex would call and take her until we picked her up from school Monday afternoon.

A few times she ran away causing Lucy extreme stress. She always went to Alex's place so I wasn't overly concerned: but then something happened that changed my mind.

I was upstairs when Lucy, who had been playing with Anna in the backyard, yelled out that she had gone.

'We know where she's going,' I said. 'You cut under the tunnel and across the park and I'll drive to the highway where she has to cross to get there.'

When I reached the main road I saw her, waiting for a break in traffic. I parked half on the street, half on the footpath and, with the motor running, ran across and grabbed her just as she began to cross. I threw her across my shoulder and ran to the car.

'Damn!' she said.

I put her in the front seat, fastened her seat belt and drove off.

No one took any notice! The realisation sent a chill through me. I could have been a predator!

I told Lucy: 'This can't go on. From now on one of us watches her every moment.'

THE MITTAGONG BANK ROBBERY

1998

In early August 1998, Alex requested permission from the court to have a copy of my criminal record. Because his daughter spent five days a week living with me he argued he was entitled to ascertain whether or not I had any convictions for drugs or sexual assault.

'I can assure Your Honour that he has no convictions for either,' my lawyer said.

But the judge allowed him to have a copy on the proviso that it was private and he could not reveal its contents to anyone.

Alex went to the place where I hired cars and showed it to them; he went to Anna's school and showed the teachers; and he sent copies to police in every state asking if there was a warrant out for me.

He hit the jackpot in Queensland. They did a little checking and decided that I owed them time over the 1983 bank robbery that I had been released on parole for in February 1992. The bond I had received in 1993 for possession of a pistol had technically broken my parole – even though the parole had finished in 1994 and it was now 1998. Queensland always get their man.

On the night of 27 August 1998, the Federal police came to our house and told me they had a warrant for my arrest. I would be extradited to Queensland the following morning. I had to take my hat off to Alex, his persistence had paid off. With me out of the way Lucy would be at his mercy – although she did have the little Derringer...

The cops knew me and were a little sympathetic. They had been involved in some of the situations when Anna ran away and I knew most of them had no time for Alex.

'Tell you what we'll do, John. You present yourself at court tomorrow at 9.30 am and we will leave you here with Lucy tonight.'

'That's decent of you,' I said. 'This has come as a big shock.'

'Well, we know who you are and we know you have been playing a straight bat, so we are giving you this break. Don't make it worse on yourself by not turning up.'

'My running days are over,' I said.

After they had gone, Lucy looked at me. 'We have to run, Boy.'

'I'll ring Bruce Miles first.'

I explained the situation to him. 'They have you cold,' he said. 'If it was a court matter we could fight it, but it is a parole matter – in their eyes you are still a prisoner and they can put you back in gaol and you can't appeal it.'

I thanked him and hung up. 'Well, Luce, we can go on the run, or I can go to gaol for a couple of years. Not a good choice is it?'

'I'm with you, Boy. You can't go to gaol. Anna is now my big worry.'

'We can't take her with us on the run. If you go with me, Alex wins.'

'I can still fight for her, she is my child.'

'Maybe I can get this straightened out. We'll go into hiding, and I'll write to the authorities and try to get some type of deal.'

After dropping Anna off at school we drove to Sydney and booked into a motel. Lucy rang Alex and told him he could have Anna until the custody battle was finally resolved.

Alex was well aware of the situation and laughed at her. We were in a tight spot. We had lost our $1000 bond, left our furniture and most of our belongings at the house and I had to sell the car because it was known to police. I still had a few thousand dollars left but expenses would now be high. We had no other income and it's not as if we could go to Centrelink. I wrote a four page letter to the Director General of Brisbane Corrective Services explaining that I had not been in hiding and had been in Family Court hearings at least a dozen times. I wrote that I had applied for and been accepted for a position with the Juvenile Justice Department and they did a police check on me. Were these the actions of a man on the run? I stated I was prepared to hand myself in to the authorities with a lawyer if he insisted. I concluded by saying I hoped he would reply to the letter and advise me of what should and could be done. I gave Gloria's address but I never received a reply. Instead I received a phone call from a Queensland cop who told me there would be no deals and if I didn't surrender he would hunt me down like a dog. I told him to carry on dreaming.

We were now under enormous pressure. I knew that it was only a matter of time before I was forced out of retirement and hit a bank. Security was a lot tougher these days: apart from CCTV everywhere, most of the banks had pop-up security screens. I had known a guy who was trapped by the neck when one was activated in a bank at St Leonards – he died a horrible death. Two other would-be bank robbers I knew – both Romanians – were trapped by a pop-up screen, one by the neck, the other by the arm. Fortunately for them the staff deactivated the screen and with the aid of customers arrested them. The young guy who had been trapped by the neck and wore a brace for about three months often complained to me that the customers laughed at him while he was helplessly hanging there. The humiliation bank robbers have to go through at times...

I remembered what the lady in the cafe at Mittagong had told me about the local Commonwealth Bank – a large amount of money had been stolen and the police station had been closed down. I decided to drive there and check it out. My main concern was the security guard. If the bandit had disarmed him last time he would no doubt have a contingency plan.

To my surprise, there was no security guard in the bank or outside it. There were also no security pop-up screens. It looked too easy. Maybe the security guard had a day off. I decided to check it again in a few days' time. I also walked around to the old police station – it was deserted.

Two days later, same scenario. At the rear of the bank there was a side street. I followed it until I came to a passageway that led back onto the main street near the post office which had a small car park. I figured I could run out of the bank into the side street, down to the passageway and then walk onto the main street and into the car park where I could drive away. If I wasn't followed no one would have any idea how I got away. If someone did follow me I would have to waylay them in the passageway and make them an offer they couldn't refuse.

Robbing a bank is a big decision. If I did it and came unstuck, I would probably, this time, die in gaol. My son John had recently gone to China and was engaged to be married. I would probably never see him again. My mind urged me to hit this bank...my heart told me to first try something else.

I borrowed another $10,000. I had nearly paid the last lot back and had no problems borrowing. I always paid top interest. My lender had no idea I was on the run or he probably would have turned me down.

Within hours I was at Star City Casino. I would play $1000 a hand at baccarat and either win $10,000 or lose $10,000. If I won I could pay back the money and we would have a good bank to live on. If I lost, well I always had Mittagong.

With Lucy by my side I played for about three hours. At one stage I was $7000 in front, another time I was down to $1000 and pulled back to be $3000 in front. It was about 3:00 am when we walked out in to the cold night air with only a few hundred dollars to our name.

'What do we do now, Boy?'

'I have to pay the $10,000 back and then get some cash for us. I'll have to rob a bank.'

For a few moments she was silent as she walked beside me. Then she said: 'Count me in.'

I had no intention of getting her involved but she needn't know that yet. 'Okay. We have a lot of planning to do before we reach that stage.'

Borrowing another $2000 from a different friend, I bought an old Toyota for $800.

'This will be the getaway car,' I told Lucy. 'It can't be traced to us.'

A few nights later an extraordinary thing happened. Driving the Toyota, we went to Canterbury Leagues Club for dinner. We stayed for about an hour then on the way out, Lucy asked me if she could drive. After the rabbit incident at Goulburn I had been reluctant to let her drive the rental cars we had been using but she thought she was going to be the getaway driver during the bank robbery so she argued she needed the driving practice.

'Okay,' I said, handing her the keys. 'But you must drive straight over any rabbits, cats or dogs that run out in front of you.'

'Boy is a comedian.'

'No, I'm serious.'

She walked over to the car, opened the door and got inside. Getting into the passenger seat I gave her a few instructions.

'Boy, I know how to drive.'

'I know, but you don't have a licence. The cops are red hot at this time of night around here and I'm a wanted man.'

'Poor, poor Boy is frightened.' She drove out of the carpark, just missing a stationary vehicle.

'Slow down, Luce, we aren't in a hurry.'

She drove steadily for a few kilometres when I realised there was something wrong. 'This isn't our car!' I said.

'What are you talking about?'

'This is not our car! Turn around and drive back to the club.'

'This is big mystery, Boy. Maybe it's a trap.'

'No trap, you got into the wrong car.'

'So did you.'

'Just drive back.'

'Seems to me strange. Two cars same type, same colour, same key, parked in same place at same time. Seems to me this is trap.'

'A trap for what? Stealing a car? They already want me in Queensland for a more serious matter. This is just one of those extraordinary coincidences.' And it was. We returned to the carpark, locked the vehicle and drove away in our own Toyota. No one was any the wiser that we had actually stolen their car and taken it for a short drive. Later when I told people about this, they were skeptical that it happened. But Lucy and I will never forget it.

My main concern about robbing the bank in Mittagong was to be able to get out of town and on to the freeway before they could put up any roadblocks. With the police station closed down, the odds were in my favour. Police coming from other areas wouldn't know what they were looking for. I had no doubts that even at fifty-six years of age I was still capable of successfully robbing a bank.

In early October I bought a blond wig that would give me a younger appearance. Maybe the police would think the young guy who had robbed the bank in May had struck again. I borrowed a pistol from a guy who never asked questions. I had thought about using Lucy's Derringer but figured there was a chance someone might think it was a toy and jump me.

When Lucy saw the pistol she knew what I was up to. 'Whatever you are going to do, I am with you, Boy.'

'Okay. All I'm doing today is checking everything out. No need for you to come.'

'But I need to know area, Boy. I should come.'

'We can do that later, when I am sure of what I'm doing.' I gave her a hug. 'I'll be back later, we'll go for dinner and I'll explain it all to you.'

I walked out, got in the car and drove to Mittagong. I figured that as a getaway driver, Lucy would be a handicap.

Driving into the post office parking lot I got out of the car and walked to the passageway where I put on the wig and a cap. Under the wig I had a stocking ready to pull down over my face as I walked into the bank. When you do something like this your senses are on high alert, you notice everything and everyone around you. I knew that if anyone took a good look at me it could arouse their suspicions. But the only person who took any notice of me was a little girl who looked to be about six. She was staring at me from the back seat of a car, parked at the side of the bank. She was alone in the vehicle and I figured the parent must have gone into one of the shops. I was only 20 metres from the entrance around the corner. I waved at her and she waved back. I pulled a funny face at her and she gave me one back. Wonderful rapport between a little girl and a guy about to rob a bank.

Slipping the stocking down over my face, I walked into the bank. There were a lot of people inside. I looked for the security guard – he wasn't there.

Holding the pistol in my right hand I placed a plastic shopping bag on the counter. 'This is a hold-up everyone! I'm here for the bank's money, not yours.' I looked at the two female tellers. 'Fill the bag up, big notes, no fives or coins!'

I stepped back, surveying the customers. An old guy, who looked to be about eighty, walked towards me. 'You don't scare me!' he said. 'I'll take that gun off you and ram it.'

What do you do? I had to demonstrate I was in charge here. 'Get back old man or I'll shoot you!'

He stepped back and said nothing. I later received more criticism for the way I spoke to him than for robbing the bank. But I did what I had to do. I had no intention of shooting him. Of course he didn't know that, but it is not a good idea for eighty-year-olds to be tackling desperate armed robbers.

One of the tellers handed me the bag and told me that was all there was.

They all say that. I don't think I've ever argued – I just grab the money and run.

'If anyone comes after me, I'll shoot!' I said as I backed out the door. I ran as fast as I could, past the little girl who was still in the vehicle. I didn't have time to give her a wave. Good luck to the cops if they tried to get a description from her, she'd tell them about the funny face.

They said the last guy who robbed this bank was very fast; I wouldn't have been as fast as him, but in less than fifteen seconds after exiting the bank I was in the passageway. Pulling off the wig, stocking and cap I placed them in the bag and walked out to the main street – a grey-haired gentleman. Walking casually to the car park, I drove out of town without incident.

After paying all debts I still had more than $10,000 to play with. Although Lucy was aware I had made a hit, I refused to give her any details. 'If I'm ever caught, you can't be charged with withholding knowledge of a crime,' I said.

'We are always the team, Boy. Next time I'm in. Promise me.'

'Okay, I promise.'

I was hopeful there wouldn't be a next time.

WHERE WAS LUCY?

1999

Despite being out of debt and having more than $10,000 to spare, our situation was dire. Because Lucy was with me, a man on the run, Alex was in the box seat regarding the custody battle. Lucy was still fighting and a final decision hadn't been made by the court, but we both knew that while she was with me she wouldn't have custody. Christmas and New Year were particularly stressful times for her.

I seriously considered handing myself in to the Queensland authorities. We had enough money for Lucy to rent a place and with the aid of Centrelink she could revert to having shared custody of Anna. Every few months she could travel to Queensland to visit me. With luck I would be out in a year. It would be tough, but at least everything would be legal. But Lucy feared for her safety if I was in gaol.

'I could go missing and Alex would say your criminal friends got me.'

So we carried on. Lucy's divorce came through in January 1999. Expenses were heavy and by early January we were down to less than $3000. I had stopped going to the casino and racetracks knowing these venues would be the first place police would look for me.

In mid-January I told Lucy I would have to hit a bank. 'This time I will come with you,' she said.

I thought about it. 'Maybe you could dress up as a boy. As long as you didn't talk it would completely fool them.'

She was excited. 'This is brilliant idea, Boy. I will take my little toy.'

'First I have to find a bank, probably in the country. Security is too tight in the city.'

I figured Bowral, 6 kilometres south of Mittagong, would be worth the risk. I had previously checked it out and unlike the city and suburbs of Sydney, there were no security pop-up screens or bulletproof partitions separating customers from the tellers. Although there was a police station a few blocks away, I anticipated being in and out before they could get organised. I would be on the freeway before they could set up a roadblock. Too many people had seen me driving the Toyota so I sold it for peanuts and rented a sedan. Deciding to leave Lucy out of it, I set off for Bowral.

There was no way she could pass for a boy. I would do the job alone....

• • •

When they took me to Bowral Police Station the old sergeant told me I had been unlucky. 'He's the only cop in Bowral who would chase an armed robber unarmed,' he said.

'It wasn't my lucky day,' I said. 'The dye bomb did the damage.'

'Well, there's a gang who have been hitting banks from Wollongong to Moss Vale lately, so that's probably why they were prepared this time. Must say, it's the first time I've seen one used. You've certainly livened up the town. Usually not much happens around here.'

I didn't mention the backpacker murders. (In January 1990, the serial killer Ivan Milat tried to kidnap an English tourist, Paul Onions, who had hitched a ride with him south of Mittagong. Although Milat fired a shot at him, Onions managed to get away, flagging down a passing motorist. They drove to Bowral Police Station where Onions, supported by his rescuer, Joanne Berry, made a statement detailing the crime. But the police didn't follow up on it and it wasn't until 1994, when Superintendent Clive Small asked for the original report, that it was discovered it was missing from the files. A constable had made detailed notes of the statement in her notebook and Small and his team were able to access these notes in 1994. But the seven murders Milat was later convicted of occurred between 1989 and 1993.)

Detectives MacDonald and Pascoe interviewed me electronically.

We had come a long way since the bad old days of police verbal and unsigned records of interview which were often fabrications.

These two cops were fair, but convinced I had robbed the Commonwealth Bank in Mittagong twice.

'If that was the case where is the weapon you said was stolen from the security guard?' I asked.

'We will find it when we search your place.'

I refused to tell them where I lived. I had to give Lucy a chance to hide her Derringer.

After about four hours of stalemate, Lucy rang Bowral from Gloria's place asking if I was there.

'Yes, he is,' was the reply. 'How did you know?'

'Heard it on the news. Can I come and see him?'

'He will be going to Silverwater tomorrow; you will have to arrange a visit with him there.'

The detectives began to suspect that Lucy might have been in Bowral and escaped with the money.

'Wouldn't be much good to her,' I said. 'It was covered in dye.'

'There would be some she could use,' Pascoe said.

'She wasn't in town.'

'We'll check her mobile,' MacDonald said. 'If she was in the area we will find out.'

'Lucy had nothing to do with this,' I said. 'She has enough problems with custody battles over her daughter without being dragged into a bank robbery that she knows nothing about.'

'Look, John, we didn't give your name out to the media. How did she know it was you when she heard the news?'

'I told her I was visiting a friend in Bowral. She knows my history for robbing banks. When I didn't come home and she heard about the bank robbery she would have put two and two together.'

'Well, we will have to check her out.'

'Leave her out of all of this and I'll do a deal with you.'

'What sort of deal?'

'I will plead guilty to the Mittagong bank robbery in October if you drop off Lucy and just leave her alone. She had nothing to do with any of this.'

'We know you did Mittagong twice, John,' MacDonald said. 'Plead to both and you have a deal.'

'No way will I plead guilty to something I didn't do. From all accounts the guy who robbed it in May was a young guy and a very fast runner.'

'The bloke who robbed it in October looked young and was also a fast runner,' Pascoe said. 'That wig you had on today made you look like a young bloke.'

'Look, I didn't do it. There's no deal.'

MacDonald sighed. 'Okay, John, here's what we'll do. You give us a statement confessing to the October robbery and we will take your word that Lucy wasn't involved in anything.'

'You won't hassle her?'

MacDonald nodded. 'You have my word. But we will also charge you with the Commonwealth Bank robbery in May.'

'That's your prerogative, but you will get nowhere with it. I didn't do it.' They didn't charge me with it that night. No doubt they tried to find more evidence than what they had – which was a big zero. I admitted to the Bowral robbery and the Mittagong robbery in October. I also admitted to shooting with intent to avoid arrest. Some media outlets reported it as 'intent to murder'. *The Australian* reported that I shot and wounded a cop.

This was later picked up by author Paul B. Kidd, who erroneously wrote the same fiction in his book *Australian Crime File.*

When I found out about it I wrote to Paul and his publisher The Five Mile Press, complaining that they should check their facts and not rely on newspaper reports.

Both the publisher and Paul wrote to me apologising. The error would be rectified in the next reprint. Paul wrote that 'as much as I strive for perfection...'

So I didn't push for the book to be pulped. When I had O'Mealley's book pulped I felt justified because he had deliberately lied about me as well as plagiarised another book. It was different with Paul who strove for perfection but failed.

A TRIP TO QUEANBEYAN

1999

At Silverwater, nearly all the cells held two prisoners each. My cellmate was only eighteen – a total mismatch. He had reddish hair, was thin and I noticed a few pimples on his face.

As I entered the cell he stared at me, obviously disappointed that he had an old guy for a cellmate.

'Hi,' I said. 'I'm John. What's your name?'

'Brett,' he said and continued to watch the television.

He obviously wasn't interested in small talk which suited me. I was in dire straits and was aware that I may never be a free man again. What would Lucy do? What a mess! That night I didn't get much sleep.

The next day I filled out the forms for a phone call, but I was told it would take a few days before the numbers were checked allowing me to ring. The cops had told Lucy where I'd be so hopefully Gloria would explain to her how to ring and book a visit. I was confident she would come to see me on Saturday.

Late on the Friday night, Brett decided to watch the music programme *Rage*. Although it was nearly midnight, he turned up the volume.

Over the years I had spent in prison I had learnt to switch off. But there was no way I could sleep with the music blaring and the kid occasionally singing along with it.

After about half an hour I got up, grabbed the remote and turned down the sound. Jumping out of bed he tried to take the remote from me. 'Give it back!' he said.

I pushed him back. 'Listen, fuckwit, you are lucky you're in a cell with me and not a few guys I know. If you want the TV on you will show respect and keep the volume low.'

He glared at me. 'I was in this cell first.'

'I'm not going to argue with you. I need some sleep. Either you keep the sound down or I'll switch the TV off.'

'I can't listen to Rage with the sound down.'

Now I was in a rage. I switched the TV off. 'You can watch it in the morning with the volume up.'

He lunged at me, trying to snatch the remote. I grabbed his arm and twisted it behind his back. He had the strength of a kitten. He began to scream out. I let him go.

'Get out of this cell in the morning,' I said. 'If you are still here tomorrow night they'll carry you out on a stretcher.'

He was close to tears. 'Who do you think you are?' He ran over to the intercom near the door and pressed the emergency button.

'What's your medical emergency?' a guard asked. 'My cellmate is threatening me!'

'All right, we'll be there shortly.'

When the guards arrived I let Brett give his version first. One of the guards was an older guy, close to fifty. I looked at him: 'Put yourself in my position, it's well past midnight, I'm an old man and I need some rest. Would you let a pimply faced adolescent have the TV blaring all night?'

He was obviously in charge. He turned to the kid. 'You'll leave the TV off until breakfast time tomorrow. If there is any more trouble from you I'll put you in a safe cell where there are no televisions.'

They locked the door and left. I heard one of them laughing.

The kid stared at me, unable to believe what an unfair world he was living in. Older people just didn't understand. 'I'm going to another cell tomorrow,' he said.

'Good idea. Try to get someone your own age.'

Later that morning Lucy visited me. I came back on a high – with her help I would find a way out of this hellhole.

When I returned the kid was gone. I spent the next few nights on my own. Sheer bliss in gaol.

• • •

While on remand I was allowed three visits a week. Although Gloria was working, she came with Lucy on the weekends and Lucy visited me on her own twice during the week.

I had taken a good look at the gaol and its security. Unlike the old English-style prisons such as Long Bay, Goulburn, Bathurst, Parramatta and Maitland, the MRRC was a modern facility based on the American designs where security was the priority. To me it looked close to escape-proof.

Lucy and I seriously discussed trying to replicate my escape from Queensland. But even if I managed to get them to take me to hospital, the security would be heavy due to the fact I had done it before. The small Derringer Lucy had may not be sufficient to hold them at bay. The chances of her being seriously injured or even killed trying to rescue me were high.

A few weeks after my arrest the guards came into the visiting room while Lucy was with me and told me I had to terminate the visit. I was on escort to Goulburn.

'What for?'

'No idea. But you have to be on the truck in half an hour.' You couldn't argue with them. I kissed Lucy goodbye.

'I will come to Goulburn to see you,' she said.

When I arrived at Goulburn I discovered I had been brought 200 kilometres for a traffic matter in Queanbeyan, another 100 kilometres away. After sitting in a cell for about an hour I was driven to Queanbeyan Police Station where I stayed in the cells overnight.

The next morning to my surprise and delight I was taken to the visiting section where Lucy was waiting for me. She had rung Goulburn Gaol and when they told her I was at Queanbeyan she had caught a train.

'I have the gun,' she said.

It wasn't a good idea to walk into a police station with a loaded weapon.

'Why did you bring it?'

She gave me a look that implied I was stupid. 'To get you out, Boy.

This could be our chance.'

I had to admire her spirit. 'Luce, say we get out of the court – where do we go? Do you have a car waiting? I am well known in Queanbeyan. Can you imagine the drama if you slipped me a pistol in the courtroom and I escaped? Cops everywhere. We aren't organised. We would never get away.' She looked tired, deflated. 'I can never get you out of this Silverwater.'

'I know how tough it is on you,' I said. 'But we will only get one chance at this – we need to plan it like a military operation. I promise you I will find a way.'

She brightened. 'Okay, Boy. When you are finished in court I will bring you T-bone steak and milkshake.'

'Be careful with that toy. If they catch you with it you will also go to gaol.'

The magistrate dispensed with the traffic matter, stating I had more serious matters to deal with and that the entire process of bringing me from Silverwater to Queanbeyan had been a waste of time and resources.

As promised, Lucy brought me a steak with chips and vegetables, a milkshake and a sweet. She knew that, compared to the food I had been existing on, it was a king's banquet.

The cops at Queanbeyan knew me and were decent enough to let us have another quick visit before I was driven back to Goulburn Gaol. Looking back, it is hard to believe she visited me twice with the Derringer in her bag.

Lucy, at my request, had bought a blue Sigma station wagon from one of the car salesmen we knew. He gave her a good deal. It was too arduous for her to be travelling everywhere by public transport. And if we could pull off an escape we would need wheels.

WHY WAS THE BACK DOOR UNLOCKED?

1999

While I was at Goulburn a prisoner whom I had known for decades approached me and loaned me a TV. Unlike the MRRC at Silverwater, you had to buy your own TV at Goulburn and the process usually took at least a month.

This particular prisoner went out of his way to be friendly and we usually paced the yard together for at least an hour a day talking the talk.

After a few days he said: 'You could easily escape if you wanted to.'

I was taken by surprise. I hadn't even hinted that I was interested in escaping. But he was well aware of my background and he knew about my 1984 escape from Queensland.

'I'm not figuring on trying to escape,' I said, 'but even if I was I think it would be extremely difficult. Security is tight these days.'

'From the gaols, yeah. But you are going to these country courts and the police cells are a joke. You just get someone overnight to cut the bars and when they put you in the cell you climb out and away you go. You'll be in your civvies, have a car waiting. Easy Campese.'

'They probably check the bars,' I said.

'No way. When was the last time someone cut the bars in a police cell and escaped? And the coppers in country towns, they haven't got a clue.'

I grinned. 'I don't know about that, I'm here now because of a country cop.'

'That sheila I saw you with on the visit, she won't wait for you.'

'I wouldn't want her to.'

'Well, what do you reckon? Get her to cut the bars the night before you go to court. You said you are going to Moss Vale – that would be easy.'

I had to kill the idea that Lucy could or would assist me in an escape. 'Lucy cut the bars? Mate, she is a meek little librarian, and is horrified about what I did. If I suggested something like that she would have a panic attack.'

'You must have someone who would do it for you.'

'None of my friends would do something like that.'

'You're a bank robber, you must have money. Pay someone to do it.'

I felt it might be in my interests to let him think I had money. 'Yeah, well they never found the money from that last robbery.'

'Your girl's got it!'

I laughed. 'I didn't say that. But if I really had to get money, I could.'

'Well, if you need a weapon, I'm your man.'

'I don't need a weapon. To be honest I'm not interested in escaping. But in case I know someone who is interested, how much for a sub-machine gun?'

'For you, $2000. Anyone else, $3000.'

I nodded, more to myself. Lucy's little Derringer may not be enough to scare off guards during an escape attempt – but who would argue with a sub-machine gun? I figured even the rock-throwing detective would have second thoughts about that. But was this guy for real or just a talker? He was a serious criminal and as far as I knew staunch. I would discuss it with Lucy, but if she was going to help me escape, I liked the idea of her being equipped with heavy, intimidating artillery.

The next day I said to the guy: 'I have a friend in Queensland who will be visiting me soon. He is the type of guy who might buy a sub-machine for $2000. He wouldn't pay three.'

'Okay, for you I'll do it. I'll give you a phone number to give your friend. Tell him to mention my name so my friend will know it's genuine.' Within a week Lucy had arranged to meet his friend. She gave him $2000 and he gave her a parcel which he assured her was a sub-machine gun in perfect working order with a full magazine clip.

When Lucy took it home and checked it, she thought it might have been an old Thompson gun – and everything appeared to be in order.

On our next visit she gave me the news. She was quite excited. 'How do you know it looks like a Thompson?' I asked.

She was enjoying this. 'You forget, Boy, I come from military background.' I held her hand. 'We said this would be a military operation and it will be. If you say it's a Tommy gun then that is good enough for me. It doesn't really matter anyway – as long as it works.'

'Do you want me to test it?'

I nodded. 'I think you should.'

Before Lucy could visit me again I was driven to Moss Vale Police Station for another court appearance. This time the security was heavy. The Goulburn Special Squad provided a personal escort for me.

'I should warn you,' the head guy said, 'that we know your history and that if you try to escape I will have to shoot you.'

'As you do,' I said.

On arrival at the police station I was uncuffed and placed in a small Perspex-covered cubicle which contained a wooden bench to sit on. A steel bolt was slid across the door safely ensconcing me inside. Anyone outside the cubicle could slide the bolt open. Almost immediately my special escort went away.

A uniformed cop remained. He came to the cubicle and said: 'We had a call from your girlfriend Lucy – she is on the way.'

Reliable Lucy. 'Thanks. Can you let her in to see me for a while?'

'We can do that.'

He walked away leaving me alone with my thoughts. Where was my special squad escort? The back door was unlocked, only the steel bolt was preventing my escape. No doubt when Lucy arrived someone would keep watch.

After about an hour there was no sign of the special escort or anyone else. Then the friendly cop returned. 'How you doing, John? Just got another call from Lucy, she got a flat tyre and is running late, but she will be here within the hour.'

Gee they are nice here at Moss Vale, I thought. 'Okay, thanks. Keep me up on things.'

Before Lucy arrived my special escort came and walked me over to the courthouse. There were a couple of journalists there. I suppose, locally, this case was big news.

The magistrate naturally remanded me and just as naturally refused bail. Some things in life are certain. After returning me to the police station and my little cubicle the special escort guys again disappeared. Only the friendly cop remained.

'Lucy shouldn't be long now,' he said. 'Would you like a glass of water?' He was alone. He would have to unbolt the door. Back door still unlocked. Where were the special escort guys? Where were all the other cops? When I arrived there were about eight of them.

Fifteen years ago I would have asked for the glass of water and tried my luck. Not now. If I escaped it would be because I outfoxed them, not overpowered someone.

'No thanks. Knowing Lucy, she will probably bring me some food and drink.'

He left. The animal instinct that I had developed over the years of living dangerously was now on high alert. I could smell a rat. Were they setting me up?

These were my thoughts when Lucy came through the door smiling and rushed towards me. She looked beautiful. At her best, she was a stunner. The friendly cop was standing near the door a big grin on his face.

'I'm going to give you two lovebirds some time alone,' he said. 'Now I know you would like to get in there with him, Lucy, but it's not allowed. Don't unbolt the door or I will have to send you away and there will be no more special visits in police stations.'

Lucy looked at him, using all her womanly charm. 'Oh come on, officer, one little cuddle and a kiss wouldn't be so bad, eh?'

'Sorry, Lucy. Rules are rules. Be good. I'll be popping in now and again to check you out.'

He went away. Lucy looked around then said, as I knew she would: 'Boy, they have made the mistake. This back door is unlocked. I can get you out!'

'It's a trap, Luce. I came with the special squad – where are they? Did you see a lot of cops when you came through the front?'

'Yes. Very friendly.'

'Too friendly. Why isn't at least one of them watching us?'

'So, they try to trap you?'

'Not just me, both of us, Luce. I'm certain this is a trap. Where is my special squad escort? I think they are waiting out the back for me.'

'In this case I will go out the front and get you the T-bone with chips and milkshake. They can wait out the back with nothing.'

As if by magic my special escort came in to see me. One of them said: 'We'll be going back soon, Killick. But because she has come all this way we will wait for your girlfriend to bring you dinner. Enjoy it: it will probably be the last T-bone you see for another decade.'

I thought the police were in charge here but it looked like Corrective Services was calling the shots. Oh well, be nice to prove him wrong about the decade he thinks I'll spend in gaol.

Looking at it realistically, it was going to be difficult to keep me in for another month – let alone a decade. I had Lucy...she had a vehicle...she had a Derringer...she had a sub-machine gun...and we both had the will and the desire. All I needed was a chance, a flaw in the system somewhere. I knew it was there, I just had to find it...

When Lucy returned she had one of the biggest T-bones I had seen on a large plate with chips, onions, peas and gravy. She had also brought me a container filled to the brim with chocolate milkshake.

The guard who had predicted a decade in gaol for me took the milkshake from her. 'He can't have this,' he said.

Lucy gave him her nicest smile. 'It's only milkshake. Not alcohol.'

'Let it go, Luce,' I said. 'After this steak and chips I won't have room for a milkshake.'

I knew why he had confiscated it. Back in the seventies when it was a common occurrence for visitors to send food into the prisoners while they were in the police cells, a woman gave a tough old sergeant in charge at a suburban police station some sandwiches and a milkshake filled to the brim to be given to her boyfriend. The sergeant gave the guy the sandwiches but, it being a hot day and he being thirsty, he drank the milkshake.

The woman had tried to do the right thing by her boyfriend who had been refused bail and was feeling depressed. She had laced the milkshake with a strong dose of the best LSD in town.

After a while the sergeant began acting strangely, screaming out that he was growing and the walls were about to crush him. He ran out of the police station and down the road babbling nonsense.

Now, quite a few people saw this and thought he might have been chasing an escaped criminal but he was travelling too slowly to catch anyone.

I ate the meal Lucy had brought me while my special escort and two cops looked on.

Suddenly security was again a priority.

I'll never know who forgot to lock the back door...

THE CONMAN PILOT

1999

In late February I was returned to the MRRC and allocated a cell in 'Goldsmith' – one of about fourteen wings, each containing about fifty prisoners. My cellmate was a kid aged nineteen who was in for drug offences. He was quiet and we got along okay. One of the residents there was the former Kings Cross Kingpin, Bill Bayeh. He was refused bail on several charges of commercial drug trafficking for which he told me he was expecting to do 'two or three years'.

'It's all fixed up,' he said, giving me a wink.

Bill served fifteen years before they gave him parole...

The day after my arrival Lucy visited me. She was stressed.

'I am getting phone calls in early hours calling me slut in Russian language and saying now my gangster is in gaol I will be dead.'

'Alex?'

'No, Boy – he's too clever. But it is definitely Russian person.'

'Okay. These people are cowards just trying to scare you.' I paused and smiled at her. 'If they come to your place you have a Tommy gun.'

'No, Boy! I took it to the forest – it doesn't work!'

I should have been surprised but I wasn't. Were we being set up? A prisoner approaches me, tells me how easy it would be for me to escape... offering to supply firearms...then provides one, which has had the firing mechanism dismantled, to a female librarian who probably wouldn't know how to test it.

Was it just a rip off to get the $2000? Or was it more devious? Had he approached the authorities and involved them? Would they be waiting for Lucy to make a move at court or if I went to hospital? The consequences were too horrific to contemplate. If she tried to hold up trained, armed special squad guards who know the weapon is ineffective – bang! bang! Both of us are dead.

Would they be so diabolical and ruthless? Or was I being paranoid and my imagination was running wild?

I guess we will never know. But I decided then, during that visit, that the only way I would be able to escape would be to think laterally.

How much could I ask of Lucy? Only one way to find out. 'Luce, we may be getting set up. I know how we can beat them, but it is risky.'

She gripped my hand. 'Whatever it takes, Boy.'

'They are building the Olympic site next door to this place. Every day I see helicopters flying over, bringing tourists to look at it.'

'Boy! This is brilliant!'

I grinned. 'If you hire one and show the pilot your Tommy gun, he will do what you tell him to do. He won't know it doesn't work.'

'I will do it.'

'You will need a good disguise and try to change your accent.'

'Doesn't matter. Main thing is to get you out.'

'If we do it they will try very hard to catch us. We will have to disappear for a few months then try to get overseas.'

She nodded. 'We can do it, Boy. They won't be ready for it.'

'Well, it has never happened in Australia. But guys often talk about it. The authorities would be aware of the possibilities. The main thing will be speed, like a bank robbery – in and out before they have time to react.'

'When do we do this?'

I looked at her. Could she carry it out? Instinctively I knew she could. 'It could take a month to set it up. First you should go for a trial run. While you are in the chopper you can rehearse it in your mind how you will do it.'

After Lucy had gone I analysed the situation. Life had taught me that wisdom is the ability to choose alternatives. Fearful of a trap on the ground, we had formulated a bold plan to surprise them by taking to the air. To succeed it would need a lot of planning, precision timing and a bit of luck. But with Lucy on board I could see no reason why we couldn't pull it off. Why not? Others had dreamed and talked about it. We would do it.

Sometimes when you gamble for big stakes and the odds are against you, fate steps in and deals you an ace.

My ace was in the form of thirty-six-year-old Kiwi chopper pilot, Paul Bennett. It had to be fate that Corrective Services allocated him a cell in Goldsmith. He was an international conman with 4000 hours of experience flying choppers. A few years later he would convince the Oscar winning actor Russell Crowe to give him a job as a pilot. But true to his nature he betrayed the actor's trust and was sacked.

Two days after his arrival in Goldsmith I arranged for him to be transferred into my cell.

'I can't handle having a teenager in my cell,' I told the Wing officer. 'Bennett is more mature and he's also in a cell with a young guy.'

He shook his head. 'The things I do for you blokes. Do you have an electric jug and a remote?

I grinned. 'Yes, thanks, chief. But we don't have a TV guide.'

'Get out of here! Tell those kids I told them to change cells.'

I soon discovered that Bennett was a shifty piece of work. He had been extradited from South Africa to Scotland where he spent two years in gaol.

After that they extradited him to New South Wales on fraud charges. He had been at the MRRC for six months.

He had been told who I was and it didn't take long before we were talking about the possibilities of an escape by chopper.

'I could get you out of here in twenty seconds,' he said. 'I'd fly straight in, hover, you jump on board and we fly out. I have the contacts to get you overseas.'

But I had my doubts. He had engaged the top lawyer, Chris Murphy, to defend him, but soon ran out of cash and Murphy told him to get a Legal Aid lawyer.

The next few weeks developed into a game of cat and mouse between us. He was convinced that he would soon be released and he tried to persuade me to get Lucy to pay him $10,000 to break me out. To keep the game alive I pretended Lucy had the money from the Bowral bank robbery. She occasionally put some money in his gaol account and arranged for his court clothes to be dry cleaned. While he was conning me I was reading his chopper magazines and trying to pick his brain without arousing his suspicion.

The magazine I was reading had an illustration of a helicopter dashboard and one of the items was a transponder.

'What's a transponder?'

'It's a tracking device. If a pilot is in trouble he turns it on and it sends a signal showing exactly where he is.'

I managed to extract enough information from him and the magazines to enable Lucy to be cognisant with the controls and gadgets of a helicopter. In mid-March Lucy visited me after taking a flight over the Olympic village.

She was excited. 'It can be done, Boy.'

'Did they check your bag?'

She smiled. 'No. Poor innocent little lamb is no danger.'

I laughed. 'Not much. Did you take a look at the control panel?'

She nodded. 'Don't worry, Boy. It's all under control. We will do this.' We set a date: Thursday, 25 March 1999.

THE LAST ESCAPE

1999

On 24 March Lucy visited me for the last time. A few of the prisoners and their visitors who knew us came across and said hello. If Lucy was nervous she didn't show it.

When we were seated alone she said: 'It's all set, Boy. I have booked a flight for 9.00 am.'

The plan was for her to force the pilot to land on the oval. There were two huge trees at one end – I would be standing near the fence at the other end.

'The only tower is situated quite a distance away,' I said. 'Anyway they can't shoot at aircraft over a prison.'

I had read Robert Lindsey's *The Flight of the Falcon* about Christopher Boyce, sentenced to forty years in the US for selling information about US spy satellites. (See also *The Falcon and the Snowman* by the same author.) Boyce escaped and went on a bank robbing spree. He mentioned in *The Flight of the Falcon* that he and a friend were planning an escape by helicopter. They were counting on their belief that guards weren't allowed to shoot at a helicopter because there may be a hostage inside. When I queried Bennett about this he said it was a stipulation in the Geneva Convention.

'In the morning I will call you when it is confirmed we are going to the oval. You will need to be close to the airport.'

The men in our wing were permitted one hour on the oval every Monday and Thursday from 9.00 am to 10.00 am. But if there was a staff shortage or a lockdown the recreational time on the oval would be cancelled.

She nodded. 'I've booked motel for us tomorrow night in Ashfield.

Chinese people run it – they won't bother us.'

'Did you book the place in Goulburn?'

'Yes. Three nights from Friday.'

It was a cheap motel where we had stayed the night she had crashed the car. The rooms were at the back of the building and out of the way of prying eyes.

'Okay. You will need to park your car near where we will be landing at Macquarie Park. You should do that tonight and get a taxi back to your motel.'

We looked at each other. This was it. She was about to take on something that some of the toughest prisoners in Australia had talked about and dreamt about, but had never been capable of achieving. She had to do it all alone – no one to finance it or even help with some of the minor tasks such as leaving the car in a strategic place or organising a safe place to hide out. Yet I was confident she could and would come through. This was the girl who hadn't panicked when she fell through the ice into the freezing water, or lost her nerve when being chased on horseback in the snow by starving wild dogs...the girl who wasn't afraid to enter a cemetery at midnight and examine tombstones despite fears from her friends that she would be grabbed by the walking dead. These were the qualities I was aware that this quiet Russian librarian possessed. Hijacking a helicopter was not a quantum leap for her – nor for me. We would do it. And if they had set a trap for us, re the hospital or court, they would be screaming blue murder when we flew away using the harmless weapon that had been deactivated.

It was time for her to go. I hugged her to me. 'I will bring Bennett onto the oval with me,' I said. 'Just in case your pilot jumps out and runs away when you land.'

She grinned. 'Trust me, Boy. This poor pilot won't be going anywhere until he takes us to the park.'

'Okay. Now don't forget, first thing you do when you show him the gun is to disconnect the transponder.'

She kissed me. 'Everything is under control, Boy.'

The planning and the fine tuning were completed. Tomorrow they would be put to the test.

• • •

At 8.22 am on 25 March the guards unlocked the cell doors. They were twenty-two minutes late and I had been pacing the cell while Bennett watched me. He could see I was on edge but said nothing. But the first objective had been achieved: no lockdown...

I immediately rushed out to the area where the two phones were situated. Both of them were already in use. A few guys were lined up waiting to make a call. In gaol phone calls are very important.

'Listen everyone! I need to make an important phone call regarding postponing a court date. I have to ring my lawyer in five minutes. I'll only be one minute.'

The guys waiting nodded. One of them said: 'No problems, bro.'

'Thanks, guys,' I said, and hurried across to the office. The guard was going through some paperwork.

'Are we going to the oval today, Chief?'

He didn't look up. 'Yep. Be ready at five to nine.' Second objective achieved: Oval was on!

Three minutes later I was on the phone to Lucy. I didn't know her whereabouts. She was on a train, close to Bankstown from where she would take a taxi to the airport.

'Hi, Luce. I'm going out for some exercise for an hour. I'll call you when I get back.'

'Okay, Boy.'

I hung up. 'Thanks again, fellas,' I said and went to the cell.

Objective three achieved: she knew it was on. Now it was all up to her. The previous night I had selected a few of the letters she had written to me, another one from Gloria and one from Lyn. I would take them with me. The others I had to leave. Bennett didn't miss a trick. I sensed he was already suspicious of my behaviour. He had confirmed he would come to the oval. What were the odds of having an experienced chopper pilot as a backup during a planned helicopter lift-out? Of course he was totally unaware that he was 'first reserve'.

At 8:55 am about forty of us lined up to be escorted to the oval. One of the guards had a muster book and checked each one of us as we exited the wing into a passageway where we were joined by men from another wing which shared our oval times. We walked to another barrier, which was opened electronically from a control station. From there we walked to another gate which led to the oval.

One of the guys from my wing was arguing with a much bigger guy from the other wing.

'You think I'm scared of you, bro?' the smaller guy yelled.

'Keep your mouth shut – we'll sort it on the oval,' the other guy said. 'What, you think I'm fucken scared of you?'

He looked scared to me. This fool could destroy all our plans. One of the guards had turned to look in our direction. If a fight broke out we would all be returned to the wings and Lucy would hijack a chopper only to find the oval empty! What would she do?

Turn to the distraught pilot: 'Sorry, I was only kidding. Can we take a look at the Olympic site now?'

'Any problems back there?' the guard asked. 'No problems here, Boss,' the big guy said.

I looked at the little guy. I figured he didn't want to go out to the oval.

Probably he didn't know the big guy would be coming.

I stepped close to him and said softly: 'Don't worry about that guy. Me and my mates will straighten him out.'

He looked relieved. 'He doesn't worry me, bro.'

'Sure. But we'll talk to him, anyway.'

We reached the oval without further incident. Then I approached the big guy, who until today I had never seen before. 'Hi, champ. I need you to do me a favour.'

He stared at me, a little nonplussed. 'What's that?'

'That bloke you were arguing with, he's in my wing.'

'So?'

'So he's arranging something for me and the boys this afternoon. I don't care what you do to him next time, but until this afternoon me and the boys need him. I'll give you two packets of White Ox on Monday if you postpone things.'

He thought about it. It was a slow process. 'Yeah, well if you don't pay I'll be coming for you.'

I smiled. 'I wouldn't want that. Do we have a deal?'

We shook hands. 'Deal,' he said. He still looked a bit uncertain. 'My name is John Killick. Ask around. My word is my bond.' He nodded. 'Might do that.'

I looked for the little guy. He was standing outside the weights room near a bored-looking guard.

I walked over to him. 'Everything is fixed,' I said. 'If I were you I wouldn't come to the oval on Monday.'

He shrugged. 'He doesn't scare me.'

I walked away. Bennett was waiting for me and joined me. 'Let's do a few laps,' I said.

For about fifteen minutes we did laps of the oval. Although I tried to act normal my pulse was racing.

During that time four choppers passed over. I knew it was too early for Lucy. The occupants of the two wings had picked their teams and were playing rugby league. We watched one indigenous guy sidestep around three or four opponents and race away for a try.

'Some of these guys are talented,' I said. 'They could probably play first grade.'

'Nah,' Bennett said. 'They can't tackle. All they do is play touch.'

It was 9.25 – time to get near the designated fence so that Lucy would be able to see me.

'I'm a bit tired,' I said. 'Let's rest here.'

'I'll carry on for a while.'

I had to keep him nearby. 'This is a good opportunity for us to get a realistic view of how you would bust me out of here. The next chopper that comes past – tell me how you would do it.'

Maybe he still believed he would soon be released and he could con Lucy out of $10,000 with the promise he would break me out. When the next helicopter flew over he explained how he would come from a different direction, and sweep in, pick me up and be out in seconds. He was very plausible. It gave me more confidence that Lucy would be able to orchestrate a similar scenario.

Suddenly we were interrupted by Bill Bayeh.

'John, Kevin wants to see you. He's collecting his buy-up.'

Kevin Geraghty, nicknamed 'The Teacher' because he had been a physical education teacher at Randwick Boys High, was on remand on charges of smuggling commercial amounts of cocaine for which the following year he would be sentenced to twenty-five years. I had met him a few times in early 1997 at a friend's place. I had no idea he was involved in a huge cocaine importation scheme and that police had been watching him for some time.

'Tell him I'm busy, Bill.'

Bill shrugged and walked away.

Another chopper flew over. I sensed it wasn't coming for me, too high, too big.

It was 9.40. They usually began to call us back at 9.55. She had less than fifteen minutes to arrive and cause bedlam.

It was a mild autumn day but I wondered if Bennett caught the stench of my sweat. I did.

I could see another chopper coming towards us. It was lower than the last few. Was this it? My heart was racing. No. False alarm. Nine choppers so far. At least no one would take much notice of Lucy's intrusion until it was too late.

Bennett was watching me. 'You haven't got a chopper coming have you?' He was half joking.

'That will be your job,' I said.

Bill Bayeh was back. 'Kevin insists on seeing you.'

I looked at my watch, 9.43. Bloody hell. My blood pressure must be sky high.

The buy-up section was about 60 metres away, fenced off from the oval. I could see a large group of guys lined up waiting to collect their buy-ups – consisting of tobacco, groceries and sweets.

'I'll be back in thirty seconds,' I said to Bennett and ran across to the buy-up section.

Kevin was waiting for me on the other side of the fence.

'John, you nearly missed out. Here's a couple of chocolates. Can you get to the library on Wednesday? I need to talk to you.'

'Okay, Kev. Keep the chocolates. I have to go. See you Wednesday.'

I jogged back to where Bennett was waiting. I had no idea why Kevin wanted to see me. It was irrelevant to my situation. It was 9.47. Where was Lucy?

(Less than an hour later, after the entire gaol had been shut down and the prisoners locked away, a team of special squad guards rushed into Kevin Geraghty's cell, handcuffed him and drove him to Lithgow, where he was placed in segregation for a year. The same day more than seventy prisoners – some of them my friends – were placed in vans and transferred to various gaols around the state. Many of them cursing me and swearing vengeance.)

Another five minutes passed. No sign of any helicopter. Something must have happened to Lucy. Had she been overpowered by the pilot? Had he activated the transponder before she managed to disable it?

It was 9.55. Time to return to the wing. My mind was racing like a mouse on a treadmill. What if Lucy arrives minutes after we have gone and there is a new batch of prisoners on the oval? What will she do? She has already hijacked the chopper. I visualised the scene.

'I can't see him...can you get a bit closer?' Pilot: 'Can't get any closer without landing.' Lucy: 'Can you see a grey-haired man?'

Pilot: 'No. What was that? I think we've been shot!' Lucy: 'Hmm. Seems to me Boy isn't here yet.'

I only had one option. When they called for us to go back I would wait until the inevitable stragglers had reached the gate then I would fall to the ground clutching my chest. Heart attack! Gaol protocol was to leave me on the ground and call for medical assistance. It would take three or four minutes for a nurse to arrive. If Lucy arrived I could jump up and run to the chopper before any of them recovered their wits...

9.56. The guards were running late. With the exception of emergencies they were never late in the old days. You could set your clock on them being on time. It was a different era.

This time their lack of punctuality would prove costly.

Lucy had arrived! I saw it before I heard the unmistakeable sounds of the approaching rescue machine. But unlike Bennett's account of how he would zoom straight in, hover, pick me up and zoom out again, this one was circling around the oval, gradually decreasing in height. 'You cunning bastard!' Bennett said.

I looked across to where four of the guards were standing near the trees at the opposite end of the oval. Instead of spreading out to cover all directions, they stood staring up at the chopper.

I was concerned it was taking too much time. I knew the dog unit, armed with carbines, regularly patrolled the perimeter in a vehicle. They could be here in seconds. As the chopper finally began to ease downwards while hovering about 40 metres away, I ran towards it, yelling. 'See ya!' to Bennett.

'Good luck!' he shouted. To my left I saw a guard running towards me from the gym room near the buy-up section. The four guards near the trees also began to run in the direction of the chopper which was hovering about a metre from the ground. The passenger door was open and I scrambled inside. Lucy handed me the sub-machine gun.

I pointed it at the pilot, Tim Joyce. 'Hi mate! I'm a lifer. You can make a lot of money out of *60 Minutes* or you can be dead. Your choice.'

'Go! Go!' Lucy yelled.

'Don't worry, mate. I'll get you out of here,' he said. He was remarkably cool. 'But I have to turn it around.'

The guards were getting close. I sat on the edge of the vehicle and pointed the disabled weapon at them. They lunged to the ground. Initially the inmates had stopped playing footy and were staring wide eyed at the chopper. Then most of them dived to the ground. As the guard running from the gym drew closer we lifted up and around and headed in the direction of the trees. I slid back inside. A guard from the dog squad arrived on the outside of the perimeter. Jumping from his vehicle he aimed a Ruger carbine at the chopper. But at that moment the guard in charge of the Central Control Tower, where the gaol's monitors are stationed, took aim with a .223 Ruger carbine and fired three rounds. Thinking that I was shooting at him, the dog unit guard immediately threw himself onto the ground. As you would.

I heard the phht! phht! phht! The first one hit the skid landing pad; the second one missed Tim Joyce by, he later estimated, 16 centimetres; the third hit the cyclic pitch control which prevents a helicopter from dropping its nose or tail when in the air. That one nearly brought us down. So much for the Geneva Convention stipulation: No shooting at aircraft over a prison. These guys don't play by the rules. (Fancy me complaining about that!)

The huge trees saved us from any further danger of being shot as we flew away from the prison complex.

'Where do you want to go?' Tim asked. 'Is the transponder off?'

'Yes. I tried to change the frequency but she stopped me. Now it's off.'

'We go to Macquarie University,' Lucy said.

Lucy had two pages of a street directory taped together. She was pointing to a spot she had marked at Christie Park.

We seemed to be travelling in slow motion. 'Can't you go any faster?'

'Sorry, mate – this is one of the oldest helicopters in Australia. It can't go any faster.'

Lucy had already taken his headset off and ripped out the leads and put them in her bag. I took off his cap which had 'Eurocopter' written on it and put it on.

I liked him. He was cool under pressure. I was unaware that he was deliberately flying too high to attract attention on the radar. Airspace is controlled over the city and suburbs and he hadn't logged a flight path obtaining clearance to fly to Macquarie Park. But our run of luck continued: the radar didn't detect us.

At one stage Lucy leaned across and whispered: 'I forgot the keys to the car.'

I nodded. She had managed to get us this far. I would take it from here. 'Not a problem.'

As we approached Christie Park, Lucy pointed to it. 'There!'

'Just land on the oval down there,' I said.

Tim eased the chopper down until it hovered less than a metre from the ground. 'You can get out now,' he said. 'Be careful not to hit your heads on the rotor blades.'

'Just land it,' I said.

'Just get out and go, mate. I can't get out on the slope, the helicopter will roll.'

I couldn't risk him following us in the chopper. 'I don't care if it rolls,' I said. 'Land it.'

'Well, I'll take it a bit farther up on flat ground.'

When we were on a flatter surface I told him to turn off the engine and get out.

After the three of us were on the ground, he said: 'Listen, mate, I've done my bit for you. I've got two young kids at home. I won't try to follow you. Leave me here.'

'No!' Lucy said. 'He comes with us.'

'We'll leave you here,' I said. 'But we will have to tie you up.'

Lucy did a quick job of hindering any intention he may have had of following us. She tied his hands with the radio wire, fastened his shoelaces together and tied a belt around his legs.

Carrying the two bags Lucy had brought, we jogged off towards Talavera Road. I knew I had to carjack a vehicle. When Peter Bax came out of Ericsson Telecommunications car park waiting to ease into the traffic, I ran up to the driver's side of his 1998 SS Commodore and tapped on the window.

He wound it down and I showed him the silver Derringer. 'We've struck a bit of trouble,' I said. 'I need you to take me somewhere. If you don't I'll shoot you in the leg.'

I knew he wouldn't argue. We got into the vehicle, Lucy in the back seat.

'Head down the highway towards the city,' I said.

He was calm. He did as I asked. I noticed a white van behind us. 'I don't want to hurt you, but I will if you try to attract attention. Is that one of your mates following us?'

'No.'

'Cut into the right lane.'

He did so. Shortly afterwards the van turned left. Then the low level fuel alarm went off.

'How much fuel is left?' I asked. 'Probably 20 k's.'

'Keep within the speed limit and just follow my directions. You'll be fine.'

I was expecting police cars with flashing lights and sirens to be charging up and down the highway. But I didn't see one.

I deliberately directed him to Milson's Point. The cops might assume I was naive enough to hide out around familiar territory.

Near the park on Kurraba Road I told him to stop, and take a walk in the park. 'And give me your mobile. Don't worry I'm not going to take your wallet.'

He gave me the phone.

'I'll leave the car nearby,' I said, and drove off. 'Where are we going, Boy?'

'North Sydney. We'll park the car there and catch a train to Ashfield.'

I was unaware that within thirty seconds of getting out of the car Bax flagged down a passing police vehicle. But by the time he had explained the situation to them we were gone.

I knew there would be a massive manhunt for us. But until they found the Commodore they wouldn't be thinking about trains.

As always, the traffic was heavy in North Sydney. Not good when you are in a hurry; but also, not conducive to trying to find another vehicle.

I've always been lucky finding a parking spot. Never was it more welcome on this occasion when I found a space in Miller Street – not far from the railway station.

Walking briskly, we entered the station where Lucy bought tickets. Two minutes later we were on a train. First stop Milson's Point. Then Wynyard. By the time we arrived at Central I was confident we had, at least temporarily, slipped the net. Concerned they might track us via the phone, I took it apart and threw it off the train.

We were in the Ashfield motel by 11.15.

'The midday news should be interesting,' I said. She smiled. But I could see she was exhausted.

It was hard to believe that eighty minutes ago I had been inside a modern maximum security prison.

While all this was happening the news of the escape had already hit the media. Listeners were ringing John Laws on 2UE, who at the time had the largest radio audience in Australia, and informing him of the whereabouts of the chopper.

'It has just passed overhead!' one listener said excitedly.

Laws was giving listeners bottles of expensive wine for information.

When we landed a listener rang him with an accurate account of our whereabouts. Lawsy gave him four bottles of his best wine. Maybe if he had rung the police instead of 2UE they would have caught us then. But the police wouldn't have given him any wine – not even the cheap stuff.

News of the car-jacking was soon being broadcast on 2UE. A lot of people were ringing the station and giving misinformation. But another listener, tuned into a police scanner, was on the money: the Commodore had been found abandoned in Miller Street North Sydney. The police had thrown a net around the area.

Winding up his broadcast at noon, John Laws said: 'The most extraordinary story I think I've heard in a decade at least.'

ON THE RUN AGAIN

1999

Within an hour of entering the motel I had dyed my hair dark brown. Lucy said I looked twelve years younger. Good. Now I was forty-five and they were looking for a grey-haired fifty-seven-year-old.

Staying in the motel, we watched television, switching channels. We were all over the news. By midday they had named me. Later in the day they were openly stating that Lucy Dudko had hijacked a helicopter and airlifted me out. On what evidence?

Tim Joyce wasn't shown a photo of her until seven weeks later. Peter Bax couldn't identify her.

She was convicted by the media solely on the fact she was my lover and regular visitor.

The following morning we were sharing the front pages with the Kosovo War. Overnight NATO had bombed Serbian military positions in the Yugoslav province of Kosovo. Until this day the armed conflict between the Federal Republic of Yugoslavia (at this stage consisting of the Republics of Montenegro and Serbia) and the Kosovo Albanian rebel group known as the Kosovo Liberation Army (KLA) supported by NATO, had been a ground offensive only. The air strike would continue until 11 June 1999 when peace deals were negotiated. It was the first time NATO had bombed a sovereign country.

The *Sydney Morning Herald* led with 'John and Lucy's Great Escape'. I read it on the train to Goulburn after we left the motel Friday morning.

Lucy and I were seated apart. But without false IDs we had no chance if police came through and did a check.

Our luck held out. We arrived in Goulburn without incident and proceeded to the motel. Wearing a grey cap and dark glasses, I picked up the key and paid for three nights. The clerk didn't give me a second glance. The authorities weren't happy with stories like 'John and Lucy's Great Escape'. Nor should they have been. The Attorney-General should have immediately stepped in and stopped it. The word 'alleged' was noticeable in its absence. In the event of her arrest, it would now be impossible for Lucy to get a fair trial. But the authorities didn't seem to care about that. They were more concerned that some people were applauding the audacity of the escape. In one article, they were discussing which actors would play Lucy and I in a movie.

It didn't take long for the media to turn it around. Saturday's *Sydney Morning*

Herald had the heading: 'Killick will shoot it out, police warn'. The article stated I had been charged with the attempted murder of a policeman.

Suddenly Alex Dudko, who knew absolutely nothing about the escape, became the go-to man.

He told the media that as soon as he saw the news on the television: 'I knew straight away that it was Lucy...'

Early Sunday morning I entered a newsagency at Goulburn and saw a prison guard whom I knew well. I walked past him and feigned interest in some magazines, my back to him. He walked out with the Sunday newspapers.

In a '*Sunday Telegraph Exclusive*' titled: 'How the escapee stole Lucy's Love – 'Evil' man turned a wife into helicopter hijacker,' there were four photos of Lucy including her wedding photo, three of Alex Dudko and one of me. There was also a copy of a letter I was supposed to have typed to Lucy from a motel. A letter I had no knowledge of.

The tone of the article can be gauged by the following passage: '... Amoral and egocentric, Killick regards women as a commodity to be used like the hard-earned savings of strangers he has robbed from banks across the country...'

Even for *The Telegraph*, this was a bit over the top.

The article also quoted Alex as stating Lucy had been on drugs: '...She was in an absolutely horrible state,' he says. 'Her eyes were wide open and protruding, her hands were shaking and she was talking strangely. She could not think reasonably or concentrate on anything and she was very distressed and upset...'

This was all news to me. Lucy wouldn't even take a Panadol when she had a headache.

Lucy stared at me. 'Tell me, Boy – how did I stay with this man for fourteen years?'

I smiled. 'No comment. But now you are his cash cow. They would be paying him big money for all this exclusive rubbish.'

I told her about my near miss with the prison guard.

'We have to go, Boy. Next time one of them might see you first.'

We caught a train to Wagga where we stayed in a motel for a few days. I was confident that with my hair dyed, and wearing a cap and sunglasses, I was unlikely to be identified. Although I booked for two people, Lucy who had also dyed her hair a reddish colour and cut it shorter, was rarely seen.

When it was time for the rooms to be cleaned we would go for a walk. Before leaving Sydney I had thrown the sub-machine gun in a dumpster. We still had the Derringer and a .32 Luger that was faulty and without bullets. When we left the motel rooms we could carry the two smaller weapons with us but the other one was too bulky.

It was a simple procedure. We moved from country town to country town.

The next one was Wangaratta in Victoria. Sometimes we went to a movie. It kept us off the streets when we weren't in our rooms.

Two weeks after the escape we arrived in Melbourne. To an extent the intensity of the police hunt had eased off. We weren't in the media every day now. But from the start police had formed Taskforce Northam, with the sole purpose to catch us. They could make mistakes every day and try again the next day. If we made one mistake we were history. Even for a risk-taker like me, they were bad odds.

We stayed in various motels from one end of Melbourne to the other. At least twice a week we would go to the State Library and check the newspapers.

We read the local, interstate and even the overseas editions. I was surprised the story had been picked up overseas. Helicopter escapes had occurred on more than one occasion – in Ireland, France, Mexico and other countries. Probably the fact a female was involved is what intrigued people. There was a lot of nonsense written about us. Police were claiming another prisoner was supposed to have gone with me but I duped him. I was reported to have had $100,000 stashed away from bank robberies. Alex was in fear of his life and the Canberra police were keeping a watch over his house.

He had to be kidding. We watched him on *Australia's Most Wanted*, where he gave Lucy some advice: 'Your life is not a B-grade movie.'

(In 2000, using the agency Rick Raftos, he tried to sell his version of the B-grade movie to Fox Studios. He came up with an original title: '*Breakout*'. The idea was quickly shut down by Fox when they realised he was using a wheelbarrow full of Family Court documents and illegally obtained tapes – none of it having any relevance to the 'breakout'.)

'Once I was Alex Dudko's wife,' Lucy said. 'Now he is Lucy Dudko's ex.'

She was right about that.

It was only a matter of time before the media tired of him.

Lucy and I caught a train to Ballarat where we stayed in a grand old hotel. It was cheap and there were a lot of vacant rooms there. We did a lot of walking, ate at local cafes where the meals were cheap but nutritious and filling. Lucy enjoyed visiting the small art gallery and on two occasions we went to the movie theatre. One of the films there, *The Matrix*, was nominated by Lucy as the best movie we had seen AH (after helicopter). BH was before helicopter. Looking back, the BH days were the best!

By now we were running low on funds. I tried to increase our dwindling bank by betting at the TAB. In Ballarat I was lucky. I had a few wins and doubled our bank when Tie the Knot brilliantly won his second Sydney Cup.

But when we moved on to Bendigo I lost most of our bank during a bad day at the TAB. Now we were in big trouble.

'These banks look wide open,' I said. 'I'll have to choose one to hit.'

'Boy, are you crazy? They will know it was you. They are waiting for you to do something. We don't have a car.'

If you believe what the newspapers say, the police were expecting me to rob a bank. Any robbery involving a silver two-shot Derringer .22 similar to that which was used in the helicopter escape, would be akin to me leaving my DNA at the scene. And the Ruger .32 was no better than a toy. After the stuff-up at Bowral I accepted that there is always a chance someone will try to be a hero and chase a robber, even one who has a weapon. I figured I was already looking at fifteen to twenty years if arrested. I at least needed a weapon with which I could fire a shot into the ground to demonstrate it was not a toy. Although it had taken three shots to deter Constable Rostron, the odds of encountering another Rostron were extreme.

No. Lucy was right. To try to rob a bank in Bendigo without a proper weapon and no getaway vehicle would hinge on madness.

Which left us with a huge problem. We were still on top of *Australia's Most Wanted* list and we were near out of funds. We had no support system. The huge police hunt had covered all of my contacts. They had even visited Jackie in South Australia, and asked her where I might go. She told them she didn't have a clue.

When things go wrong it is easy to have regrets. Although Lucy had played a major role in the escape and was aware of the difficulties we would be confronted with if we succeeded in getting away, I knew she had believed that if she rescued me, I would find a way to get us out of the country. But I had failed. There is no point scoring a spectacular win in the preliminary final if you fail miserably in the grand finaI. We hadn't lost but a win was looking improbable. I had to come up with something.

On Lucy's birthday, both of us had severe doses of the flu. For two days, we stayed in a motel in the city. The only occasions I went out were to buy some food and the newspapers. I also brought back the May edition of *The Australian Women's Weekly*. It contained a comprehensive story 'Hijacked Pilot's Hell Flight,' in which Tim Joyce told his story. Lucy was named numerous times in the article as the hijacker. There were a number of photos of both of us.

By this time, on her forty-first birthday, just about everybody in Australia had been told that she was the woman in the helicopter. No need for a trial. Just catch her and lock her up. And eventually that's what they did: treated her as a convicted prisoner from the time of her arrest. There was a trial. But the damage had been done.

This time they got it right. But what about when they get it wrong? Lindy

Chamberlain for one. This case is another classic Australian example of Conviction by Media.

Although Lucy had nearly recovered from her bout of the flu I was far from well when we caught a train to Footscray and booked into a cheap motel: The Midgate Motor Lodge. When the manager, John Turner, came out of his room to the office I could smell the odour of marijuana. It was indicative of what a dump the place was. As we went to our room I was already formulating a plan.

I sensed we had, by sheer luck, come to the right place.

There was a guy in Sydney, an ex-prisoner I'll call Ray, whom I had known for thirty-five years. The last time I saw him he was in a TAB in Eastwood.

We went for a drink at the nearby hotel. After a while he asked me if I could get him a couple of pistols.

I grinned. 'Planning to knock over an armoured van with a mate?'

He gave me a stern look. 'Don't even joke about it. Can you do it, or can't you?'

He was one of the few last hard men I knew. He would never rat on me to the police. But I wasn't prepared to sell what I had. 'Can't do it.'

He shrugged. 'Well, if you come across any, give me first option. I'll give you ten per cent on top of the cost.'

He didn't have a mobile phone, believing the police could track his movements. But he still had the same home phone number and I remembered it. I agreed to call him should the situation change.

Now, two years later, I phoned him. I was certain the police hadn't made the connection between us.

'Mate,' he said, 'I can't believe it's you. Be careful, mate, they want to kill you.'

'I am being careful,' I said. 'That's why I rang you – a man I can trust.' Although there was talk in the media about a $50,000 reward for information leading to Lucy's and my arrest, the reward still hadn't been announced. There would be no incentive for him to turn me in. 'Why are you ringing me, mate?'

'I've got two for you.'

'Two? You mean what we spoke about in the pub?'

'Yes.'

'How much?'

'Five. That includes my ten per cent.'

'I'll take a look. Where are you?'

'I'll be there in a few days. I'll call you then.'

'Okay, mate. Be careful.'

I figured that, short of robbing a bank, selling the two weapons was our best chance of survival. I knew that once he saw the Ruger he wouldn't pay $5000 for the two, but on the black market the Derringer would be in demand. Maybe

I could persuade him to loan me the difference. He knew my dire situation.

I explained my plan to Lucy. 'It's dangerous, we are going back into the lion's den,' I said.

She shrugged. 'They look for us everywhere. It's probable they don't look for us in Sydney anymore.' She paused. 'Boy, can you trust this person?'

'Yes. He hates police. He would never tell on me.'

'So, we sell these toys then what do we do when money is gone?'

'We get some honest work somewhere. Out where no one will take any notice of us. Maybe fruit picking – even washing dishes. We survive for a few months then we take it from there.'

We looked at each other. It wasn't much of a plan. We both knew that eventually I would have to rob a bank.

And for that I'd need a new, effective weapon.

I would worry about that when the time came. Right now, we had to go to Sydney and see Ray.

BACK IN SYDNEY

1999

My main concern with returning to Sydney was the danger of travelling long distances by public transport now that our images had been so prevalent on the media. *The Women's Weekly* article had brought it home to me that if a person sees an image of someone once they might not recognise them if they saw them in public. But after weeks of seeing the image in various media outlets, there was a good chance they would make the connection.

We needed someone to drive us to Sydney and I thought I might have the man. I had been chatting a few times with John Turner. I knew he liked to smoke a bit of pot, so I threw him a bait.

'John, I've a contact who gives me the best pot in Sydney at bottom rock price. But I've lost my licence.'

'Why are you telling me?'

'I need someone to drive me to Sydney, pick up a car load and drive back. It's worth a thousand bucks to you and I'll throw in a bit of pot. But it has to be today or tomorrow.'

At first, he resisted, stating he didn't have any rostered days off that week. But he wasn't hard to persuade. He agreed he could ring his boss and call in sick in the morning.

On the night of 5 May, the three of us set off for Sydney.

Turner and I shared the driving and, apart from a short break in Albury, where he withdrew some cash from an ATM and filled up with petrol, we drove non-stop to a motel in West Ryde. It was too early to book in. Turner made a call from a public telephone to his boss stating he was sick and couldn't do the 5.00 pm shift that day. At this stage, he had realised who we were. Maybe he read the *Women's Weekly*. I was now wary of him.

'There is no reward for us, John,' I told him. 'When I introduce you to my friend he can arrange for you to be supplied with as much pot as you want. You can make a good living from it.'

'I've knocked around,' he said. 'I've been in trouble with the law. I won't put youse in.'

'I know that. You will be glad you made this trip.'

After we booked into the motel, Lucy went for a shower. I decided to dangle another carrot. 'Did you notice the way she looks at you?'

He looked alarmed. 'What do you mean?'

'She fancies you, mate. She likes the strong, silent type.' Despite himself, he was interested. 'You serious?'

'Why wouldn't I be?'

'Yeah, but she's with you.'

'John, I'm getting old. Sometimes I turn a blind eye.' He stared at me, not really believing it, but wanting to. 'Just don't rush it,' I said. 'It's all about good timing.'

That time would never come for John. He had as much chance of bedding Lucy as I had of the Queen granting me a Royal pardon.

'I'm going to ring my friend now,' I said. 'We'll arrange to pick up the pot and you can meet him.'

We drove to a phone booth a few kilometres away. 'Come in with me John. You can listen to the conversation.'

He stood near me as I called Ray. 'Do you have the money?'

'Yes. You bring the items?'

'Of course.'

I arranged to call him at 6.00 pm to fix a meeting point.

Turner spent most of the day watching television. When he showed interest in a book I was reading, 'Never to be Released' by Paul B. Kidd, I told him he could have it.

'Would you sign it for me?' he said.

'We'll both sign it for you.'

After I inscribed it Lucy also signed it. He seemed happy about that.

Now he had the proof that we were with him.

While he was watching a soap opera I took Lucy aside. 'I think he will turn us in first chance he gets,' I said. 'You will have to go and meet Ray while I stay with this guy.'

'Be careful, Boy. He might think there is a reward for us.'

I nodded. 'Once we give him some money he'll be involved. He won't go to the police then.'

After watching the headlines on the five o'clock news to ensure we weren't suddenly of interest again I drove the three of us to West Ryde railway station. Turner didn't know the Sydney area and agreed that while he was here it was best that I drove. It was risky without a licence. But if the police stopped us for any reason, it wouldn't matter who was driving, I was certain at this stage Turner would give us away. If he was driving he could easily bring attention to us.

Leaving the others in the vehicle I called Ray. 'I am sending Lucy to make the deal.'

For a few seconds, there was silence. Then he replied: 'All right. You know what you're doing. Whereabouts?'

'Strathfield. On the left side travelling to Sydney. There are bus sheds there. She will be wearing a grey cap and jeans.'

'Believe me, I'll know Lucy when I see her.'

I had briefed Lucy on what to expect. When he realised the Luger wasn't functional he would refuse to pay the $5000. But I was certain he would be desperate to take the Derringer. I was hopeful Lucy could persuade him to pay $4000 for the two. But $3000 was the bottom line. Otherwise she would walk away.

After picking up some takeaway Turner and I returned to the motel to wait for her to call.

Two hours later she hadn't called. Had I sent her into a trap? My mind was racing with negative thoughts about what could have happened. I rang the desk to check in case the phone was malfunctioning.

No. The phone wasn't the problem.

By now I was certain Lucy was in trouble. What do I do? There was nothing on the news about her. But of course, there wouldn't be. If the police had her they wouldn't want me to know. If Ray had set her up they would now have his phone tapped. I couldn't ring him from here.

Turner had fallen asleep on his bed. I shook him. 'John, time to go. I need to drive across town and make a phone call.'

'Can't you do it here?'

The phone rang. I grabbed it. Lucy was stressed: 'Boy, he didn't come. I waited ninety minutes then I saw Russian woman from Ryde. She knew me. I had to get away and make certain I'm not followed.'

'Okay. Where are you?'

'West Ryde.'

'I'll be there in ten minutes.'

Why had Ray said he'd be there and then not come? I knew he wanted the weapons. Did he think that when I told him I was sending Lucy it was some type of a trap? He was a paranoid guy. But why would one of the most wanted fugitives in Australia try to set him up buying a few weapons? There was no logic to it.

I discovered years later that when I arranged the meeting with him he only had $3000. Ray was a heavy gambler. He went to a TAB and tried to win the other two, but lost the lot.

He had simply been too embarrassed to meet Lucy.

Turner gave me an inquisitive look. I told him that my marijuana friend had arranged to supply the goods tomorrow. I could see he wasn't happy but he had come this far, another day wouldn't matter. He would just have to call in sick for another day.

When we arrived at the station Lucy was waiting.

Turner wanted to go and have a beer. I told him it was risky for me, people in this area knew me.

Back at the motel we had a crisis meeting in the bathroom while Turner watched television. We had $340, nowhere to live and when I told Turner there was no money or pot for him he would be looking for the nearest police station.

'We don't have a choice,' I said to Lucy. 'We have to buy a tent and go bush for a few weeks.'

'You think we survive in this bush?'

'It was a huge mistake coming here with this guy. If we had have sold the guns we would have had enough cash to hide out. When we part company with this guy he will bring the heat right back on us.'

'Then it is settled. Maybe we eat kangaroo for a while.'

'First, tomorrow we have to leave some false trails.'

Overnight the tension was affecting the three of us. Turner was either watching television or sleeping. But sometimes I saw him watching either Lucy or me. Maybe he was trying to work up the courage to make a move on Lucy. He knew she liked him...

We drove out of the motel at about 9.00 am. I told Turner we were going to meet my friend. After about half an hour I stopped at Terrey Hills and pretended to make a phone call.

I told Turner: 'We have to meet him at Hungry Jacks.'

I drove to the Bass Hill outlet where the burgers are better and stopped in the car park. I had already arranged with Lucy for her to walk to the nearby Tourist Park and book a cabin for two nights.

Turner and I entered Hungry Jacks and ordered burgers, chips and drinks. This was the test. Although he knew I was carrying the Derringer I had never threatened him. There had been no reason to. But we were now playing a game of chess. I figured he probably believed the hype about me being a dangerous criminal. If he tried to expose me here, what might I do? He wasn't an overly brave guy. I gambled that he would say nothing. He still believed he would be collecting $1000 and some pot today.

Lucy joined us. She whispered to me that she had booked a cabin. She didn't want anything to eat and we left.

'Where's your friend?' Turner asked.

'He wants to transfer the stuff from his car to yours where nobody will see it,' I said.

It was time to part ways with our Footscray friend. I drove to Lane Cove National Park where the three of us alighted. There were a few people scattered around but no one was taking any notice of us.

I held out my hand. 'My friend isn't coming, John. Looks like he ripped us all off.'

He shook my hand. 'You brought me here for nothing. I could lose my job.'

'John, I know you are going to the police. We can do a deal. You can tell them the truth, we promised you a thousand dollars to drive us to Sydney. At some stage, you realised who we were. You were too frightened to run away because you saw my little silver revolver and thought I might shoot you. But I never actually threatened you.'

'You didn't have to.'

'John, I wouldn't hurt a kitten. Now listen, you can be a media star. You are big news. On the road with John and Lucy. You shared a motel with us.' I paused, and smiled.

'Make sure you show *60 Minutes* the book we signed for you.'

'You think they'll pay me?'

'Are you kidding? You will be the hottest ticket in town. And you might be able to sell that book for a sizable sum.'

'How much?'

'Thousands. Get Harry M. Miller to sell it for you.'

'Who's he?'

'A promoter. But focus on *60 Minutes*. You have to do us one favour in return.'

'What's that?'

'Tell the police I have shaved my hair off to look bald. And Lucy has dyed hers black and is wearing contact lenses.'

'Okay. I hope you both survive.'

We shook hands again. 'We have to use your car to get away. We'll leave it a couple of miles away. You can say you went into that toilet over there and when you came out we had driven off.' I paused. 'You'd better walk over into the toilet now, in case police check with witnesses.'

John Turner, the hottest ticket in town, walked towards the toilets. He didn't look back.

Driving out of the parkway, I headed towards Macquarie Shopping Centre which was about 4 kilometres away. We parked on one of the levels inside the giant shopping centre and hurried towards the taxi rank. There were a lot of people in line and it took about five minutes before we were inside a cab and on our way across town. We changed taxis then caught a train to Bass Hill. From there we walked quite a distance down the Hume Highway to our cabin and temporary safety.

Now it depended on what John Turner did and said.

That was Friday night. There was nothing on the TV news that night. 'I have no doubts Turner went to the cops,' I said to Lucy. 'For some reason, they are keeping a lid on it. Probably trying to lull us into a false sense of security.'

'So, we still go bush?'

'I'm afraid so. But only for a week.'

Early on Saturday morning we bought some camping gear. After returning to the cabin we remained there for most of the day, only going out to buy some takeaway.

But the animal instinct for danger I had developed over the years was sending signals to me.

'We'll leave at 6.00 am, Luce. It will be tough for a week.'

She grinned. 'I am Spartan by nature. Besides, I want to watch Boy catch this kangaroo.'

What we didn't know was that the Sunday newspapers had already printed in their early editions, available in some outlets at 7.00 pm, a major 'scoop'.

'44 hours of terror with jailbreakers' (*Sun-Herald*, 9 May 1999.)

Turner had claimed we kidnapped him from his motel at Footscray and forced him at gunpoint to drive us to Sydney where we held him hostage for forty-four hours.

He also told the police we had robbed him of $800 which police later found hidden under his mattress at the motel.

He did an interview with A Current Affair. They paid him $500, flew his wife up from Victoria and paid for a suite for two nights at Sydney's Star Casino.

John Turner had indeed become the hottest ticket in town. The only hotter ticket was the Killick and Dudko one – and that was red hot.

Especially as Turner had given police a detailed accurate description of how we looked.

At 8.00 pm the manager of the Bass Hill Tourist Park saw a newsflash on Channel 9, with a quick summary of Turner's accusations and a detailed description of how we had changed our appearance. There were also recent media pictures of us.

The manager thought he recognised Lucy and rang Bass Hill Police Station claiming he was eighty per cent certain that Lucy Dudko was in cabin fourteen.

By 11.00 pm our cabin was under surveillance by police in the cabin opposite us. By 1.00 am the State Protection Group police were in command. Roadblocks went up on the Hume Highway and the tourist park was surrounded by forty police, including the dog squad.

A bit after 2.00 am twelve SPG officers wearing bulletproof vests surrounded our cabin. Others were waiting behind bushes and shower blocks. Some were armed with machine guns. They still believed I had the machine gun.

At 2.20 am the call came on the loudspeaker: 'John Killick, Lucy Dudko, this is the police. The place is surrounded. Come out with your hands in the air.'

In my life, I have experienced many shocks, but to be woken by this booming message was comparable only with the unexpected death of my mother almost forty years previously.

Lucy, usually calm and collected, was also shaken. This was it. I had failed her.

'They've got us, Boy.'

I nodded. She still had a chance. 'Don't say anything when we go to the police station. They haven't got any real evidence you did it.'

The loudspeaker was in action again ordering us to come out.

Years later a prisoner – considered by some as a 'heavy' – asked me: 'Why didn't you try to shoot your way out?'

I preferred to stay alive. Maybe down the track I'd get another chance to escape. The priority now was to try to get Lucy out of it.

We took our time leaving the cabin – about fifteen minutes. I never considered suicide. Did Lucy? She later said she thought fleetingly about it, but decided against it.

I went out first. Lucy followed. We were quickly handcuffed and taken to Bass Hill Police Station.

Surprisingly on arrival they sat us in adjoining cubicles where we could see and speak to each other.

'We are almost certainly bugged,' I said. 'Don't answer any questions without a lawyer present. You have been convicted without evidence by the media. There is every chance a court will set you free.'

'Poor Boy. He still believes in fairy tales. They are out to get us, Boy.'

'They got me. But you didn't do anything wrong except came with me when I escaped.'

'We will see, Boy.'

'They will separate us soon and you may not see me again until we go to court. I will write to you every day. I will number the first letter number one. A month later you will get letter number thirty-one.'

'I will do the same, Boy.'

She was holding up remarkably well. She had an inner strength that would see her through the next seven years of tough times.

SPECIAL TREATMENT

1999–2004

The punishment meted out to both Lucy and I was far in excess to that of most criminals, including murderers.

Although she was an unconvicted prisoner, she was given the highest security of any woman in New South Wales prisons. She was informed that the orders came from the highest level. For ten weeks she was confined, under constant surveillance, in solitary confinement in a cell containing two cameras. The shower curtain was removed, leaving her with no privacy.

They brought her out of the cell daily for an hour's exercise. It was more than two months before anyone was permitted to visit her.

I was taken to the Goulburn High Security Unit (HSU) and placed in a cell next to serial killer Ivan Milat. I remained in segregation for nearly four years. Eventually after about twelve months I was allowed twice a week to walk in an exercise yard for ninety minutes with another prisoner. Sometimes that prisoner was Ivan Milat. I found him to be intelligent and persuasive. He tried to convince me that he was innocent – set up by the police who planted items of victims' clothing on his property. But after I was out of segregation and able to get to the library I managed to get a copy of his Supreme Court Appeal. What he hadn't told me, but what was undoubtedly damning in the eyes of the judges, was the fact that every time one of the young victims went missing Milat had taken a day off work.

Even today he insists he is innocent. He has a history of going on hunger strikes to protest his innocence. It is hard to imagine the horror, pain and suffering those young victims must have gone through. Ivan Milat will die in gaol.

When Lucy was allowed out of segregation she was still classed as an Extreme High Risk (EHR) inmate and would remain so for at least three years.

She was placed in a special wing, Kipling, that according to Lucy mainly housed child killers. She was forced to share a cell with at least one of these women and if one of them went on escort for a day or two Lucy would have to go to another cell with two other prisoners, where she was forced to sleep on the floor.

During her seven years of incarceration she, despite reaching minimum security status, was not once permitted outside the perimeters of the walls or fences without being handcuffed and escorted. No day leaves, work release or any other form of leave was granted to her. A privilege granted to many murderers towards the end of their sentences.

Despite opposition from a lot of the guards, we were given one privilege: a fortnightly, six-minute inter-gaol phone call. The Governor at Goulburn told me that the Governor at Mulawa, a decent man, was concerned about Lucy's mental state while she was in isolation. He also gave her a Walkman. He obviously felt that the stimuli from the Walkman plus the contact with me would help to counter the extreme conditions of her segregation.

These phone calls, later extended to ten minutes, became the highlight of each fortnight.

Some of the guards at Goulburn – unofficially the gaol where prisoners were sent for extra punishment – were furious about the phone calls.

'You two shouldn't be allowed any contact at all,' I was often told.

Sometimes, by pre-arrangement I always felt, most of the six minutes was taken up by the difficulties encountered getting Lucy to the phone.

An example: 'Who is this?'

'John Killick. I'm calling from Goulburn. I have a pre-arranged phone call with Lucy Dudko. She should be there waiting.'

(Lucy was always waiting outside the office for the scheduled call.) 'Who?'

'Lucy Dudko.'

'Oh, I know the one. You have the wrong wing. She's in another section.'

'Could you put me through, please?'

'Just a minute, I'll try.' Another minute goes by.

'Are you there? I'm putting you through.'

'Thank you.'

'Hello, is that John Killick?'

'Yes. Could I speak to Lucy please?'

'I'll just get her.'

Another thirty seconds go by, then Lucy all out of breath says: 'Hi, Boy! I was worried sick. I thought something happened to you.'

'A bit of a stuff up, Luce. We only have two minutes left.'

It was only when I was transferred to Lithgow in 2003 that phone calls became less of a hassle.

Lucy always worried that something would happen to me. In a letter she wrote on 18 July 1999, she explained how she thought I had killed myself.

A girl sang out to her: 'Hey, sweetheart! Your bloke committed suicide hanging himself in the cell.'

She told Lucy it was on the news. Another girl also heard it. Lucy asked them what was the name of the guy? They didn't know but told her it was the 'bloke that escaped from Silverwater'.

'I thought it was you, Boy!' Lucy wrote.

She ran to the officers' post and asked the guard. He said he knew nothing about it.

It took about thirty minutes before one of Lucy's friends persuaded another guard to ring Goulburn where they confirmed that John Killick was still alive.

The poor wretch who died had escaped from the minimum security section of Silverwater and after being recaptured, hanged himself in a cell. Lucy wrote: 'I know that this is not your style, I know, but when something like that is told all reasoning dies away and nothing is left except horror. Jesus! I love you!'

She later alarmed me when she wrote: 'If you go, I go...'

I went to great lengths to convince her that no matter what, I would survive and be with her again. But if something, inexplicably, did happen to me she had to focus on surviving, get out and tell our story. She agreed to that.

The letters we sent, combined with the phone calls, held together the strong bond between us against almost impossible odds. Even though we knew every word we spoke and every word we wrote would be scrutinised and analysed by guards. But not once did we mention that taboo word 'helicopter'. Although I did slip up once and say 'chopper'. I think I got away with it.

The agreement, that first day of our arrest, to write every day and date and number letters proved to be a thorn in the side of those guards, and there were many, who resented our being able to maintain regular contact. It often became a stressful battle to receive mail. Occasionally it would arrive in a batch of ten or twelve – three weeks after the first one was written. Sometimes there would be one or two missing.

A typical scene. Me: 'Numbers 1127 and 1131 are missing.'

Guard: 'You never stop whingeing about mail, Killick. Blame Australia Post.'

It upset them when I rang and wrote to the Ombudsman on dozens of occasions complaining about missing mail. A lot of the guards wrote reports stating that I was a 'whinger'. It didn't matter what gaol I was in – letters went missing. Lucy had the same problem.

The Ombudsman proposed that our letters be logged when sent and when they arrived. Problem solved. But the guards refused to do it, stating they didn't have the time.

Between 10 May 1999 and December 2005, we wrote 4676 letters to each other plus dozens of cards. Of that amount, at least 250 never arrived. At least another 1060 simply 'disappeared' from Lucy's property.

In late October 2004 Lucy had been transferred from Mulawa to Dillwynia at Windsor. When she was given her belongings she discovered that about 1000 of my letters, which were packed in a plastic tub used for prisoner escorts, were missing. She wrote: 'They lost about a thousand of your letters!!!!

Despite complaints by both of us to the Ombudsman and the Commissioner Ron Woodham, no explanation was ever given.

I was told it was just one of those unfortunate things. Although every precaution was made to ensure the safety of both prisoners and their property during transport, sometimes things got lost.

'They just disappear into a black hole,' one guard joked.

I wondered if he would be so jovial if, rather than my letters that had disappeared during escort, it had been Lucy.

Imagine the headlines: 'Helicopter Lucy disappears during escort!' And the Ombudsman and Ron Woodham couldn't find her.

'She just sort of disappeared into a black hole,' a spokesman for Corrective Services said.

But if we accept that somehow the guards did manage to lose a tub containing 1000 letters – over 3000 handwritten pages – a 'It fell off the back of the secure prison van' sort of thing and we blame Australia Post for the 250 letters that never arrived, it still doesn't explain what happened on 24 February 2005 when Lucy complained to me in a letter:

'Just went through all your letters which are in my possession and found out that all your letters for October & November (up to 4.12/04) are MISSING! I keep your mail in a special box on a top of my wardrobe. Well, those letters are gone. Last time I checked them – was about a month ago and everything was here. I keep my room locked all the time I am out, so...I don't want to talk about it. I am so sick of some scumbags stealing my mail. And when tomorrow I'll go and ask for those letters, they'll tell me that it's impossible to say what happened.'

And impossible to say what happened to the thousand letters. And impossible to say what happened to the 250 letters that never arrived.

For me, the answer is glaringly obvious. You don't need to be Einstein to figure it out. Not all the crims in prison wear green...

Although I can understand the heavy security placed on me, I was stunned by the similar amount of security placed on Lucy.

On numerous trips to court from Goulburn to Sydney, I was always placed in the back seat of a car with three armed 'special squad' guards. I had my legs shackled and a leather security belt placed around my waist with handcuffs attached to it. During the 400-plus kilometre return trip I couldn't even scratch my nose. A 'back up' vehicle with another two armed guards would follow us.

Even though she hadn't escaped and was unconvicted, Lucy had a similar escort procedure – except they didn't put leg cuffs on her. During her trial, she had four 'special squad' guards standing nearby. One can only guess as to what influence this would have had on a jury.

After she was found guilty the judge sentenced her to ten years with a seven years non-parole period. For someone who had no convictions it was a heavy sentence. On her appeal for a reduction of sentence she cited the case of Heather Parker:

A married guard at Melbourne's Remand Centre, Parker fell in love with a prisoner, Peter Gibb. On one occasion, they were discovered in a broom cupboard. She left the prison service and her husband left her.

In March 1993 Gibb and Butterley used explosives smuggled in by Parker to blast a hole in the wall of the prison and used a makeshift rope to lower themselves to the street. As he dropped to the pavement the overweight Butterley damaged his leg. They hurried to a nearby vehicle left for them by Parker who had also placed a loaded pistol in the glove box. With Gibb driving and being chased by a guard who had hailed down a taxi, the vehicle collided twice with other vehicles as they dumped the car and commandeered a motorcycle. Gibb must have panicked: he crashed the motorcycle as well.

When two police officers tried to arrest them, Butterley shot one of them, John Schoenpflug, twice wounding him in the chest and the arm. The other one, Warren Treloar, hit Gibb with a baton, breaking his arm. With his other hand Gibb grabbed Treloar's revolver and threatened to shoot Schoenpflug again unless Treloar retreated.

Seizing the advantage, they stole the police van and drove off. After a few kilometres, they changed to a waiting vehicle owned by Parker and drove to Frankston where she had stored a 4-wheel-drive Pajero. After dropping into La Trobe Regional Hospital at Moe to attend to the injuries sustained by Butterly and Gibb, the three of them journeyed on to bushland.

On March 11, they booked into a hotel at Gaffney's Creek, 175 kilometres out of Melbourne. Before leaving the following day, they set fire to their room to destroy all traces of their identities. The entire hotel was destroyed.

On 13 March police tracked them to Picnic Point. Gibb and Parker were arrested without a struggle. Butterley was found dead with a bullet wound to the back of his head – fired by the pistol he had stolen from the police officer.

Police claimed he committed suicide.

In dismissing Lucy's appeal against the severity of her sentence, Justice Spigelman stated: 'Dudko's offences are more serious than those committed by Parker.'

I could never understand the logic there. Explosives used to blow a hole in the side of the prison...a police officer shot twice...a police vehicle stolen... another officer assaulted and his pistol taken...a motorcyclist held at gunpoint and his motorcycle stolen and an escapee shot dead.

Parker, a trusted prison officer, supplied the explosives, the weapons and the vehicles and was even involved in the burning down of a hotel that had people in it at the time.

Parker served four years in gaol. Lucy served seven years.

When Parker and Gibb were released they were immediately reunited and were married.

The conditions of Lucy's parole stipulated that she couldn't contact me. Fifteen years after the escape, one of the conditions of my parole was that I couldn't contact Lucy.

It's a medical fact that stress can increase the risk of heart attack and stroke. Certainly, it helped to increase my blood pressure to alarming levels. It was not unusual for my BP to soar to 200 – 120. According to specialists such a reading is unacceptable and necessitates being in a hospital bed with monitoring by medical staff.

But the Corrective Services had a different policy – at least where I was concerned. Although the doctors had prescribed medication for me, it didn't prevent my BP soaring to dangerous levels.

In May 2000, I had been brought from Goulburn to the segregation unit at Long Bay. I was there due to medical concerns about my uncontrolled hypertension. A specialist wrote that my BP was often at 'unacceptable' levels. He arranged for tests and increased my medication.

On the night of 19 May my cell door opened and a team of special squad guards came in. Another guard was videoing the procedure. I had to wait outside while they searched the cell. Trashed is a more appropriate word. All my court documents were strewn on the floor and the cell was left in a mess.

After ten minutes, I returned to my cell and before leaving one of the guards said: 'Tidy your cell up!'

It took me about thirty minutes to get some semblance of order with my court papers and personal letters.

Then the door opened again. The boys were back! Another search ensued. This time they used a spanner to unfasten the connecting water pipes running to the toilet. They again 'searched' the cell, with my court documents once more visiting the floor.

When they couldn't find any unauthorised item, the guy in charge said: 'Pack your gear, you're going on escort.'

I stared at him. My head was pounding with a severe headache. Gloria and my lawyer had both arranged to visit me in the morning. There was no way I could let them know I wouldn't be here.

Among all the special squad guys standing around I noticed the wing officer. He was a fair man and had ensured that the last scheduled phone call with Lucy had gone through.

I caught his attention. 'Chief, could you get the nurse for me before I go – I feel a bit crook.'

He nodded. 'I'll see what I can do.'

The special squad guys were watching me as I began packing my property into two plastic tubs.

After about five minutes the nurse arrived. The first thing she did was take my BP.

'It's 200 over 120,' she said to the guard in charge. 'If it gets any higher his head will go through the roof.'

'If you put me on the escort and I survive,' I said, 'I'll have you in court charged with malicious abuse of duty of care.'

'I'll give him some more medication,' the nurse said, 'but he probably shouldn't go tonight.'

'Security overrides medical,' he said. 'We'll see about that in court,' I said.

He looked a bit uncertain. 'I'll go and check.' They locked me in the cell and went away.

Ten minutes later they returned.

'You have to go,' the head guy said. He sounded apologetic. 'Orders from up top.'

They placed the leg cuffs on me, fastened the security belt then ordered me to push a trolley with my tubs of property on top.

Feeling lightheaded and dizzy, I shuffled along pushing the trolley with great difficulty. As I passed Neddy Smith's cell (he was in the top end of the wing, sectioned off by a locked gate from the segregation unit) I yelled out: 'Hey Ned and the rest of you guys! It's John Killick. I'm seriously ill and being taken away in chains to Goulburn. If I don't survive get the truth out there!'

The guards didn't even try to stop my rant. At times during the drive to Goulburn I thought I might die.

On arrival, the Goulburn guards told me they had nowhere to house me except in a cell upstairs in the strict protection unit. A nurse came to my cell and gave me more medication. It wasn't long before I was asleep.

The following morning when they opened the door I asked for a phone call to Gloria to inform her of my whereabouts. Three hours later I was given the call. By then she was at Long Bay trying to visit me.

Later that day I was transferred to a security cell in the segregation unit. But somehow the news I had been in the strict protection unit was circulated all over the prison.

I wasted no time in making a complaint to the Ombudsman. What was the 'security' reason that overrode the medical duty of care?

It took about three months before the Ombudsman informed me that I had been transferred to Goulburn because a shiv (a knife) had been found in the shower yard which I shared with one other prisoner. There had also been 'vague' rumours of 'taking a hostage'. The Ombudsman noted that there had been no notes concerning these incidents made in the log book at the time.

Strange. Usually if someone hits the buzzer and asks for an aspirin it is entered in the log book.

In February 2004, the special squad came to my cell at Lithgow and told me to pack a few items – I was on escort to Goulburn. That morning I had already complained of being sick.

'We can't do anything about that,' a guard said. 'Security overrides medical.'

'What security?'

'You know damn well what!' I had no idea.

I was shackled and placed alone in the back of a van. The escort was just for me. But the van needed petrol. They stopped at a service station a few kilometres from the gaol.

As the guards were refuelling, I began kicking on the side of the van and yelling out. One of them came to the rear.

'What's your problem?'

'I've got bad pains in the chest!'

He had no option. He made a call to security.

Five minutes later I was back inside the gaol and escorted to the medical room.

A short, solidly built matron in a nurse's uniform stood with her hands on hips. 'And what's supposed to be wrong with you?'

'I've got a shocking headache and a pain in the chest. I think my blood pressure is through the roof.'

'Oh, do you? I'll be the judge of that.' She was a no-nonsense type of nurse.

She rolled out the electronic blood pressure monitoring machine and strapped the sleeve to my arm. The monitor read: 200–120.

She glared at me. 'You are bringing it on yourself! I can do that. Just relax and stop stressing.'

'I'm being shanghaied to Goulburn and I don't know why. Wouldn't you be stressed?'

'I'm not in gaol.'

I looked around. 'Well, where are we?'

One of the guards laughed. But in this room, she was in charge. She took my BP again: 200–120.

She disconnected the machine. 'It's not working properly.'

She then proceeded to take my BP manually. 'One-fifty over 100,' she said to the guard. 'It has come down. He is safe to travel.'

I couldn't believe that this woman was a nurse who had a duty of care to her patients. 'I'll be seeing you in court,' I said. 'You'll soon be out of a job.'

'Do what you want. He can go officers.'

The guard in charge seemed genuinely concerned. 'What, immediately?'

'Yes. He is fit enough to make the trip.'

The journey, often around tight mountain bends, took nearly three hours. This time, shackled as always, I truly believed I would die. My headache was so severe that I thought my head would burst. The chest pain had subsided but I was experiencing dizziness and nausea.

When I arrived at Goulburn I was placed in a reception cell. Shortly afterwards a male nurse arrived and took my blood pressure.

'Two hundred over 120,' he said. 'You need to rest, you are as pale as a ghost. How's the chest pain?'

'Just about gone. But my head is killing me.'

After he gave me some more medication, I was again handcuffed and walked through the gaol to the segregation unit where I was placed in a cell. This time the reason given for my transfer was more extraordinary than the one proffered in May 2000.

'Someone' had informed the authorities that Kevin Geraghty and old Joe McClean (a major drug importer) had financed Lucy to jump the wall at Berrima, hijack a chopper and fly into Lithgow and rescue us Silverwater style.

Kevin and Joe were placed in segregation at Lithgow, Lucy transferred from Berrima to Mulawa segregation.

After two weeks, I was returned to Lithgow. Lucy returned to Berrima and Kevin and Joe were released from segregation. It was the second time Kevin Geraghty had been placed in segregation over me.

When I returned to Lithgow the governor, whom I always found to be fair, came into my cell and told me 'unofficially' that he was sorry it happened. The authorities hadn't really believed the story but because it involved four very high-profile prisoners, they had no choice other than to be 'proactive' on the matter.

He assured me it had nothing to do with the fact Lucy and I had been refused permission to go to court to make our verbal submissions to the High Court during the time we were in segregation, because as the newspapers reported we were 'flight risks'. Both of us had our High Court appeals rejected. Justice Kirby, one of the justices presiding over the case, commenting that in this day and age of digital electronics he saw no reason why prisoners shouldn't be given the opportunity of personally presenting their arguments if not in person then by video link.

This time I gave the guards who complained that I was a 'whinger' plenty of ammunition. I rang The Ombudsman and the Health Care Complaints Commission (HCCC) as well as writing to Justice Health complaining about the nurse who gave the okay for me to be placed on the escort. HCCC asked me to send a letter detailing the incident. Justice Health simply ignored my letter. But both the Ombudsman and HCCC investigated. After about four months the HCCC ruled in my favour, stating my concerns of having a stroke or a heart attack while on the trip to Goulburn were justified. The fact my BP was 200–120 on arrival at Goulburn indicated that the original reading twice on the electronic monitor at Lithgow had been correct. Negotiations were now under way to ensure that 'security overrides medical' would be rectified.

Tragically, months after this finding, the nurse involved died during an operation. It had nothing to do with my case but a few of the nurses at Lithgow seemed to think I was responsible for her untimely demise and treated me accordingly.

If the policy of 'security overrides medical' was overturned, I saw no evidence of it. On at least four occasions I was forced to travel in the backs of escort vans on long trips while my BP was at dangerously high levels.

HARD TIMES

1999–2006

In late 1999 Lucy and I, after discussing the matter with the Salvation Army officers, applied to the Minister, Dr Leo Kelaher for permission to get married.

We didn't hear any more about it until January 23, 2000 when *The Sunday Telegraph* published another 'scoop' about us.

'How can I marry Helicopter Lucy from my jail cell.'

There were photos of both of us with a reprint of half of my letter.

Despite complaints to the Ombudsman and the Commissioner, no-one was able to find out how the letter managed to find its way into *The Sunday Telegraph* office.

They couldn't blame Australia Post for this one.

The last time I saw Lucy while I was in gaol was during our committal hearing at Downing Centre in July 2000. I had been brought to Silverwater for a week to save the exorbitant costs of paying five or six special squad guards to escort me each day from Goulburn.

The committal hearing saw John Turner totally discredited. He admitted signing a police statement claiming I had stolen $800 from him when he had actually hidden it under his mattress. He had spent time in a psychiatric unit, had a conviction for marijuana possession and had contradicted various parts of his original statement to police. The magistrate had no hesitation in dismissing the charges we faced over Turner.

Although Lucy and I were usually brought to court in separate vehicles, on the last day of the committal they placed us together in a small van, separated by steel mesh but able to see each other and talk.

'Be careful, Boy, they are listening.'

I grinned. 'You Russians are all paranoid.'

But I had no doubts they had us bugged. She was as pale as I had ever seen her. After ten minutes, she was car sick. I was going to start banging, kicking and yelling to get them to stop, but as she pointed out: 'They won't stop. They will think it is a trick.'

On the return trip, despite the court victory, she wasn't much better. I knew it could be a long time before I saw her again and it saddened me to see her this way.

Towards the end of the trip she made a valiant effort to brighten things up.

'Today we won, Boy.'

'Yes. And soon you will win and go free.' She gave me a sad smile. 'And you?'

'I won't get as long as everyone thinks,' I lied. I knew they would make an example of me.

We arrived at Mulawa. I watched the woman I loved, pale and drawn, step from the van in handcuffs and my heart cried out for her. I had done this to her.

She smiled, then disappeared from my view.

It would be fifteen years before I saw her again.

On 23 December, Acting Judge Mahoney gave me twenty-eight years for Christmas. He imposed a non-parole period of fifteen years.

Although Professor Ian Plimer travelled from Adelaide, and Lyn Warner and solicitor Bruce Miles all testified on my behalf, the judge had made up his mind. A reference from the Pope wouldn't have helped.

Naturally I appealed to the NSW Court of Criminal Appeal. I was confident that the sentence would be considered too harsh when compared to sentences handed down for other serious crimes. Most murderers received lesser sentences. Eventually the CCA reduced the sentence to twenty-three years and six months with a non-parole period of fourteen years.

Lucy's trial began in March 2001. When Tim Joyce admitted that he might have been influenced by media images when he identified police photos of Lucy seven weeks after the event, the trial judge Morgan had no option other than to exclude his identification of her. This swung the scales in her favour.

But after deliberating for over three days the jury returned a verdict of guilty.

When we lost our High Court appeals in February 2004 she wrote to me that all she could see ahead was 'darkness'.

Only weeks before experiencing that setback she had suffered a traumatic experience that most male prisoners don't encounter. The following signed statement by Lucy explains it:

> I am Lucy Dudko. I am currently in custody at Mulawa Training and Detention Centre, Locked Bag 130, Silverwater, NSW, Australia 1811. I am 46 years of age.
>
> On the 25th January 2004, a cell search of entire wing I am housed in, was conducted due to some incident I did not take part in. The search was conducted by a number of officers.
>
> During the search, I obeyed all orders and followed all procedures inmates have to follow. During the search one of the officers proceeded to explain to me certain issues regarding to inmate property procedures which I excepted (sic).
>
> Suddenly another officer rushed towards me and pushed me hard against the wall. He started twisting my arms behind my back whilst

forcing my arms towards my neck. He was doing this with a great force causing me a great deal of pain.

Then he handcuffed me. The handcuffs were applied very tight, the pain in my wrists and my shoulders became unbearable. At some stage I started loosing (sic) feeling in my hands. The officer continued the torture by twisting my arms with one hand. He also started jerking violently on the handcuffs to increase the pain I was dealt. At some stage I experienced lightheadness (sic) and almost lost consciousness. He said to me 'You are a fucking bitch, you won't win'.

Then continuing the torture by twisting my arms, pushing them towards my neck and jerking violently on the handcuffs the officer pushed me out of the Wing saying: You won't win, you won't win...'. After a while he led me into my cell, took off the handcuffs and locked me in. I inspected my wrists. I had bruises and cuts on my wrists, I lost feeling in my thumb because I think, while jerking on the tightly applied handcuffs the officer damaged a nerve. My shoulders were aching severely.

I strongly believe that he was talking about the result of my Geneva appeal, because I obeyed all orders, and in all my time in custody I had never been subjected to anything like that. I have been always polite and respectful towards officers all the time. There was no issue of 'loss or win'. The search team supervisor was present and approved the torture by not intervening in any way; therefore I believe it was approved action. My Geneva appeal was made public by media and is a common knowledge throughout the gaol.

On my request later I was taken to the prison clinic. Again I was handcuffed and I remained handcuffed during the time I was given medical assistance by a nurse. The nurse put in writing only the description of unrelated injury and carefully avoided to mention any injures (sic) inflicted by the officer. No photographs were taken, no X-ray was conducted. I believe it was a cover-up.

25.01.2004 (signed by) Lucy Dudko

The Geneva Appeal Lucy was referring to was an application being launched on her behalf to the UN Human Rights Committee under the Optional Protocol to the International Covenant on Civil and Political Rights complaining that she wasn't given a fair trial due to pre-trial publicity from the media and remarks made by Judge Mahoney when he sentenced me and stated that she was the woman in the helicopter. At the time, he made those remarks in December 2000 she was awaiting trial.

She also complained that Legal Aid wouldn't help her with her High Court appeal despite the fact the Corrective Services wouldn't allow her to appear before the court to make her submissions.

Justice Kirby was on record stating that in a case in Western Australia he would not have granted leave to appeal on the written application.

But when the prisoner appeared before him and stated his case the court granted leave to appeal.

The Human Rights Committee rejected her article 14(1) claim concerning pre-trial publicity as inadequately substantiated, but found a breach of the same provision, namely her right to a fair trial and equality before the law, which includes the right to be present in person during a criminal appeal. The HRC said Australia should provide Ms Dudko with an unspecified remedy. No remedy has been forthcoming. (see Dudko v Australia July 2007)

Lucy's letter to me claiming she could only see darkness ahead alarmed me. But when I spoke to her on the phone she had become positive again. We were 'the team'. We wouldn't allow them to break us.

At that stage, I had nine years to go before I was eligible for parole...

Our relationship faced impossible odds. Somehow, it was still strong in early 2005. But the disappearance of a thousand letters from her property, followed by the disappearance of another sixty-plus after we complained about it, hurt her. Then we were given permission by both governors for her to visit me. For over two years she had been told that when she was classified as a minimum security prisoner she could visit me if she paid the overtime for two officers. That amounted to $600 and she had more than that amount in her account.

The visit was set for January 2005. They would bring her to Lithgow from Dillwynia and she could spend two hours with me. Two days before the scheduled visit I was handed a letter from the assistant commissioner. The visit had been cancelled for 'security' reasons.

The department had dealt a mortal blow to our relationship.

Still recovering from the shock of the loss of over a thousand letters, she wrote to me stating she doubted they would let her see me again. Her parole officer had already told her that she wouldn't be given parole unless she admitted her guilt and agreed to break communication with me.

Lucy then did what thousands of other prisoners have done when they begin losing hope. She turned to God. By the time she wrote and told me about it in May she had 'rediscovered' her faith.

Over the next five months she wrote letters trying to convert me. She knew I wouldn't buy it but she tried. She even sent a pastor from the Seven Hills Baptist Church to see me. He brought me a Bible and we had a long discussion about the Bible. He then reported back to Lucy that there was zilch chance of my joining the flock.

I knew the John and Lucy story was over when she refused to take a phone call from me in December 2005.

'She doesn't want anything to do with you,' a delighted guard yelled out so the whole wing could hear it.

I was humiliated. At first, I didn't believe him. She wouldn't end it this way. We had fought them every inch of the way for nearly seven years.

The guard was enjoying it. 'Well, that's the message she gave to the officer when I rang.'

'Can you ring again? Someone might have their wires crossed.'

Most of the guys who had heard him yell out to me were watching and listening.

'All right. I'll ring again.'

I didn't care what the inmates thought. Most of them had been dumped long ago by their women. I was shattered that the hard-line authorities who had tried so hard for nearly seven years to break our relationship had finally succeeded. With the help of God.

This time the guard was more discreet. He looked at me and shook his head. 'She's serious.'

'Okay.' I walked away. A few guys came up to me with commiserations. 'Forget it,' I said. 'It's over. End of story.'

On 8 May 2006, I watched the news as she was released on parole from Dillwynia. She had signed parole papers agreeing she was guilty of committing the crimes and that she would have no contact with me. She looked good. Much healthier than the last time I had seen her nearly six years ago.

Regardless of the way our relationship had finished, she had survived. I was thankful for that...

LIFE WITHOUT LUCY

2006–2014

After Lucy's release, she kept in touch with Gloria for a while. She was living with Mary, a woman she had met through the church. She told Gloria she was having difficulties with the arrangement and would soon move out. When she did, she cut all ties with Gloria, who only realised it when Lucy didn't contact her again. Considering Gloria had regularly visited her for seven years it was, in my opinion, shabby treatment of a friend. Maybe she did it to break all connections with me. Whatever the reason, she owed it to Gloria to explain her actions.

Over the next eight years I was sent from Lithgow, to Goulburn, to Wellington, to Long Bay, to MRRC, to Bathurst, to Wellington, to Parklea, to Nowra, to Dawn De Loas Silverwater, to Nowra and back to Dawn De Loas.

I became a pilgrim of the prison system, but there was nothing religious about it.

It began in March 2007 at Lithgow when a young guy came to me and handed me a thin package about 26 centimetres in length, bound in tape.

'I thought you could do something with these, mate,' he said.

Although I had already guessed what they were, I asked anyway. 'What are they?'

'Six new hacksaw blades. Good luck.' He walked away. My mind was racing. Was this a trap? No. This kid was staunch. He had probably given the blades to me because he thought I would organise a breakout.

The blades could each be cut in half leaving twelve blades that could be passed around to a dozen dangerous inmates who had nothing to lose by attempting a mass break out.

The odds of it being successful were about one per cent, maybe less. Some of them would tell their mates who would tell their mates, etc. They would walk into a trap. But if they did manage to cut through the bars in their cells without the authorities being aware of it, they still had to get over two razor wire fences, then climb a much higher fence that had metal barrels on top covered with razor wire. There were electronic sensors placed near the fences which would pick up the movement of anything larger than a rat. And if by some miracle they managed to get through all that without detection, they were stuck in town 140 kilometres from Sydney. I still remembered being arrested late at night with my two mates in Lithgow forty-seven years ago.

Aside from the almost certainty of failure in any escape attempts, who would the authorities blame for it? I would be nominated for certain. Experience had taught me that the authorities didn't concern themselves with evidence in these matters, they just picked a suspect and threw him in segregation. If these hacksaw blades were either used in an escape attempt or were found during a routine search of the gaol, I would be given a one-way ticket to Supermax.

I had to get the blades out of the system. How? A lot of the guards disliked me, I couldn't trust most of them.

But there were a few whom I liked and would trust enough to hand them the blades.

Taking a huge risk, I took them to the library and slid the blades down behind a steel cabinet. Returning to the wing, I rang Gloria and asked her to visit me on the weekend.

When she came, I outlined the situation. 'If I reveal where they are to a guard and he double crosses me, it will be all over the media that I was planning a mass escape. I'll never get parole.'

She gave me a concerned look. 'What do you want me to do?'

'I'll try to find the right person to give them to. If I don't call you by noon on Monday, I want you to ring Head Office, tell them who you are and ask to speak to someone in authority. Tell them you have some important information regarding security at Lithgow Correctional Centre.'

'How do you know we can trust this person?'

'We don't. You record the conversation. Simply tell him or her that I know the whereabouts of six hacksaw blades and need someone I can trust to get them. But when the crap hits the fan the first thing the authorities will want to do is send me to Goulburn Supermax. Head Office has to ensure that I am kept out of it.'

Gloria had misgivings about the entire situation but agreed I had to do something. Apart from everything else, there was the possibility the young guy who gave them to me might tell one of his mates and after a while half the gaol would know.

On the Monday morning one of the two guards who were in charge of the wing that day was a man I believed I could trust. I decided to take the risk. First, I rang Gloria and told her not to bother Head Office. Then, waiting until the other guard had left the office, I approached the one I trusted.

'Chief, I'm going to reveal the whereabouts of some heavy contraband to you. I need you to tell the governor that I was the one who gave you the information and for me to be kept out of it.'

For a few seconds, he sat there staring at me. No doubt he was a bit stunned. 'Okay, Killick. You have my word. What's the information?'

'There are six hacksaw blades hidden behind the steel cabinet outside the classroom in the library.'

'Why are you telling me?'

'They can only lead to big trouble for everyone.'

'Okay, John. Leave it with me. You will be kept out of this. And thanks.

You've done the right thing.'

But he didn't have the power to keep me out of it. The gaol was quickly locked down, the blades retrieved and I was taken to segregation. No explanation given.

The following day the deputy governor visited me in my cell. A couple of security guards stood outside. 'We know you play chess, Killick, but what exactly are you up to this time?'

'I was trying to avoid a possible mass breakout for which I'd automatically be blamed.'

'Where did you get the blades from?'

'I found them behind some books in the library. It was a good hiding spot – most of the guys in here don't read books.'

'I want the truth, Killick. Where did you get the blades from?'

'I told you.'

He walked out and locked the door. A few days later I was taken to Goulburn and placed in the segregation unit.

It is my experience that in the eyes of most of those at the top in Corrective Services, if they don't like you, then no matter what you do right, it will be ignored. They only judge you on what you did wrong or what they think you might have done wrong, or even what they think you might do.

I remained at Goulburn for two years. It was the gaol where they kept, in their assessment, the worst of the worst.

When I came out of segregation I was placed in the Aussie/Asian yard with up to fifty of us crowded into a small enclosure with nothing to do all day. One of the men was my old mate Robert 'Bertie' Kidd. His sentence was similar to mine. 'They don't like us old crooks,' I joked.

I wrote a short story and entered it in a competition run by the Bridge Foundation. I was awarded second prize. But there was no mention of that in my case notes. I completed writing courses, earning distinction passes. No mention of that either. I completed a programme designed to cure gambling addiction. No credit for that. I was classed as a manipulator trying to manipulate my way through the system. In fact, in late 2012 when I was approaching eligibility for parole, an article appeared in *The Sunday Telegraph* titled 'A crime to set them free'. It had a photo of a murderer, another guy who was convicted of the manslaughter of a policeman, a woman convicted of torture and me.

The article stated that we hadn't completed any courses, had no remorse and wouldn't accept responsibility for our crimes.

I wondered who had fed that information to the chooks?

Maybe the article carried some weight. My parole was held back for fourteen months.

While I was at Goulburn I received the tragic news that my good friend, Lyn Warner, had died. I was shattered. She had on quite a few occasions accompanied Gloria to visit me at Lithgow and Goulburn. She had Chronic Fatigue Syndrome and eventually it wore her down.

In 2009, I was transferred to Wellington Correctional Centre – nearly 400 kilometres from Sydney. The more time I spent in gaol the farther away they sent me. It made it difficult for Gloria to visit me. But she still made the trip on occasions. While there I worked in the bakery. Some of the young guys were simply too lazy to work and I was made foreman, working six days a week. The bakery supervisor wrote in my case notes that I was 'an asset' to the bakery. I wonder what Head Office thought about that?

When Lucy finished her parole on the 8 May 2009, *The Sun-Herald* had a big photo of her on the front page with the caption: 'Lonely Lucy'.

It quoted her as saying: 'Back then my life was a soap opera.'

Ouch! Some soap opera. I had to smile when it revealed she was working in a bakery. Here we were, ten years after our capture both working in a bakery. A bit of irony there.

As much as I found the prison system to be geared more towards punishment and retribution rather than rehabilitation, there was, in my opinion, one shining light: The Violent Offenders Therapeutic Programme (VOTP). Undoubtedly it is the jewel in the crown of the programmes run by NSW Corrective Services. It is run solely by psychologists who work one on one and in groups with prisoners convicted of violent crimes. Not all prisoners, even extremely violent ones, are accepted into the programme. They have to undergo a psychological suitability assessment before they can participate.

In 2010, I was transferred to the VOTP unit at Parklea. About eighty of us were housed in two wings separated from the remainder of the gaol. A lot of guys don't make it through. In my group of twelve, only five avoided expulsion.

Inmates are thrown out of the programme for a variety of reasons: a dirty urine, fighting, not attending groups, disobeying orders, etc.

While I was there two guys decided to escape. They told everyone and one guy rang his girlfriend to say he would be getting locked in early. The phone calls are monitored and the guard who listened to that must have been wondering why the VOTP was getting locked down early.

When I walked into the Wing one of the would-be escapees was knotting some sheets together. I went to the top floor and arranged for a game of chess with one of the best players there. Both of us were aware of the situation and we played a poor quality game.

When they were satisfied that the knotted sheets were sufficiently long enough to get them over the wall the two would be escapees cut through some wire on the roof of a shed. It took about five minutes before they were able to clamber down to the concrete drain channel which ran alongside the wall. By this time, they had been seen by a guard and were quickly apprehended and taken to their cells. From there they were transferred to Goulburn.

As an escape attempt, it would rank one out of ten.

I found the VOTP and the psychologists working there to be of great assistance in my being able to reassess my attitude about robbing banks. After many hours of both group work and one on one with a psychologist I accepted that I had a lot of victims due to my crimes. Although I always took the attitude that it was me against the banks, in reality it was me with a weapon against employees and customers. Some of them would have suffered trauma. In turn, their family and friends would be affected. I am thankful to the tireless workers in the VOTP who helped me to turn it around. Today, six years after completing the programme, I still attend the meetings on a voluntary basis.

I believe that programmes such as this should be extended to include certain non-violent crimes. A person who embezzles millions often leaves many of his/her victims not only traumatised but sometimes suicidal. A housebreaker can leave his/her victims feeling violated and fearful of going out in case it happens again.

Crimes don't have to be violent to destroy lives.

If the government wants to reduce the crime rate, rehabilitation and educational programmes should be increased in prison – not decreased as seems to be the present policy in NSW. The recent decision to take most of the qualified teachers out of the system and replace them with less qualified people is in my opinion a retrogressive step that will backfire.

In July 2011, I was transferred to the minimum security section at Nowra Correctional Centre.

For the next nineteen months, I worked in the buy-up section where we packed and supplied the inmates in both the minimum and maximum security sections with their buy-ups. There were fourteen of us working alone with one female officer. She was a good boss respected by all of us. And she knew she was safe. If one of the men stepped out of line the other thirteen would step in immediately.

Bertie Kidd was one of them. We had travelled similar paths. Met in the late sixties in Pentridge. Both of us confined in H Division during the riots there in the early seventies. Together at Long Bay in 1978. Bumped into each other at Boggo Road in 1984. Met again at Long Bay in 1985. Twenty-two years later at Goulburn. Now here we were in minimum security at Nowra.

In February 2013, the Parole Authority gave an intention to grant me parole on my due date, 3 March 2013. Apart from a charge of 'intimidation' in May 2005 when I slammed an office door breaking the lock, when a guard refused to allow my fortnightly phone call to Lucy, my record was flawless. On paper, I was a model prisoner. But I had spent a total of nearly five years in segregation, been shanghaied to gaols all over the state and caused much grief to many guards by making complaints about lost or stolen mail, etc. I knew I wasn't popular with most of the Corrective Services staff.

The new commissioner, Peter Severin, opposed my intended release.

Lawyers acting for him argued that I had to be 'eased' back into society by doing some external leave. The only fly in the ointment being that the commissioner wouldn't grant me external leave because I had impending extradition to Queensland on the old parole matter for the 1983 bank robbery. The Corrective Services policy was no external leave for anyone facing extradition.

This catch-22 situation kept me in custody for another six months until the Parole Authority concluded:

'Either give him external leave or we'll have to release him.'

It took until October before the commissioner allowed me four hours a month external leave with an electronic bracelet on my ankle.

At this stage, I was housed in the minimum security unit at Dawn De Loas. Once a month Gloria would pick me up and drive to Westfield Parramatta where we would have a meal and walk around and go into a few shops. On the first occasion, we were being followed by prison guards dressed in civvies.

It was my first taste of freedom, if you could call it that, in more than fourteen years. Was I a bit apprehensive or intimidated? Not a bit. I felt as though I had never been away.

In December, the commissioner took a risk and extended the monthly leave to six hours. This gave us enough time to drive home to Milson's Point.

In January, the commissioner threw caution to the wind and also allowed me four hours a month to go into town via public transport to the VOTP with two other prisoners. When I applied for weekend leave he denied it.

When I was again due for parole in February 2014 the commissioner opposed it. He stated that I should have to complete weekend leaves to prove I could adapt to normal society. He said that after I completed a series of weekend leaves he wouldn't oppose parole in 2015. (When I would be extradited to Queensland.)

This time, anticipating his response, I was ready. I immediately made an application to the Supreme Court arguing an abuse of process. Within a week I was before Justice Garling via video link. After I outlined the case to him the Judge remarked:

'If Mr Killick is correct, we have a man in custody who shouldn't be in custody.'

The press picked up on it. Soon afterwards the Parole Authority granted me parole.

I would be released on 15 April 2014.

QUEENSLAND GET THEIR MAN

2014–2016

On the afternoon of 14 April, I was transferred from Dawn De Loas minimum security to the MRRC maximum security.

'Why?' I asked. 'Security risk.'

That night I slept in a one out cell in the gaol where fifteen years and three weeks ago I had left in a hurry.

At about 8.30 am I was taken to the front offices and signed my parole papers. Two plainclothes cops were waiting. The taller of the two said: 'Good day, John. You know why we are here?'

'Do I get three guesses?'

'You only need one. We have a provisional warrant from Queensland.'

'You might as well throw it in the bin. I'll be going home today.'

The other cop who had an old-fashioned crew cut, laughed. 'You're dreaming, John.'

They drove me to Central Police Station and I was placed in a cell. Last time I had been here Lucy was in the cell next to me.

Soon I was called up to see Barrister-at-Law Joe Crowley. He had flown from Queensland to do my case pro bono. Aware that I might eventually need a good lawyer in Queensland, a friend had made the connection for me in 2010. During the past four years I had established a good friendship with him via telephone and letters. He had put a lot of work into my case, studying up on extradition laws. He was of the opinion we could get the extradition stayed on the grounds that it was an abuse of process.

Magistrate Jane Wahlquist presided over the case. Assisting Joe was solicitor Eidan Havaas, a former student of his from Bond University.

One of Joe's arguments was that when the warrant had been issued for me in August 1998 my parole had expired in June 1994. I had not been in hiding, having received a police clearance to work for Juvenile Justice as well as attending Family Court in Canberra on at least a dozen occasions. I had fought two AVOs in court against Alex Dudko, one against Tom (Faye's ex-husband) and been arrested and bailed for driving without a licence. I had even appealed the licence suspension. Hardly the actions of a man 'on the run'.

When the prosecution realised it had a real fight on its hands, they asked for a week's adjournment.

This was granted. The prosecutor then insisted I be refused bail and remain in custody as I was a flight risk. (They all enjoyed saying I was a 'flight' risk.)

The magistrate disagreed, pointing out that I had too much to lose. She granted me $5000 bail. I had to report to North Sydney police station before 8.00 pm daily.

I was taken to Surry Hills Police Centre. When Gloria arrived at about 7.00 pm with the cash she was asked to prove where it came from. She had to return home and get the bank receipts.

It was after 9.00 pm before it was sorted. After signing the bail papers, I was in for another shock. Two Corrections officers were waiting for me inside the police station.

'We will follow you home,' the female officer said. 'When we get there, we'll be putting an electronic monitor on you.'

As I walked out into the light rain, I was approached by a Channel 9 news reporter. 'How does it feel to be free, John?' He had to be kidding.

'I'm not free,' I said. 'I can't talk. The matter is sub-judice.'

When we arrived home, the electronic bracelet was clipped on to my left leg above the ankle. Then a small black box was plugged into the corner of the room. 'Don't ever turn this off,' the female said. 'If you do, it will send an alarm to headquarters.'

Then she gave me some paperwork.

'These are schedules. Before you can leave these premises, you have to fill out where you will be every minute of the day for the next week. If you go somewhere where you aren't meant to be you'll be in trouble.'

After fifteen years inside, it was intimidating stuff to be immediately confronted with, but she was only doing her job. This was all orchestrated from the very top. She explained that until I did the schedules and had them faxed through for approval, I could ring a number she gave me to get permission to go to certain places such as the police station to report on bail or the local shopping centre, or a walk in the park, etc. As long as they knew in advance and approved it.

It wasn't easy to live under these conditions. I was fighting an extradition to Queensland, reporting to police every day and had to figure out where I'd be every minute of the day for the next week. But with great support from Gloria I managed.

The first movie we went to see was at Roseville. While we were in the theatre they rang me on three separate occasions.

'We've lost your signal. You'll have to go outside for five minutes.'

I missed about twenty minutes of the movie. But eventually this type of harassment eased.

Eventually the magistrate ruled against us. She said that it was close to an abuse of process but it was out of her jurisdiction. She held the extradition over and continued bail to enable us to appeal to the Supreme Court.

Thus followed a series of short hearings and adjournments as technical issues and points of law were debated. A few times when Joe couldn't make it, Eidan stood in and did a great job.

John and his wife Julia came over from Shanghai for a few weeks. That was a terrific boost for me.

I did a long interview over a two-week period with Mike Willesee for Sunday Night. I had always liked him and I enjoyed the entire process. They even brought Tim Joyce to meet me at a helipad, where he and Mike landed in a helicopter. Tim accepted my apologies, we shook hands and sat down and had a beer. He offered to drive me home but I showed him the ankle bracelet.

'I have to go home by train, Tim. If I go by car they'll panic and arrest me.'

After all the arguments by both sides had been presented, Justice Carol Simpson finally ruled in favour of Queensland. She also said it was close to an abuse of process but the matter had to be heard in the jurisdiction of Queensland. When the prosecution applied for costs against me because it was a civil case, not criminal, she dismissed the claim stating it was a criminal case dressed in civil clothing. The end result was that I was going to gaol.

A few days later Eidan flew with me to Brisbane. Joe met us at the airport and we drove to the city and had coffee and sandwiches. We then walked to the City Watch House with a dozen journalists and camera crews tagging us.

I spent six months in Queensland before they paroled me. For most of that time I was held in the maximum security prison, Woodford, where I saw quite a few fights. A couple of them as bloody and brutal as any I'd seen. Smoking had been banned and there was a bit of the drug ice floating around. I suspected that a few of the combatants were fuelled up on it. But no-one bothered me. Old age has its advantages.

On 22 January 2015, I was released on parole. Eidan was there with a friend of his to pick me up.

We had to go to the parole office to sign the interstate transfer papers.

While there we were besieged by journalists outside.

I simply said I was sorry for any trauma I may have caused victims of my crimes. You can't take it back and I believed I had paid for my crimes.

I concluded with: 'As far as I'm concerned it's over and we've broken about even.'

When we arrived at Sydney airport two correction officers were there to greet me. They escorted me through the airport away from the media.

They drove me home and we went through the same procedure as the first time.

A few months later we applied to have the electronic monitoring and daily scheduling taken off me. The Parole Authority assented to our request. I simply had to report to a parole officer once a fortnight. Life was again beginning to gain some semblance of normalcy for me. It had been a long time coming.

In July, I had my first book, *Gambling for Love* published by Connor Court. My good friend Professor Plimer, with whom I had kept in contact throughout the years, had organised the publication and flew from Melbourne to attend the launch at the Camellia Grove Hotel opposite Channel 7. Mike Willesee also came along to say hello. John Kerr flew from Melbourne to host the proceedings. I had worked with John via visits, letters and phone calls on his excellent book *Wanted: John and Lucy* published in 2003 and now a collector's item.

Lucy had done some translating for him.

THE FINAL MEETING

2015

About eighteen months after my release in April 2014, I received a phone call from Russia. It was a woman stating she worked for Channel 1, the main television channel there. Her English was only fair as she explained that a Russian film crew wanted to come to Australia and interview Lucy and I for a special programme. They would even pay Lucy's accommodation and fare to Russia so she could see her daughter.

I told her I doubted Lucy would participate. She pushed me for Lucy's phone number and address. I replied that I would provide the information to Lucy and if she agreed to the proposition I would also be happy to co-operate.

A few months prior to this phone call I had done some spring cleaning and found an old steel box containing hundreds of letters and photos belonging to Lucy. The letters were from her father, written during 1993 – 1998. The photos were treasured family pics dating back nearly a century. Gloria had taken them to Lucy's work place and given them to her during the lunch break. For a while they sat in the car talking.

'These are so precious to me,' Lucy said. 'I thought they were gone.'

She told Gloria that Vitali had had a stroke. 'I'm going to Russia this week to see him.' As they parted Gloria could see she was quite distraught, as was Gloria who had enjoyed his company both in Australia and when visiting Russia.

Although I hadn't seen Lucy for fifteen years, for most of that time we had been forcibly separated. Now I was permitted to see her – but only if she agreed to it.

I felt this was the right time to set up a meeting. I could give her the option of replying to the Russian journalist. If she refused to talk to me then so be it.

She had told Gloria she normally finished work at 2:00 pm. At 1:45 I parked down the street from where she was employed. An hour passed. No sign of her. But her car remained on the premises. I began to feel conspicuous. Had she seen me and was waiting for me to leave? Or was she simply working overtime?

I decided to drive to the main street. She would have to come that way. But would she turn left or right? I parked in a northerly direction on the opposite side of the bus stop on the corner.

Another thirty minutes passed. Did she know I was here?

I recalled the day when I watched her favourite movie with her when we lived in Queanbeyan – a hundred years ago. Near the end she was close to tears when Omar Sharif, while standing in a tram, saw his lost love Julie Christie walking past. He hurried off the tram and clutching his chest, began to run then stagger after her before collapsing to the ground and dying. Unaware of his presence, she never looked back.

'It was in their destiny never to meet again,' Lucy said sadly. 'There is much tragedy in Russian literature because of its history.'

Even if it proved to be the last time, I was going to see Lucy again.

Then I saw her car. She was turning left heading towards me. Jumping out of my vehicle, I ran across the road as she approached and waved her down. I could see a female passenger seated beside her.

Although she had to double park, she stopped and opened the window. 'Oh my God.'

'Drive 50 metres up and park for a minute,' I said. 'It's important.' She complied. By the time she got out of her vehicle I was there.

For a few moments we stood there, a metre apart, staring at each other.

There were no hugs.

Here we were, at one time on top of *Australia's Most Wanted* list. Separated by prison walls for more than fifteen years. Finally, the moment we had often written about during our exchanging over 4600 letters, the anticipation, the dreaming, the waiting – that moment was here.

The great anti-climax.

You have to confront it, see it, feel it, to be certain that the magic was gone. This was the reality. The authorities hadn't beaten us – time had. The authorities had psychologically battered us. But time and separation had killed the emotions, eroded the love and made the thousands of letters seem, in retrospect, a waste of time.

And the helicopter? No doubt the infamous escape would forever remain a dot on the landscape of Australian history. That was the remaining legacy of our relationship. They couldn't kill that.

I smiled at her. She reciprocated with the faintest of smiles. 'You look good,' she said.

'So do you.'

But I was shocked at her appearance. Still dressed in her work clothes, she looked pale and drawn. Always slim, she was thinner than ever. And she was so much older than the Lucy I once knew. I wanted to cry. You can cry without tears, without expression, you cry inside. That's how I felt. I shouldn't have come. I should have just remembered the way it had been. The way we were. We stood staring at each other, strangers, and a multitude of thoughts were flashing through my mind...the infamous ride...the terrible times in prison...the joys we had together and finally the love that went where? That dropped into a black hole just like the thousand letters had in what seemed like another lifetime ago.

I was responsible for all of this. No matter what I did from here, I could never bring it all back. I had disillusioned her – the man she had believed in and loved. The man she had proudly told the Russian magazine Ogonyk: 'John is my general, my soldier, my lover...'

'I'm illegally parked,' she said.

I could see her passenger still in the vehicle staring at us. She was obviously wondering what this was all about.

'How is your dad?'

'He died.'

I was stunned. Another blow. 'I'm sorry, Luce.'

'It doesn't matter.'

'It does. Did you see him before he died?'

'Yes. I was in Russia for two months. I only returned this week.' Suddenly the reason I was there became irrelevant.

'The reason I pulled you over, a Russian film crew want to do a documentary about us. They will pay your expenses to Russia.'

She gave a faint smile again. 'I would have to think about it.'

I nodded. She wouldn't do it. I handed her the details with phone numbers, etc. I included my number. 'Give me a call, let me know what you decide.'

'You should stay away from the media,' she said. 'You make it difficult for me. My friends talk.'

'Then they aren't your friends.'

'I have to go. I'll get booked.'

I handed her a copy of my book. 'Here, you helped me write some of this.'

She took it. Another smile. 'Hmm.'

I laughed. It was easy now. Emotion was gone. 'Don't worry, you aren't in it, but you will be in the next one.'

'No, I don't want that.'

'What happened to your book?' I asked. 'It would be a bestseller.'

'No. It's too painful.'

'It has to be done, Luce. Ring me. Even if you don't want to do the documentary. We will talk about what I can and can't put in my book about you.'

Without looking back, the woman I no longer knew got into her car and drove away and out of my life.

She never rang.

EPILOGUE

A few weeks after handing this manuscript to the publisher I had to deposit some money in a city bank. I was the only customer. The young female teller was immaculately groomed, friendly and attractive.

It flashed through my mind that there was a time when I might have pointed a loaded weapon at this young woman and threatened her in the process of robbing the bank. A chill ran through me.

How could I have done it? Not once but many times. I tried to imagine how this girl would feel; the fear and the trauma.

I felt ashamed. No doubt I had terrorised people just like her. Somebody's daughter...Somebody's wife...Somebody's mother...

My justification? It had been me against the banks. Wrong, Killick. It had been you with a loaded weapon against unarmed, innocent people.

The young teller handed me my receipt and, with a beautiful smile, said: 'Thank you, John.'

Did she know who I was? No. She had simply noticed my name on the statement.

'A pleasure,' I said, meaning it.

It was a great feeling to walk rather than run when exiting a bank.

All of those bank robberies occurred last century. Three of them fifty-one years ago. But these events will always live with me. I can recall in detail how each one played out. And I'm sure that for those victims still alive they too have total recall of the robberies and how they were affected by them.

I have paid a heavy price for the mistakes I have made. But that comes with the territory. Specialists recently revealed to me that in 2007 I suffered a stroke. Neither Corrective Services nor Justice Health revealed this information to me. My family has also suffered. But you have to move on. I feel that overall, I have broken about even with just enough time left to finish ahead. If I can do good things from here that goal will be achieved. Earlier this year I was interviewed by a journalist who approached me offering to write an article about this coming book. But she didn't do that. Instead, she misquoted me and gave the impression to anyone who read the article that I considered my life of crime to have been great fun and thus my total disregard for victims. This was in contrast to twenty-five previous radio, television, newspaper, magazine and online interviews and articles I have done since my release in April 2014. I suppose if she had written the same old story it wouldn't have been worth printing. So, suddenly I am renouncing not only all I have said in those interviews but everything I have said in all of the counselling groups I have attended in the past seven years, as well as one on one discussions with psychologists. I have lectured university students and kids caught up in the juvenile justice system. Some of them would have seen the article and lost faith in people like me. Not to mention the many victims of armed robberies who would have been angered by what I was supposed to have said.

If the article was written with the intention of harming me and the message I have been trying to get across about the damage that can be caused through crime, then it has achieved its objective. Those who know me regarded it with the contempt it deserved.

In July 2016, I received an email from Cathy. I hadn't heard from her since 1971 when I had been in H Division. She said that from time to time she had checked me out online. When she saw a picture of herself on the cover of my first book she had, after recovering from the shock, obtained my email from my publisher. At first, I was skeptical, thinking it might be someone who had read my book and was pretending to be her. But when she mentioned the gold tooth that I had lost during my fight with O'Mealley in 1969 I knew she was the real deal. Divorced from her attorney husband, she has three children who are all doing well and four beautiful grandchildren. We now have regular phone contact. Hard to believe that fifty-five years have passed since I walked into that housie game in Fairfield, saw this big-eyed beautiful girl and was immediately smitten.

The Cathy and John story is a remarkable one with its many twists and turns. So too, in a totally different way, was the John and Jackie story. There is no question that the John and Lucy story is not only remarkable but unique. Urthboy even put out a song about it called 'The Long Loud Hours'. The story will live on long after we are gone. Three totally incredible but different women who impacted immensely on my life over the past fifty-five years. And no doubt I impacted on theirs.

But to me, the most remarkable story is the one least known to the public: The John and Gloria story. For forty-two years she has never been out of my life. The mother of my clever son, she was always there for me when I crashed heavily. We had a great marriage, until I spent three and a half years in South Australian prisons for robberies I didn't commit. The marriage was over after that. Now she is my best friend. I owe her more than I could ever repay.

And my son, John? He is a very private man. He is married and now works overseas. In May 2014, I did a comprehensive interview with the great Mike Willesee for the *Sunday Night* programme. At the time my son and his wife were here on holidays.

I said to him: 'John, no one blames the son for the sins of the father.' He replied: 'Some do, Dad.'

I nodded. 'I am doing this interview with Willesee. I'll make sure you are kept out of it.'

'No, Dad. Julia and I want to show our support for you. You have paid for your mistakes.' Both of them appeared on the programme and left no doubts that I had their support.

Albert Facey beat me to it when he called his classic book *A Fortunate Life*. But I still think my life has been an incredibly lucky one. Sure, I have spent over thirty years in some of the toughest prisons in Australia. But I survived and am able to write about it. Australia is a great country with a convict heritage it doesn't hide. My story, warts and all, also needs to be told. I should be dead...shot at on three separate occasions spanning thirty-nine years...but the friendships and the loves in my life have been as good as it gets.

From here on, I look forward – not back. I tell every person out there who is involved in or considering a life of crime the same thing: Don't be stupid.

Crime doesn't pay.

The ripple effect of crime is immense. It is better to be poor than to be in gaol. And gaol is all but inevitable for criminals. It is the great destroyer of relationships, families and self-respect. gaol is where you can be brutalised, bashed and buggered.

You can't put a price on freedom.

ACKNOWLEDGEMENTS

Sincere thanks to the law under-grad, Maria Morris, at Bond University who suggested the name 'The Last Escape'. Why didn't I think of that?

As always, Gloria has been of great assistance in the typing and editing resulting in an improved final product.

A special thanks to prolific writer Alan Whiticker, who persuaded me to write this book and when needed, gave me moral support.

My old friend, Emeritus Professor Ian Plimer, who edited the first draft despite numerous overseas trips and writing another two books of his own. Well done, Ian.

My good friend Dean – supportive as always – who helped out with another laptop when mine was destroyed by fire.

My son John, who told me to write the story warts and all. "You paid the price, Dad." All my family did.

My brother David encouraged me throughout the writing. Thanks Bro.

Cathy, the American girl, who has given me her blessings to include her photo in this book.

Thanks to my legal team: Joe Crowley, Barrister-at-Law, and Solicitor Eidan Havaas for helping me to come home for good. Still there when I need them.

Thank you John Kerr, author and raconteur extraordinaire, for supplying me with some details I didn't have. Saved me a lot of research.

Finally, thanks to the psychologists, Aleesha, Fiona and Georgina at the VOTP meetings which I still attend. You do a difficult job well and you *do* achieve some positive results.

ABOUT THE AUTHOR

A lot of people assume that if you have been in gaol you would have trouble writing a letter. And some prisoners are illiterate. Something that should be attended to by prison authorities. If an illiterate prisoner comes out of prison with the ability to read and write, that person's chances of employment and a lawful life are increased manifold.

I would encourage anyone thinking about becoming a writer to first enrol in a writing course where you will realise you had a lot to learn. I was taught how to write during a TAFE course while I was in the notorious H Division in Pentridge in the late 60's and early 70's by the renowned author and poet, the late Ian Mudie. He made me realise that until I did that course I knew nothing about writing. Ian, himself, had to drive taxis and tutor students to supplement his income.

As for me, I missed a lot of schooling and failed my final exams but I was always top of the class in English due to all the reading I did. And I was also a good storyteller. So writing stories, articles and even books was never a problem for me. But when I was younger I preferred to do it rather than write about it. Although I have had spasmodic periods of writing and being published over the past five decades usually my long stints in prison (for doing it rather than writing about it) curtailed my career as a writer.

Nevertheless, there have been some successes … various articles, short stories and now this book. Seeing your work published provides enormous satisfaction.